The Crabby Cook

COOKBOOK

135 ALMOST-EFFORTLESS RECIPES
PLUS SURVIVAL TIPS

by Jessica Harper

Illustrations by Ingo Fast

WORKMAN PUBLISHING · NEW YORK

Library of Congress Cataloging-in-Publication Data

Harper, Jessica.
   The crabby cook cookbook / by Jessica Harper.
      p. cm.
   Includes bibliographical references and index.
   ISBN 978-0-7611-5526-3 (alk. paper)
   1. Cooking—Humor. I. Title.
   TX652.7.H35 2010
   641.5—dc22
                                   2010032801

Design: Janet Vicario
Cover photograph: Gabrielle Revere
Book illustrations: Ingo Fast

Workman books are available at special discounts when purchased in bulk for premiums and
sales promotions as well as for fund-raising or educational use. Special editions or book excerpts
also can be created to specification. For details, contact the Special Sales Director at the address
below or send an e-mail to specialmarkets@workman.com.

Workman Publishing Company, Inc.
225 Varick Street
New York, NY 10014-4381
www.workman.com

Printed in the United States of America
First printing November 2010

10 9 8 7 6 5 4 3 2 1

ACKNOWLEDGMENTS

S WE KNOW, it takes more than an author to create a book. In this case, it took a crabby multitude. When I stop and think about all the people who helped make *The Crabby Cook Cookbook* happen, I feel giddy with gratitude.

For starters, I am especially grateful to Peter Workman, and to my editor, Suzanne Rafer, for tidying up my crabby ramblings, binding them beautifully, and sending them forth, buoyed by the support of the amazing Workman Publishing team, especially art director Janet Vicario and production editor Irene Demchyshyn. Thanks also to my agent, Jennifer Griffin, and to my super webmeister, Concetta Halstead at Lord Creative.

I'm grateful to the friends (some crabby cooks, some stove-huggers) who gave me their recipes and support: Cynthia Beckler, Arlene Zeichner, Susan Helmrich, Jeffie Lee Fiskin, Hannah Hempstead, my book group, my mahjong group, Richard Rubin, Amy Taubin, Abby Shaw, Carla Hacken, and Irma Henriquez.

I'm grateful to my family, without whom I would have nobody to complain about. My cheerleader sister, Lindsay, and my older sister, Diana (oatmeal cookie queen), Anna McDonnell, Julie and Ellen and Lily and Bette Rothman and hummus-lovin' Katy. I send a big shout-out to Susan Bolotin, whose encouragement and expert advice meant so much to me. Thanks to Scott for being so irritating and to Sam for the lamb. Thanks to Dad and Mom for the three squares and for the love.

Most of all, I am grateful to Elizabeth and Nora, my lifelong recipe testers, who, in spite of years of picky eating, have grown into spectacular young women, and to my husband, Tom, who makes me crabby sometimes, but mostly, well, he rocks.

CONTENTS

Are You a Crabby Cook?

MANY OF YOU (AND I) can answer that question unequivocally, but some of you may be uncertain. To determine just how crabby you are, do this simple self-check. Read the following six statements. If any of them sound like something you might say or think, then, I'm sorry, but most likely you do *not* qualify for crabby cook status.

1. I can't think of anything I'd rather do at five o'clock than cook dinner.

2. I'm always one to read a recipe thoroughly before I begin cooking. You never know when, say, a unique browning method might be called for, and you'll need to run down to Home Depot to pick up a blowtorch.

3. I never curse while cooking, even when the recipe requires that I chop seven vegetables and flour and sear fifty cubes of beef. I also do not curse when, in mid-recipe, I am distracted by a phone call from the PTA lady and I burn my finger with the blowtorch.

4. When the PTA lady calls to ask me to contribute food to their annual luncheon, I love the fact that she entrusts me with making a chicken entree for forty, instead of one of the no-brainer donations like bottled water.

5. If a family member doesn't care for what I've prepared for dinner, I thank them for their feedback and offer them an alternative entree.

6. After dinner, I love the solitude of kitchen cleanup, while my family scampers off to watch *American Idol.* It gives me precious time to consider what I'll cook for dinner the next day, and the next . . .

For a long time I thought I was the only crabby cook I knew. While I complained my way through daily cooking for my picky family, I envied my friends who seemed so Martha Stewart-y, all rushing around recipe-swapping and table-decorating, searing tuna and braising beef cheeks.

I had not always been so irritable. I was an actress for many years, in the days B.C. (Before Children), and between gigs, I enjoyed collecting cookbooks and buying shallots, concocting fabulous food to please boyfriends and family. But back then I cooked what I wanted, when I felt like it, which, of course, is not remotely how a family food agenda works. When I found myself cooking several times a day, including two dinners—an early one for kids who would eat only six things and a later one for their father who would eat only eight things, none of which correlated with the kids' six—my positive feelings about menu-planning and execution imploded, and I became a full-fledged crabby cook.

Ashamed of my inability to experience the "joy of cooking," I kept my gnarly attitude to myself. While I pretended to be Julia Child-like, I secretly honed my cooking-avoidance skills. I ripped easy recipes from the magazines in my doctor's office, trolled the city for take-out options, even invited my mother-in-law for dinner and handed her an apron.

Then one day, not so long ago, I had my mahjong group for dinner. (N.B.: This is a subgroup of my book group, which is itself an offshoot of my PTA special events group.) Between bites of take-out sushi, my friend Kathy announced, "You know, I am just *so over* cooking dinner every night."

I was stunned. I'd thought Kathy was a regular Rachael Ray. She makes killer stroganoff, freezes pesto in the ice cube tray, and owns monogrammed coasters.

"Oh, I know," my friend Lynn said. "Doesn't it suck?" I was shocked: I'd thought Lynn was the next Nigella.

But these revelations were just the tip of the iceberg lettuce. Later, I got confessions from Denise and Mimi and Patti. They were all fed up with daily cooking. Even my sister-in-law Julie, who writes a newspaper food column no less, had this to say about daily food prep: "I HATE IT!"

It was then I knew I was not alone; apparently the world was full of crabby cooks.

The day my friends and I outed ourselves, I got the idea for *The Crabby Cook Cookbook.* While it wouldn't be my dream cookbook (that would be the one that just pops open and produces a meat loaf or a chicken dinner), its recipes and survival tips would make life easier for those of us who are kitchen-challenged. That's why the recipes here are not complex or glamorous. This is everyday, family-friendly (and chef-friendly) food, home-tested for acceptability by very picky people (my relatives). Pay special attention to recipes marked as a **Miracle Food,** which absolutely *everyone* will eat without complaining.

Speaking of my relatives, you'll notice that I've loaded this book with stories about their care and feeding, to amuse you while you cook, or even for reading on a night when you're not cooking (like that'll ever happen). The cast of characters you will meet on these pages includes the following:

TOM: My chocoholic husband, who says, "I'll eat anything," neglecting to note that his "anything" excludes onions, garlic, peppers, scallions, eggplant, squash, shellfish, most meat, spices, all non-chocolate desserts . . . I can't go on. It's making me too crabby.

ELIZABETH AND NORA: My darling daughters, who have lately become much more adventurous eaters than their father, although they once would eat no food that was not white.

OLIVER: My pesky golden retriever, an expert at counter-surfing, the rewards of which have ranged from a tuna sandwich to an entire roasted chicken.

MOM: My mother (Eleanor), who cooked for her husband and six children (including two sets of twins) every day for way too many years but was never visibly crabby, a fact that puts me to shame most days.

BETTE: My mother-in-law, who, although not related to me by blood, shares with me the distracted cook gene. She has been known to put soup on the stove and go out to buy a bathing suit.

BILLY: My twin brother, my partner in childhood crime. (Once, in a fit of sugar deprivation, we stole a Mounds bar.)

LINDSAY: My sister and kindred spirit, who is at least as crabby a cook as I am.

Other passers-by include SCOTT, my brother-in-law (whose food aversions include ground turkey, chicken soup, and panini),

MARTHA, my fake grandmother (who cooked for us grandkids even after Billy shot her in the butt with an arrow), and THE FAMOUS WIFE (a fancy dinner guest who found my cooking inedible), RICHARD GERE (to whom I once fed an appalling pot pie), MRS. KERRY (*not* the politician's wife—the one who came over the night I discovered the hell of lasagna), JACK NICHOLSON (all he wanted was some whiskey), plus a whole circus of other siblings, in-laws, and extras.

Okay, it's time to face the inevitable. Unless you have my dream cookbook, you're going to need to make dinner tonight, so start reading. (If you *do* have my dream cookbook, call me. I'll make you an offer you'll probably refuse.)

ONE
Breakfast,
Slow and Fast

I N THE EARLY YEARS of our family life, when household chores were assigned, my husband, Tom, got dog poop and soccer. I got cooking and carpooling. The latter was easy in the preschool days, when you could straggle in with the children at 10:30 and nobody minded. But when the kids were older and school got serious, the frantic dash to the school bus was a duty I'd gladly have swapped for the dog poop.

In middle school, my daughters were required to travel to school by bus, although (much to my perennial annoyance) it was almost as far to the bus stop as it was to the school itself. We needed to leave the house by 7:00 to make the 7:23 in a relaxed manner. If we missed the 7:23, I'd have to drive the girls to school and make a contrite appearance in my morning attire (not pretty) before Mr. Wogens, the attendance officer. My fear of this humiliation was such that when the clock struck 7:06 and a daughter was still looking for clean underpants, I'd become, well, unbalanced. Propelled by caffeine, I'd ricochet between the girls' bedrooms, shrieking, "Let's GO! Let's GO!" like some kind of deranged cheerleader.

By the time the kids finally emerged with untied shoes and ponytails askew, any kind of real breakfast was out of the question; I'd shove frozen waffles into the girls' hands. On a good day they'd be toasted. (The waffles, I mean, not the children.)

I'd charge out the door, my bathrobe flapping. By the time the girls caught up, all car doors would be open and the ignition ignited. "Let's GO!"

I'd already be backing the car out of the driveway when the girls sleepily clicked their doors shut. "Watch out, Mom," they'd say in unison as we did our daily near-miss of my husband's car, which he'd parked in the danger zone, i.e., within a hundred feet of me driving in reverse.

We'd rocket around the corner to pick up Garrett and Marissa (whose routinely punctual mom would glare at me from the kitchen window), then we'd tear down the hill, airborne over speed bumps, praying the cops were still at Starbucks, and pull to a whiplash stop just as the bus was leaving. Arturo, the driver, had gotten used to the sound of my screeching tires thirty seconds after his departure. He'd stop, probably hurling a curse in my direction, and reopen his doors for my carsick passengers.

We always gave Arturo a large box of peppermint bark for Christmas.

I'd return from the morning's madcap outing, emotionally spent, hair bent. I'd collect the remnants of the girls' waffles from the back seat, invariably wondering whatever happened to the slow, civilized breakfasts of times gone by.

I'd walk into the house as Tom was walking out, off to work, all showered and crisp, scarfing down a muffin. He would occasionally (annoyingly) note that his mother had never let him leave the house without a proper breakfast.

"Every school day, Bette would set the table and cook up some eggs and bacon," he'd say in a tone of loving awe, apparently forgetting that his mother has always had what might be called a flexible relationship with time. When you describe someone as "late," Bette thinks you mean they are deceased. The L-word has no other meaning for her. Tom may have had good breakfasts, but on Bette's carpool days, he'd be lucky to get to school by lunchtime.

That was in the early '60s, in slower times when there was more tolerance for a relaxed attitude. With all the tardy slips Tom would accumulate if Bette were driving him to school today, his life would be over. Well, certainly college would be out of the question. At least Harvard would be. But then, nobody gets into Harvard these days anyway, according to people I know whose kids didn't get into Harvard.

Bette's Tardy Slip Special

AS YOU WILL SEE in Bette's recipe for eggs and bacon, they cook (and should be eaten) at a leisurely pace. If you don't mind that your kids miss first period and get detention and will therefore neither go to Harvard nor amount to anything much, go right ahead and let 'em eat eggs.

✳ SERVES 4

8 slices bacon
8 eggs
¼ cup half-and-half
1 teaspoon salt

¼ teaspoon freshly ground black pepper
2 tablespoons unsalted butter

1. Heat a large skillet over medium heat. Add the bacon and cook, turning it once or twice, until it's very crisp, about 10 minutes. Place the bacon on paper towels to absorb the excess drippings. Tent the bacon with aluminum foil to keep it warm.

2. Whisk the eggs, half-and-half, salt, and pepper together in a bowl until they are well blended.

3. Wipe out the skillet, heat it over low heat, and add 1 tablespoon of the butter. When the butter has melted, add the egg mixture and stir gently with a whisk or fork until the eggs are cooked the way you like 'em. (I like them a little bit moist.) Then stir in the other tablespoon of butter until it melts, and serve immediately, with the bacon on the side.

VARIATIONS You can sprinkle the eggs with ¼ cup freshly grated Parmigiano-Reggiano cheese toward the end of cooking, or mix in ½ cup chopped ham or prosciutto. You can also add fresh herbs: chopped parsley, basil, or dill is great, as are chives or scallions—unless your family faints at the sight of green things in their eggs.

Ix-nay the Acon-bay

UNLIKE BETTE, my mother did not cook eggs much, nor did she like to cook bacon.

"All that stink for a few sticks of crispy fat?" she'd say with a snort. "Ix-nay the acon-bay!" (Pig Latin was a second language in our house, and seemed especially appropriate when discussing pork products.)

Although we whined that all our friends ate bacon daily and were perfect human specimens as a result, I couldn't blame my mother for her anti-bacon position. It was pre-microwave, and there were eight of us. She'd have been at the stove for hours, inhaling pig smoke, her sweat and tears hissing as they hit the frying pan.

In Chicago in the late '50s, nobody'd yet heard of exotic breakfast choices like bran muffins or yogurt or granola; so if you didn't make eggs and bacon like Bette did, your options were limited. My family ate a lot of Cheerios and Kix and Wheaties (although I refused to eat Wheaties because I had an idea that if I did, I'd grow up to be a baseball player). But I think my early childhood was mostly powered by oatmeal.

From the age of five, my twin brother, Billy, and I walked to school together every morning. On the chilly days that dominated the school calendar, Mom filled us with oatmeal, served with cream (half-and-half to be exact) and brown sugar, and sent us off.

In my memory I see myself in a plaid wool skirt and Billy in a plaid flannel shirt. Perfectly plaid, we're holding hands, mutually protective. We're careful not to step on a sidewalk crack for fear that we will, per the old cautionary rhyme, break our mother's back. Halfway to school, we pass a gingko tree, which we never cease to find remarkable, and then we come to the crossing guard.

We don't know his name, but wiry, stooped, and gray-haired, with a neon chest banner to indicate his assigned duty, the crossing guard is always there. He's so consistently a part of our route, we have a hard time imagining him anywhere else, like in a house or at the beach. He never fails to ask, in his Scottish accent, "How arrrrrre ya, boys and girdles?" (His pronunciation of "girls" sends us into giggle fits.) "Have ye had yerrrr oatmeal tuhday?" In unison we say we have, and the guard seems so delighted that Billy and I decide we should always tell him we've had oatmeal, even on Cheerios days, to keep his spirits up.

I'm guessing that when we moved to another suburb in first grade, the crossing guard must have noticed—but maybe he didn't.

Maybe he fired the oatmeal question at everyone and got enough yeses to keep him happy, even in our absence.

It's a good thing my kids had no inquisitive crossing guard at their school, or I'd have been outed as a breakfast slacker. But now I sometimes make oatmeal for Tom if he's not too rushed and I'm not too crabby. He says nothing sets him up for the day quite like oatmeal, and I know just what he means.

Tom's Oatmeal

WHEN TOM HAS TIME TO EAT OATMEAL and I have the patience to cook it, I admit that I burn it about 50 percent of the time. Even with the kids gone, mornings are an explosion of activity; after a little caffeine, I find myself doing six things at once while I'm still in my bathrobe. I'll put the oatmeal on and then go do the five other things until the smell of something burning summons me back to the kitchen.

If you have an oatmeal disorder like me, maybe you should just stick to Special K and save yourself a lot of aggravation. Otherwise, go for it. ✳ SERVES 2 OR 3 GENEROUSLY

For the oatmeal
- 1 cup old-fashioned rolled oats
- ¼ cup raw sunflower seeds
- ¼ cup sweetened dried cherries
- ⅛ teaspoon salt
- 1 teaspoon honey
- ¼ cup fresh blueberries (optional)

For serving (optional)
- Milk or half-and-half
- Unsalted butter
- Brown sugar

1. Bring 1½ cups water to a boil in a small saucepan. Add the oats, sunflower seeds, cherries, and salt,

reduce the heat to low, and cook, stirring occasionally, until the liquid is absorbed, about 5 minutes.

2. Stir in the honey, and sprinkle the top of the oatmeal with the blueberries if you're using them.

3. Serve the oatmeal with milk if you like, or a little butter, or go wild and add some half-and-half and brown sugar.

Mom's Pancakes

WHEN I WAS SEVEN, with a twin brother and two sisters, my mother unexpectedly gave birth to twin boys. Well, I mean, she expected *something,* of course, but it was pre-ultrasound, and everyone thought she was having one extra-large kid, not two mediums. With Dad at the office all day, Mom suddenly found herself almost solely responsible for six children under the age of nine.

In spite of her domestic burden, my mother always made pancakes on Sunday. She made piles of them, standing at the stove for ages, flipping, the bow of her apron flopping. She'd smash them into mush for the babies, and drench them in syrup and melted butter for the rest of us. They were the kind of delicious that makes you freeze, totally focused, transfixed by flavors.

I can't help but recall one of those Sundays when I ate seven or eight pancakes—so many that I'd have liked to lie down to allow for proper digestion. But I had to go to a birthday party, which involved riding all the way downtown in a van stuffed with children and an unlucky lady named Mrs. Kenly.

Mrs. Kenly sat next to me, all squished in. She was wearing a beautiful mink coat, which at the time was *not* politically incorrect.

On the other side of me was Donna, who was chewing on watermelon bubble gum, the fumes from which turned my stomach in the close quarters. Also, the temperature in the van must've been ninety, with all windows shut to keep out the Chicago chill, and Mr. Kling, the driver and dad of the birthday girl, was smoking a cigar.

It was a perfect setup for disaster.

Still, it took me by surprise when I threw up violently all over Mrs. Kenly's lovely coat. (She was surprised too, with a few other emotions mixed in.) The humiliation was awful, made worse by the fact that Mrs. Kenly was a terribly nice person. If I'd barfed on, say, Mrs. Landon, who once laughed at me because I had toilet paper stuck to my shoe, I wouldn't have minded so much.

That experience was a lesson in moderation; since then, I only eat two or three pancakes at a sitting. When I made these pancakes for my own young children, I often added chocolate chips, which won me at least a few hours of serious appreciation. ✳ MAKES ABOUT 16 PANCAKES

2½ cups buttermilk

2 eggs

3 tablespoons unsalted butter, melted, plus extra for cooking and for serving

2 cups all-purpose flour

1 tablespoon sugar

2 teaspoons baking powder

1 teaspoon baking soda

½ teaspoon salt

½ cup mini chocolate chips (optional)

Maple syrup, for serving

1. Whisk the buttermilk and eggs together in a large bowl until they are well blended. Stir in the melted butter.

2. In a separate bowl, sift the flour, sugar, baking powder, baking soda and salt together. Add this to the egg mixture and whisk just enough to combine the ingredients. Stir in the chocolate chips if you're using them.

3. Melt about ½ tablespoon butter in a large skillet over medium heat. Pour ¼-cupfuls of the batter into the skillet, and cook until the pancakes are bubbly and the edges dry, about 2 minutes. Flip them over and cook until golden on the bottom and springy to the touch, about another minute. Transfer the pancakes to a plate and keep them warm while you repeat, adding more butter when it's needed, until you've used all your batter.

4. Serve the pancakes immediately, with more butter and masses of maple syrup.

# ★ Killer Pumpkin Pancakes

IN THE TRADITION ESTABLISHED BY MY MOTHER, I have always (even in my crabbiest phases) liked to make a big, leisurely breakfast on Sunday mornings.

Up until recently, however, this presented the kind of challenge I grappled with in Mr. Steele's 7th-grade math class. You've got four people, two of whom will not eat pancakes, three of whom refuse to eat oatmeal, and two of whom do not like scrambled eggs. Only two will eat French toast but one prefers white bread and the other whole wheat. What (the hell) do you feed them for breakfast? Is there a common denominator here?

My answer was often Special K, which three members of my family will eat (okay, not four, but close—I'd get a B from Mr. Steele), although one uses skim milk, another prefers 2 percent, and a third likes soy with a little flurry of wheat germ.

Because I'm math-challenged, it took me years to solve this problem definitively with the discovery of these pumpkin pancakes. All four of us love them, which makes them a Miracle Food (and pumps my grade up to an A). ✳ MAKES ABOUT 16 PANCAKES

1 cup all-purpose flour

1 cup whole wheat flour

2 teaspoons baking powder

1 teaspoon baking soda

1 teaspoon ground cinnamon

1 teaspoon ground allspice

½ teaspoon ground ginger

½ teaspoon salt

2½ cups milk

1 cup canned pumpkin puree

¼ cup honey

1 egg

2 tablespoons unsalted butter, melted, plus extra for cooking

Maple syrup, for serving

1. Combine the flours, baking powder, baking soda, cinnamon, allspice, ginger, and salt in a large bowl.

2. In another bowl, whisk the milk, pumpkin puree, honey, and egg together until the mixture is smooth. Stir in the melted butter. Pour the pumpkin mixture into the flour mixture and stir just until all the ingredients are combined.

3. Melt about ½ tablespoon butter in a large skillet over medium heat. Pour ¼-cupfuls of batter into the skillet and cook until the pancakes are bubbly and the edges are dry, about 2 minutes. Flip them over and cook until they are golden brown on the bottom and springy to the touch, about 2 minutes.

4. Transfer the pancakes to a plate and keep them warm while you repeat, adding more butter when it's needed, until you've used all your batter.

5. Serve immediately with maple syrup.

Breakfast on the Fly

IN THE CARPOOL YEARS, when breakfast became whatever you could grab on your way out the door, the challenge was to come up with some ideas for portable food for the kids. Here are some of my favorite carpool breakfast recipes, for days when there's no time for pancakes but you just can't stand the sight of another frozen waffle.

Killer Pumpkin Muffins

THESE MUFFINS are the carpool equivalent of pumpkin pancakes. They're my daughter Nora's favorite, dating back to her preschool days.

My daughters' preschool was a co-op, and a daily snack was provided by parents on a rotating basis. On your day, your kid would act as the snack-bearing waiter, so you had to provide something that would do her proud or she'd be humiliated. The snack also had to be healthy enough to pass muster with Karen, the pre-K teacher. (Karen behaved like Oz's Glinda, the good witch, with the kids, but with the parents she was more like Glinda's wicked green-faced counterpart.)

When my turn rolled around, I'd spend a fair amount of time irritably bagging twenty raisin-Goldfish-cheese combo packs, which went over okay, but other parents would show up with home-baked anise-scented buns, carefully balled melon, or tiny quiches, making me feel like a loser.

Shortly before the girls moved on to kindergarten and I was relieved of snack duty, I discovered these muffins. With them, I won the contest for best snack-bringer, at least in my own mind. Now that my girls are at the other end of the educational spectrum, I just might throw some of these into a college care package.

This ingredient list may seem challenging, but that's because there are multiple spices, which don't really count. Have a cup of coffee and these muffins will be oven-ready in just a few minutes.

✳ MAKES 18 MUFFINS

1 cup whole wheat flour

1 cup all-purpose flour

2 teaspoons baking powder

1 teaspoon baking soda

1 teaspoon ground cinnamon

1 teaspoon ground ginger

½ teaspoon ground nutmeg

½ teaspoon salt

1 cup canned pumpkin puree

1 cup low-fat milk

½ cup unsweetened applesauce

¼ cup maple syrup

¼ cup canola oil

1 egg

1 apple (any kind), peeled, cored, and diced

½ cup raisins (optional)

½ cup raw sunflower seeds (optional)

1. Preheat the oven to 425°F. Place 12 paper liners in a standard muffin tin. (You could also grease the muffin tin if you prefer, but I'm too crabby to bother with that.)

2. Combine the flours, baking powder, baking soda, cinnamon, ginger, nutmeg, and salt in a bowl.

3. In a larger bowl, beat the pumpkin puree, milk, applesauce, maple syrup, oil, and egg together until well blended. Add the dry ingredients to the pumpkin mixture, mixing just until all the ingredients are moist. Fold in the chopped apple, and the raisins and/or sunflower seeds if you're using them. Fill the muffin cups about two-thirds full with batter.

4. Bake the muffins until they are springy to the touch, about 20 minutes.

5. Serve the muffins hot or at room temperature. (They freeze well.)

VARIATIONS You can use ½ cup chopped walnuts or pecans in place of the sunflower seeds.

Acon-Bay Olls-Ray (Bacon Rolls)

DUE TO MOM'S NEGATIVE FEELINGS about bacon, we never had acon-bay olls-ray. (If you do not speak Pig Latin—shame on you!—you can call them bacon rolls.) But I sometimes made them for my kids on those rare school days when I woke up early with an abundance of energy. I'd find myself channeling my mother-in-law, Bette: I'd cook up some bacon. I didn't bother with the scrambled eggs due to the school bus pressure. Besides, I preferred the format of acon-bay olls-ray for breakfast on the fly.

Here's a wee caveat: When cooking bacon, make sure to keep it out of the reach of your pet. My golden retriever, Oliver, an avid counter-surfer, ate nine pieces of bacon (not to mention a stick of butter) last weekend. He suffered no ill effects and easily dodged my airborne frying pan.

Try to use really good quality ingredients—good buns, gourmet bacon and jam— but if you just can't, don't worry about it. The kids will like them anyway. If they don't, just open your door and call Oliver. ✳ SERVES 4

8 slices bacon
4 hot dog buns
¼ cup strawberry jam
2 tablespoons unsalted butter,
    at room temperature

1. Preheat the oven to 250°F.

2. Heat a large skillet over medium heat. Add the bacon and cook, turning it once or twice, until it's very crisp, about 10 minutes.

Place the bacon on paper towels to absorb the excess drippings. (Keep it out of the dog's reach.)

3. Open a hot dog bun and smear one side with jam and the other with butter.

4. Place the buns on a baking sheet and warm them in the oven for about 5 minutes.

5. Place 2 slices of bacon inside each bun. Wrap the bacon rolls in aluminum foil and put them back in the warm oven until the kids are ready for the mad dash to school.

VARIATIONS Seedless raspberry jam or currant jelly is an excellent substitute if you don't like strawberry jam.

Liza's Luscious Scones

THESE ARE GREAT FOR CARPOOL if you mix up the batter, shape the scones, and then refrigerate them overnight to bake in the morning. The only trouble with making them the night before is that you have to make them the night before. If you're like me, after you've cooked dinner you are seldom (as in never) in the mood to start cooking for the next day. But sometimes I'd lose my mind and do it anyway, and it paid off because the kids were so grateful for those delicious scones, they'd even let me listen to NPR on the car radio. ✳ MAKES 6 TO 8 SCONES, WHICH WILL DISAPPEAR VERY QUICKLY

2 cups all-purpose flour,
    plus extra for dusting
¼ cup sugar, plus an extra
    spoonful for sprinkling on top
1 tablespoon baking powder
½ teaspoon salt
1 cup (2 sticks) cold unsalted butter,
    cut into small chunks, plus extra
    for the baking sheet
2 eggs
½ cup heavy (whipping) cream
½ cup chocolate chips

1. Preheat the oven to 350°F. Butter a baking sheet and set it aside.

2. Place the flour, sugar, baking powder, and salt in a food processor and pulse a few times to blend. Add the butter and pulse just until it is incorporated and the mixture resembles small crumbs.

3. In a small bowl, whisk one of the eggs and the cream together.

Add this to the flour mixture and pulse just until the ingredients are blended.

4. Place the dough on a lightly floured surface, add the chocolate chips, and knead the dough just long enough to incorporate the chips. Shape the dough into a round that is about ¾-inch thick. Using a biscuit or cookie cutter (or an inverted juice glass), cut the dough into 2-inch rounds. (You could also cut it into 6 wedges, like a pie.)

5. Place the scones on the buttered baking sheet. Mix the remaining egg with 1 tablespoon water, and brush this egg wash on top of the scones. Then sprinkle them with sugar.

6. Bake the scones until they are slightly golden and flaky, 25 to 30 minutes. Place them on a wire rack to cool. Serve them warm or at room temperature.

Tom-to-Go: Healthy-ish Oat Muffins

THESE MUFFINS ARE THE PORTABLE VERSION of Tom's oatmeal breakfast, designed for mornings when he, like the rest of us, is in such a big fat hurry that he doesn't have time to sit down. I like to make a bunch of these and throw them in the freezer to grab on frantic mornings. ✳ MAKES 12 MUFFINS

1 cup quick-cooking oats
1 cup all-purpose flour
½ cup (packed) dark brown sugar
1 teaspoon baking powder
1 teaspoon baking soda
½ teaspoon salt

1 cup buttermilk
¼ cup canola oil
1 egg
1 teaspoon vanilla extract
1 cup fresh blueberries

1. Preheat the oven to 425°F. Place paper liners in a standard muffin tin. (As I've said before, you can grease the muffin tin if you have no paper liners and/or more patience than I have.)

2. Combine the oats, flour, brown sugar, baking powder, baking soda, and salt in a large bowl.

3. In a separate bowl, whisk together the buttermilk, oil, egg, and vanilla. Add the buttermilk mixture to the dry ingredients, stirring just until everything is combined. Gently fold in the blueberries. Pour about ⅔ cup batter into each of the lined muffin cups.

4. Bake the muffins until they are golden brown and springy to the touch, 13 to 15 minutes.

5. Let the muffins cool in the tin for about 5 minutes. Then remove them from the muffin tin and place them on a wire rack to cool completely.

Tom-to-Go #2: Day-O Banana Bread

BANANA BREAD IS ANOTHER HEALTHY OPTION for a fast breakfast, and it's Tom's favorite. It has the added benefit of saving you from the irritation that comes with tossing brown bananas that nobody got around to eating.

Just do me a favor. If you ever meet Bette, please don't tell her Tom's eating breakfast in his car. She'll plotz. ✳ MAKES 1 HEFTY, TASTY, BANANA-Y LOAF

1 tablespoon unsalted butter,
   for the pan

2 cups whole wheat flour

1 teaspoon baking soda

¼ teaspoon salt

4 very ripe bananas

2 eggs

½ cup canola oil

½ cup honey

¾ cup walnut halves (optional)

1. Preheat the oven to 350°F. Butter a 9 x 5-inch loaf pan.

2. Sift the flour, baking soda, and salt together in a bowl.

3. In a larger bowl, mash the bananas with a potato masher until they are smooth. Whisk in the eggs, one at a time. Add the oil and the honey, whisking until the ingredients are well blended. Add the flour mixture and stir just until everything is combined.

4. Pour the batter into the prepared loaf pan and arrange the walnut halves on top, if you are using them.

Bake the loaf until a knife inserted in the center comes out clean, 55 to 60 minutes.

5. Let the bread cool in the pan for about 10 minutes. Then invert the pan, remove the loaf, and let it cool completely on a wire rack before slicing and serving.

VARIATIONS I love nuts, but I just put them on top of the bread for easy removal by those who feel differently about them. You can incorporate them into the batter if you prefer. Just chop the nuts and fold them in at the end of Step 3.

You can also add the grated zest of 1 lemon, if your family likes a little citrus accent in their Day-O bread. Tom likes no accents (except the one I use when I'm pretending to be a French chef), which is why I also do not add ½ cup raisins or dried cranberries, although I encourage you to try this if you're cooking for more tolerant people.

A POSTSCRIPT

MORNING LIFE IS CALMER now that the girls are in college, but I'm still in fast mode: I get up and drink coffee and start rocketing around, doing things. After all that carpooling, I think it will take me years of debriefing until I can adjust my pace to something more normal.

I get a glimpse of what that future looks like when I visit my parents in Connecticut these days. I get up late there (I'm on L.A. time), but Mom and Dad are still in mid-breakfast. This country's renewed interest in slow food is gaining momentum, but Mom and Dad are way ahead of the pack: they've already moved on to slooooooooooow.

For starters, my mother makes fruit salad for breakfast each and every morning. I could never face such a labor-intensive task until after I'd eaten breakfast, which of course would make for an ass-backward situation. Mom serves the salad with coffee for him, tea for her, granola, yogurt and cottage cheese, a little toast, and I forget what else, but there's a lot of stuff. Before dining, *The New York Times* must be fetched from the local general store, another task I could not perform first thing in the morning. Without nutrition (and caffeine), I'd get lost or run over a cow.

My parents take their time, munching, with their steaming cups, in a state of relaxation that at the moment looks foreign to me. Maybe when I'm in my eighties (or hopefully sooner), I, too, will be capable of the kind of peaceful bliss brought on by a long, ritualized breakfast. It seems like something to look forward to (except maybe for the fruit salad part).

After breakfast, Mom and Dad do their exercises. (They are in remarkably good health.) Then it's pretty much time for lunch . . .

TWO
Mom's Little Lost Lamb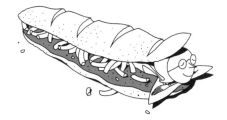
(and Other Lunch Options)

BETWEEN THE YEARS of 1948 and 1957, my mother gave birth to six kids (including two sets of twins), and she cooked all our meals until her nest finally emptied in 1975. (You do the math.) Our elementary school had no cafeteria and our secondary school served scary food, so she never even got the weekday reprieve from lunch duty. I remember the production line of brown bags in the kitchen, Mom stuffing them with tuna sandwiches and Hostess Twinkies and apples.

Even now, Mom still makes three squares a day for my father. She doesn't seem to mind—maybe because, after all the years of cooking for eight, this new routine seems lightweight. She starts with their elaborate breakfast (*avec* fresh fruit salad) and ends with a candlelit dinner, a meal for which my mother always dresses, putting on a fresh blouse, jewelry, and perfume. At midday, there's a serious lunch (*dead* serious: homemade soup and sandwich) almost every day, which is a meal composed mostly of leftovers.

Mom is a food saver and recycler. Having grown up in the Depression, she feels that nothing, not a scrap nor a morsel, should be thrown away. Two weeks after its first presentation, you'll find a bit of roast lamb jammed in the back of the fridge in a small glass dish. It'll be covered with aluminum foil which will have come loose, allowing a perfect escape route for freshness. The little lost lamb won't be enough to feed a pigeon; if I'd been in charge of that postprandial cleanup, I'd have tossed it (or fed it to our dog, Oliver) and nobody would have called the Waste Police. But my mother will have saved it, no doubt imagining many uses for it that were beyond my food-wary imagination. If it hadn't gotten lost behind the mayo and the leftover spinach, the lamb would have baaaaaaed its way into my father's lunch sandwich. The spinach was destined for his soup.

Mom's Soup

I HAVE BEEN KNOWN to make soup like Mom's (for *dinner*) when I happen to have some random mounds of leftover vegetable-y things that are on the verge of expiring but are still, as my mother would say, "perfectly good."

You throw a can of Campbell's condensed cream of mushroom (or celery) soup into the food processor with a cup of milk. Add your nearly expired veggies, a couple of teaspoons of curry powder and a pinch of cayenne pepper, and process till it's smooth. Heat it up and serve.

These days, Mom is much more likely to ditch the Campbell's and just add more vegetables to thicken the soup. But the concept remains the same, and my father is always grateful for the result.

Try pairing it with Mom's Little Lost Lambwich, as I do when I'm having a totally Mom-ish moment.

Mom's Little Lost Lambwich

IF YOU HAVE A LITTLE LEFTOVER LAMB in the fridge, as my mother often does, don't lose it, use it. Here's how. ✳ SERVES 4

4 pita breads, cut in half crosswise
1 recipe Minty Cuke Salad (page 204)
16 slices leftover roasted or grilled lamb (about 1 pound)
1 tomato, thinly sliced
½ red onion, thinly sliced (optional)
¼ to ½ cup crumbled feta cheese, to taste

Open a pita bread half and fill it with some of the salad, some sliced lamb, a slice of tomato, a slice of onion, if desired, and a tablespoon or more of feta cheese. Repeat this with the other pita halves, and serve.

Bette's Saturday Soup

MY MOTHER-IN-LAW, BETTE, is a saver like my mom. For decades she cooked for her family of six, and she had her own special way of dealing with leftovers. At the end of each week, Bette would assemble the remains of the week's meals—including meats, vegetables, macaroni and cheese, whatever—chop them into bite-size bits, and hurl them into a pot of Campbell's vegetable soup.

Now, although Bette is not my mother, I feel we share a certain gene—the one that makes a person unable to remember that something is cooking on the stove. So when Bette left her Saturday Soup to simmer, it was a dangerous thing. She'd turn on the stove and go out to buy a bathing suit (see Note). Luckily there was enough human traffic in the house that the house was not reduced to a pile of ashes. But the soup was often, shall we say, concentrated in quality.

Since I'm as distractable as Bette, I will not just set a kitchen timer. I will strap the timer to my body, in case I forget something's cooking and jump in the car to go bowling.

Bette's four children ate the Saturday Soup willingly for years, giving credence to the idea that if you start feeding children something early in their lives, no matter what it is, they will eat it forever. (How else could you possibly explain the acceptance of say, gefilte fish?)

But when the kids grew up and spouses got involved, Saturday Soup fell into disfavor. I had it only once, because my family lives far from Bette's kitchen. I loved it, but then I'm very accepting of food that somebody besides me has prepared.

But after my brother-in-law, Scott, found a chunk of hot dog with teeth marks on it floating in his bowl, he banned Saturday Soup. He was sure it was toxic, that it might impede his kids' neurological development, if it didn't just, you know, kill them outright.

If you are more daring than Scott and are also (a) a saver and (b) nuts by the end of a week of menu-planning, you might want to try making Saturday Soup. Just don't make too much; there's nothing more annoying than leftover leftovers.

Here's what you do: Prepare two cans of Campbell's condensed vegetable soup according to the not-too-challenging directions on the label. (Add water.) Then you sort through your leftovers from the week's meals, carefully removing any that smell like sewer gas or have grown fur. (When I'm in doubt as to a food's freshness, I often run it by Oliver, our dog. If he sniffs it, looks at me dolefully, and goes outside to eat grass, I toss it.)

Next, chop your leftovers into bite-size pieces. If you have foods that are likely to repulse any diners, like eggplant or Tuesday's half-eaten cheeseburger, cut them up until they're unrecognizable. Use common sense: Don't throw in, say, that half cup of leftover oatmeal or last night's cheesecake remnants.

Dump the leftovers into the soup, adding a little more water if you want to stretch this thing. Bring the soup to a boil; then reduce the heat and simmer until there is no chance that any bacteria could still be alive. This may take some time, but don't go out to buy a bathing suit. If you really want to do my mother-in-law proud, serve the soup with Bette's cream cheese and olive sandwiches (see page 24).

NOTE Going out "to buy a bathing suit" is a generic expression that Tom's family uses to explain the mysterious errands that often mean Bette's disappearance for hours. (She'll go out at 10 A.M. and come back at 3 P.M. with some shower gel and a museum brochure.) The expression was coined when the family was headed home after a ski trip. Bette went AWOL at the airport, reappearing long after their plane's departure with the explanation that she'd gone to buy a bathing suit. It was never established why she chose that time, place, or season for such a pusuit, but, whatever.

The Baltimore Special

I WISH HE'D TOLD me years ago.

Just recently, out of the blue, for the first time in twenty-one years of marriage, Tom shared a recipe with me. He'd forgotten all about it, and he doesn't know why it suddenly rose to the surface of his memory. It's his mother's recipe for a cream cheese and olive sandwich.

There's a theory that the sandwich was a specialty of Baltimore, where Tom grew up. He watched his mother make them for years and thus became a skilled CCOS chef himself. He honed that skill at college and beyond, until he walked into my life (and my kitchen) and forgot about it.

The method and ingredients are very specific; Tom will accept no variations. I did my research (I consulted with both Tom and Bette), so I now know the secret to making a perfect CCOS. Read further and you will, too.

The list of recipes that Tom can execute now numbers three. But who knows? Maybe someday he'll suddenly remember that he knows how to make blondies and then I'll be *really* happy.

✳ MAKES 1 SANDWICH

2 slices Arnold white bread

2 tablespoons cream cheese, at room temperature

1 tablespoon chopped pitted green olives

1. Lightly toast the bread. Smear each piece with a tablespoon of cream cheese.

2. Sprinkle the olives evenly over the cream cheese, and put the bread slices together to make a sandwich. Serve immediately.

★Pain-in-the-Ass Minestrone

MY MOTHER HAS THREE TIMES as many children as I have; my cooking life has been much easier than hers (although I complain about it three times as much). In my current life, things have lightened up: with Tom at the office and the girls away, I have happily taken lunch off the day's agenda. If I'm solo at midday, I just grab a piece of bread, smear it with peanut butter, and keep right on moving.

But, while I am thrilled to have eliminated one of the day's three squares, I still like to eat lunchy food . . . for dinner. I find soup and sandwiches comforting, but not if I have to cook all that in the middle of the day.

Now, I know what you're thinking. You're looking at the recipe that follows and thinking, What is she thinking? And as I reflect on the list of ingredients, I, too, wonder what I am thinking. This recipe involves an awful lot of choppage.

But then I remind myself that this soup is one of the Miracle Foods, i.e., one that everyone will eat with gusto. So, once in a while, on those now rare occasions when the kids are home and there's a group to feed, I'm willing to make it even if it *is* sort of a pain in the ass. The trick is, I make enough so that I have leftovers to serve two days later and then it's two meals for the aggravation of one.

If you are having a day when the idea of chopping a leek is beyond the pale (I've been there), you can skip right on over to the next recipe, which is for Lazy-Ass Minestrone. Whether you go with Pain or Lazy, I suggest serving the soup with quesadillas (see page 28).

✳ MAKES ABOUT 12 LUNCHTIME SERVINGS

2 tablespoons unsalted butter

2 tablespoons olive oil

1 medium onion, chopped

2 leeks (white parts only),
    well rinsed and finely chopped

2 cloves garlic, minced

½ teaspoon dried basil

½ teaspoon dried oregano

½ teaspoon dried thyme

Salt and freshly ground black pepper

½ head green cabbage, shredded

2 large carrots, peeled and diced

2 ribs celery, diced

1 medium potato (any kind),
    peeled and cut into ¾-inch dice

1 parsnip, peeled and diced

2 quarts low-sodium chicken broth
    (see Note)

1 can (14 ounces) diced tomatoes,
    with their juices

½ cup frozen petite peas

½ cup frozen corn kernels (or fresh
    if it's summer and you're not too
    crabby to scrape a cob)

1 can (15 ounces) small white beans or
    pinto beans, drained and rinsed

1 cup freshly grated Parmigiano-
    Reggiano cheese

1. Melt the butter in the oil in a large soup pot over low heat. Add the onion and leeks and cook, stirring occasionally, until the vegetables are soft and translucent, about 15 minutes.

2. Add the garlic, herbs, ½ teaspoon salt, and pepper to taste. Cook for 1 minute.

3. Raise the heat to medium-low and add the cabbage. Cook, stirring once or twice, for about 5 minutes.

4. Add the carrots and cook, stirring once or twice, for about 2 minutes. Repeat this with the celery, potato, and parsnip, in that order, adding one vegetable at a time and cooking each for 2 minutes or so.

5. Add the chicken broth and tomatoes. Raise the heat to medium and bring the soup to a simmer. Then return the heat to low, cover the pot, and simmer it for about 1 hour.

6. Add the peas, corn, and beans and cook for 15 minutes. (Are you crabby yet?)

7. Taste, and add more salt and pepper if needed. Serve hot, passing the cheese separately.

VARIATIONS If you're not too crabby already, you can add or substitute any vegetables for those listed, like green beans, broccoli, a turnip, rutabaga—anything your family will tolerate (or not notice). Also, at the end of cooking you can throw in a handful of diced cooked chicken or meat. You can also put a scoop of cooked rice or pasta at the bottom of each diner's bowl and pour the soup over it.

NOTE If I'm too lazy to make homemade, I like to use Imagine Organic Free Range Chicken Broth, which is available at most Whole Foods stores.

Lazy-Ass Minestrone

WHEN YOU DON'T HAVE THE TIME (or the inclination) to make Pain-in-the-Ass Minestrone, try this easier version. Like its more challenging cousin, it's a one-dish meal, but it has way fewer ingredients. ✳ SERVES 4 TO 6

3 tablespoons olive oil

1 cup chopped onion

2 tablespoons tomato paste

1 cup canned crushed San Marzano tomatoes

4 cups canned low-sodium chicken broth

1 can (15 ounces) small white beans or white kidney beans, drained and rinsed

About 5 ounces spaghetti, broken into 1-inch pieces

1 medium zucchini, diced

2 tablespoons basil pesto (store-bought is fine)

Salt and freshly ground black pepper, to taste (optional)

1 cup freshly grated Parmigiano-Reggiano cheese

1. Heat the oil in a large, heavy-bottomed soup pot over medium-low heat. Add the onion and cook until soft and translucent, about 10 minutes. Add the tomato paste and cook until the oil and tomato start to separate, about 2 minutes. Then stir in the crushed tomatoes and cook until the tomatoes are slightly reduced and the flavors blended, 3 minutes.

2. Stir in the broth, raise the heat slightly, and bring the soup to a simmer. Add the beans and spaghetti and cook for about 5 minutes. Add the zucchini and cook until the spaghetti is tender, about 5 minutes more.

3. Remove the pot from the heat and let the soup sit, covered, for 5 minutes. (The pasta will swell as the soup sits.)

4. Stir in the pesto. Taste the soup and add salt and pepper, if needed. Serve the soup with the grated cheese sprinkled on top.

VARIATIONS You can add other vegetables if you like: chopped broccoli or cauliflower, peas or carrots, whatever you have on hand. You can also vary the pasta.

If you don't have any pesto, add a teaspoon of dried basil to the crushed tomatoes at the end of Step 1. If you don't have dried basil, fuhgedabodit.

Full-of-Beans Quesadillas

QUESADILLAS ARE SUCH A STAPLE of our diet in Southern California, it's hard to believe I'd never heard of them in my childhood. We didn't know from tortillas, for that matter, or salsa, or guacamole, or refried beans. I think my parents once took us to a Mexican restaurant, where I was confused by the chicken mole. (Chocolate on chicken? Eeeew. A waste of perfectly good chocolate!)

A great thing to cook for picky people (you can vary the ingredients while you cook), quesadillas are an excellent accompaniment to minestrone. ✳ SERVES 4

¼ cup vegetable oil

1 cup chopped red onion

1 jalapeño pepper, seeded and finely chopped (optional)

1 clove garlic, minced

½ teaspoon chili powder

½ teaspoon salt

¼ teaspoon freshly ground black pepper

1 cup canned black beans, drained and rinsed

4 flour tortillas (8-inch size)

2 plum tomatoes, seeded and chopped

4 sprigs fresh cilantro (optional)

1⅓ cups grated Monterey Jack cheese

1. Preheat the oven to 200°F.

2. Heat 2 tablespoons of the oil in a 10-inch nonstick skillet over medium-low heat. Add the onion and the jalapeño, and cook until they are soft, about 5 minutes. Add the garlic, chili powder, salt, and pepper, and cook for 1 minute more. Add the beans and stir. Cook for about 1 minute, crushing some of the beans lightly with the back of your spoon. Transfer the bean mixture to a bowl and set it aside.

3. To assemble a quesadilla, lay a tortilla on a flat surface and spread about ⅓ cup of the bean filling over half of the tortilla. Add 1 or 2 tablespoons of the chopped tomato, and a sprig of cilantro if you like. Top that with ⅓ cup of the cheese, and fold the tortilla in half. Repeat this with the other tortillas, forming 4 quesadillas.

4. Brush the tops of 2 quesadillas lightly with some of the remaining oil, and place them in a clean skillet, oiled side down, over medium heat. While they cook, brush the tops with oil. Cook the quesadillas until the cheese starts to melt, 3 to 4 minutes. Flip them over and continue cooking until the other side is crisp and golden, 3 to 4 minutes. Place the quesadillas on a baking sheet, cover them with aluminum foil, and keep them warm in the oven while you cook two more.

5. Cut the quesadillas in half and serve them hot.

VARIATIONS Serve the quesadillas with fresh salsa and/or guacamole. Or if you're feeling beanophobic, omit the bean mixture and try making quesadillas French style, just using Gruyère cheese and ham, or go Italian, using mozzarella, tomato, and a little pesto.

Creamy Dreamy Vegetable Soup

I KNOW THERE IS A SCHOOL OF COOKING these days that's all about hiding vegetables in things so you can sneak up on your kids, nutritionally speaking. But I feel the way my mother does: children should get to know and befriend their vegetables. Otherwise, they'll be at a dinner party when they're thirty and they'll refuse to eat their peas and become socially extinct. Mom and I also reject the sneaky approach because the recipes often involve advance pureeing and other tasks that we find too annoying to perform.

With that said, we would both admit to concealing a veggie or two sometimes, if it's for the greater good, which is to say it makes our cooking lives easier. With this recipe, for example, you can collect all the neglected vegetables in your fridge and throw them in, thereby cleaning house and feeding your family in one swoop.

Serve it with bruschetta (see facing page) and you're done.

✳ SERVES 6 TO 8

¼ cup mascarpone cheese

2 tablespoons fresh lemon juice

4 tablespoons finely chopped fresh dill

3 tablespoons unsalted butter

1 onion, chopped

1 bay leaf

1 pound Yukon Gold potatoes, peeled and cut into 1-inch chunks

4 to 5 cups chopped mixed vegetables (I like equal parts cauliflower, broccoli, carrots, and celery)

5 to 6 cups low-sodium chicken broth

Salt and freshly ground black pepper, to taste

1. Mix the mascarpone cheese, 1 tablespoon of the lemon juice, and 1 tablespoon of the dill together in a bowl, and set it aside.

2. Melt the butter in a soup pot over medium-low heat. Add the onion and the bay leaf, and cook until the onion is soft and translucent, about 10 minutes.

3. Add the potatoes and cook them, stirring once or twice, for 2 minutes. Add the remaining vegetables and cook, stirring, for another 2 minutes.

4. Add 5 cups of the chicken broth, bring the soup to a simmer, and cook, covered, until the veggies are tender, about 15 minutes. Remove and discard the bay leaf.

5. Transfer the soup, in batches, to a food processor, and puree it. Then return it to the soup pot. Stir in the remaining 3 tablespoons dill and 1 tablespoon lemon juice, and heat the soup to a simmer, adding more broth if it needs thinning.

6. Taste, and add salt and pepper as needed. Serve the soup with a tablespoon of the mascarpone mixture on top of each bowlful.

Bruschetta with Somebody-Else's-Garden Tomatoes

WHEN I WAS PREGNANT with our first child and in a fit of domesticity, I decided to create a vegetable garden. Wise enough to recall the many projects I'd begun and quickly abandoned, I started small: I bought a tomato plant.

I'm not known for my green thumb; many plants have perished on my watch. But I had visions of feeding my child organic tomato sauce, and of making Tom's favorite thing, bruschetta, dripping with the chopped, perfectly red fruit of my soon-to-be robust plant. I watered, nourished, and generally cared for the thing as if it were the child I was expecting (*sans* diapers).

Sadly, the tomato plant seemed to shrink rather than prosper. So, I began talking to it. In my research on tomato care, I'd read about a study in which twenty men and women spoke to tomato plants to make them grow. After some time, the plants addressed by women grew beyond expectations while, interestingly, the men's plants grew less than normal.

I told Tom not to speak to my tomato. Aside from the study's claim that the timbre of the male voice is not tomato-friendly, I suspect it's also that men favor inappropriate topics of conversation. I mean, who doesn't wilt when forced to hear about the Lakers' winning streak or the benefits of owning a '65 Mustang?

Anyway, after the plant and I had a couple of chats about the weather and butterflies, it dropped dead (of boredom, maybe) and with it died my interest in making a vegetable garden. I moved on: I took up yoga (for a couple of weeks) and resumed buying tomatoes at the farmers' market.

Now I live in a house that has two orange trees in the backyard. I'm very grateful to my little orchard because the trees bear fabulous fruit even though (or maybe because) I do not engage them in conversation, or even pay much attention to them at all. ✳ SERVES 4

4 plum tomatoes, seeded and diced
2 tablespoons chopped fresh basil
3 tablespoons olive oil
2 cloves garlic
¼ teaspoon kosher salt
Freshly ground black pepper, to taste
4 slices good-quality country-style
    white bread

1. Preheat the broiler.

2. Mix the tomatoes, basil, and 1 tablespoon of the oil together in a bowl. Mince one of the garlic cloves and add it to the tomatoes. Season the tomato mixture with the salt and pepper, toss gently, and set it aside.

3. Cut the other garlic clove in half.

4. Place the bread slices on a baking sheet and brush them lightly on both sides with the remaining 2 tablespoons olive oil. Place the baking sheet under the broiler and toast the bread until it is lightly browned on both sides, about 1 minute per side.

5. Rub each side of the toast with the cut garlic and serve, spooning some of the tomato mixture on top of each slice.

Slammin' Yam Soup

AS I AM WRITING THIS, Sarah Palin is taking a lot of heat for writing those cue notes on her hand before speaking at a Tea Party convention. But as an avid palm writer myself, I totally get where she's coming from. I mean, when you're circling the age of fifty, who can remember anything without a little support?

In family discussions, I find it very useful to have a few notes handy (if you'll pardon the excellent pun). Like, the other night, when Tom discovered the Manolo shoebox and we had a lively debate about whether a woman really needs to own five different styles of black pumps, I was really glad I'd jotted down a few talking points on my hand before things heated up.

And when my daughter brought the Honda home with a very impressive scrape across two doors, I was pleased in the ensuing exchange that I'd had the foresight to jot down some notes on the cost of scrape repair and the wisdom of driving carefully. I felt I was able to put a sizable dent (haha!) in her defense ("the *stupid* post just appeared out of *nowhere!*"), and I felt good about that even after I paid the $1,800.

I also use palm jots as a nifty reminder system when I am multitasking at home. If I leave my office to go to the bedroom, say, to get my backscratcher, I make a note on my palm as to why I am going to the bedroom; otherwise, when I arrive there, I will often have forgotten what my mission was and I will have to return to my office and wait until that information resurfaces. Or if I make a phone call, I will write down the name of the person I'm calling before I dial, so when they answer, I will not need to ask them who they are.

Palm writing is, however, not always reliable. Knowing I would otherwise forget it, I wrote on my hand a recipe that I found in a magazine at the dentist's office. The office has an intimidating sign up, forbidding the ripping of pages from magazines, but I had no scratch paper and I really wanted this easy recipe for yam soup. I went home and, forgetting the precious information I had on my hand, washed my hair, thereby obliterating it. (The recipe, not the hair.) So, while writing on your hand is a great tool for remembering what you don't want to forget, you can't forget that you are trying to remember something, or else you'll wash your hair and screw everything up.

Anyway, I figured out my own yam soup recipe. Whether it's as good as the one in the magazine, I will never know, but I think it's slammin'. ✳ SERVES 4 TO 6

2 tablespoons unsalted butter

1 tablespoon olive oil

1 medium onion, chopped

2 cloves garlic, minced

1 teaspoon curry powder, or to taste

1 teaspoon salt

¼ teaspoon freshly ground black pepper

3 yams or sweet potatoes (about 2 pounds), peeled and cut into 1-inch chunks

1 quart low-sodium chicken broth

Snipped fresh chives, for garnish (optional)

1. Melt the butter in the oil in a large soup pot over low heat. Add the chopped onion and cook until it is soft and translucent, 10 to 15 minutes. Add the garlic, curry powder, salt, and pepper and cook for 1 minute more.

2. Add the yams and broth to the soup pot and bring the mixture to a simmer. Cook until the yams are soft, about 10 minutes.

3. Transfer the soup, in batches, to a food processor, and puree it. Return the soup to the pot and bring it to a simmer.

4. Serve hot, with a sprinkling of chives on each serving, if desired.

VARIATIONS If you're feeling a little more ambitious than usual, whip some heavy cream and put a dollop on each serving; then sprinkle the chives on top of the whipped cream.

Turkberry Sandwich

WHEN I'M MAKING PESTO for pasta, I occasionally (okay, rarely) have the culinary foresight to put aside a little extra to use for other random things like pesto mayonnaise, which is great on this sandwich. If you didn't put aside any pesto the last time you made it, don't kick yourself. Or, go ahead, kick yourself, but you can also just go buy some pesto at the market. Or you can kick your husband and tell him to go buy it. Or you can just chop up some fresh basil and add it to the mayo with a little lemon juice.

Or, if the whole exercise makes you too crabby, you can throw in the towel and tell your husband to make his own damn sandwich while you go get your nails done. ✳ SERVES 2

½ cup mayonnaise

2 tablespoons basil pesto, homemade (page 108) or store-bought

4 slices sourdough bread

8 ounces sliced turkey

¼ cup dried sweetened cranberries

2 leaves butter lettuce

1. Mix the mayonnaise and pesto together in a small bowl.

2. Spread the pesto mayo over one side of all 4 slices of bread. Divide the turkey between 2 mayo-covered slices, and sprinkle the dried cranberries over the turkey. Cover the turkey with the lettuce, and top with the other slices of bread. Cut the sandwiches in half and offer one to your husband, partner, child, or dog.

Tom's Tomato Soup

IN ADDITION TO THOSE TASTY cream cheese and olive sandwiches (see page 24), Bette taught her son Tom how to cook two other things: grilled burgers and tuna melts. He makes grilled burgers once a summer. He made tuna melts once, in 1996.

Occasionally Tom tries to step outside his comfort zone and make something he has not made before. One day, not so long ago, I was thrilled when he volunteered to make soup. Campbell's tomato soup.

After consulting me on whether to make the soup with milk or water, Tom required instructions on how to light the stove. (He had not used that appliance since the tuna melt of '96.) He also needed a walking tour of the utensil drawer, whose contents had been reinvented since his last visit, and a briefing on which was the appropriate pot for his project.

Once I'd adjusted the flame under the soup (men like high heat— is this an atavistic, caveman thing?), found Tom some soup bowls and spoons, wiped up some floor drippage, and pointed out the location of the fire extinguisher, I was free to retire to my office while Tom finished his cooking task.

If you have a husband or partner who is a cooking novice and they volunteer to make Campbell's tomato soup, I suggest you politely decline and then *you* make this homemade version. It obviously has more ingredients, but believe me, it'll be much less time-consuming.

✳ SERVES 8 TO 10

For the soup

   4 tablespoons (½ stick) unsalted butter
   1 onion, chopped
   2 cloves garlic, minced
   2 carrots, peeled and finely chopped
   1 rib celery, finely chopped
   ¼ cup finely chopped fresh basil
   1 bay leaf
   2 cans (28 ounces each) Italian plum
      tomatoes, with their juices
   2 cups low-sodium chicken broth
      (or more if you like a thinner soup)
   Salt and freshly ground black pepper
   ½ cup ricotta cheese

For the basil cream (optional)

   ½ cup ricotta cheese
   ¼ cup heavy (whipping) cream
   ¼ cup chopped fresh basil
   1 teaspoon grated lemon zest
   1 teaspoon fresh lemon juice

1. Melt the butter in a soup pot over low heat. Add the onion and cook until it is translucent and soft, about 10 minutes. Add the garlic, carrots, celery, basil, and bay leaf, and cook for about 5 minutes more.

2. Coarsely chop the tomatoes and add them to the pot, along with their juices. Add the broth, ½ teaspoon salt, and ¼ teaspoon pepper and bring the soup to a simmer. Cook, covered, until the vegetables are very soft, about 20 minutes. Remove and discard the bay leaf.

3. Transfer the soup, in batches, to a blender or food processor, and puree it. As it is pureed, pour each batch into a large bowl. When you get to the last batch in the blender, add the ricotta and blend until the mixture is very smooth. Stir that batch thoroughly into the rest of the soup. Taste the soup, and add more salt and pepper if desired. Transfer the soup back to the pot and reheat it over low heat.

4. If you are making the basil cream, combine all the ingredients in a food processor and pulse a few times, until they are well blended. (You can also just mix them by hand.)

5. Serve the soup hot, with or without a tablespoon of basil cream floating on top of each serving.

Tuna Kahuna Panini

"**WHY DO YOU BUY THINGS** for yourself right before Mother's Day?" My daughter Nora was pissed off last May when I bragged that I had just bought a panini maker, exactly what she'd planned to get me as a gift for my favorite holiday.

If I were to give *my* mother a panini maker, she'd laugh at its pretentious title. She used to have something just like it, back in the '50s, but it was just called, uh, I don't know what. It was made by Sunbeam or Hotpoint or somebody, and it performed the same function as its modern counterpart. It grilled cheese sandwiches—so many that its surfaces turned black from use. This century's foodies have just changed the name of Mom's whatchamacallit to suit our fancy-pants era.

Actually, I rarely buy small appliances. I have limited counter space (and limited patience) for cappuccino machines and waffle irons. When things like that enter my house, they usually make their way to the garage in short order, where they cure for a couple of years before heading down to the Goodwill. (I currently have not one, but two ice cream makers in the garage, biding their time until they upgrade their lodgings.)

But I'm determined that my panini maker will avoid consignment to the land of dust and spiders. Like Mom with her whatchamacallit, I have been putting it to good use. Since I sucked the air out of Nora's gift idea, I have made it up to her by showering her with panini whenever she's home from college.

The next time Mother's Day rolls around, I will ask Nora for the gift that *really* keeps on giving: TiVo lessons.

This tuna panini bears a striking resemblance to that tuna melt

Tom made back in the '90s. Now that the panini maker makes it so easy to prepare, maybe he'll make another one sometime before this decade is done. ✳ SERVES 2

1 large can (12 ounces) solid white tuna packed in water
⅓ cup mayonnaise
1 loaf ciabatta bread, 12 to 15 inches long
4 ounces Jarlsberg cheese, sliced
2 cups packaged "spring mix" lettuce, baby romaine, or arugula
1 avocado, pitted, peeled, and cut into thin slices
1 tomato, seeded and thinly sliced
2 tablespoons olive oil

1. Drain the tuna well and place it in a bowl. Add the mayonnaise, and using a fork, mix until the tuna and mayo are well combined.

2. Cut the bread in half crosswise. Split one of the halves horizontally, and scoop out a little of the bread to make room for the filling. Place half of the cheese slices on the cut sides of the bread. Spread half of the tuna over the cheese on one side, and 1 cup of the lettuce leaves on the other side. Add some avocado and tomato (as much as you like), and press the sides together to make a large sandwich. Repeat with the other piece of ciabatta.

3. Heat your panini grill, and brush 1 tablespoon of the oil over the bottom and top of one of the sandwiches. Place the sandwich on the grill, close the top, and grill until the sandwich is nicely browned and the cheese is melted, 6 to 7 minutes.Repeat with the remaining sandwich. Cut the sandwiches in half, and serve hot.

NOTE If you do not own a panini maker, do what I did for years: Place the sandwich in a lightly oiled skillet and set a heavy pan on top to compress it. When the sandwich is golden and melty, flip it and repeat on the other side.

VARIATIONS Dress up the tuna any way you like: add pepper, lemon juice, chopped onion or celery, herbs—whatever. My husband likes it straight up, so that makes it easy for me, if a tad boring.

St. Patrick's Day Soup

IN CHICAGO WHEN I WAS GROWING UP, St. Patrick's Day was always pretty lively. They'd dye the river green, and there'd be fun parades and people barfing in the gutter. Here in Los Angeles, March 17th is almost as much a non-event as Groundhog Day.

But when my children were in elementary school, the holiday did not go unacknowledged in our house. This was because if I forgot to wear green on the day (which I invariably did), they would pinch me mercilessly because they were taught at school that pinching is what leprechauns do to punish forgetful people. (That killer tuition was worth every penny.)

This year, I have resolved to be more on top of things when St. P.'s Day rolls around. The night before, I will sleep in my green Beatles T-shirt so I won't forget to put it on in the morning. I will also make green soup so I can even be green internally, further protecting myself. If Nora and Elizabeth have not lost interest in promoting leprechaun traditions, they will be pinching their college pals, not me. But if a leprechaun shows up at my house, I'll be *so* ready.

If you, too, are interested in pinch protection, try this delicious recipe, and serve it with a most appropriate Saint Patrick's Day treat: the beer bread on the facing page. ✳ SERVES 4 TO 6

2 tablespoons unsalted butter

2 leeks (white part only), well rinsed and chopped

½ teaspoon salt

¼ teaspoon freshly ground black pepper

1 medium Yukon Gold potato, peeled and cut into 1-inch chunks

1 package (16 ounces) frozen petite peas

2 tablespoons chopped fresh tarragon

4 cups low-sodium chicken broth

¼ cup heavy (whipping) cream (optional)

1. Melt the butter in a soup pot over medium-low heat. Add the leeks, salt, and pepper, and cook until the leeks begin to soften, about 5 minutes.

2. Add the potato and cook, stirring, for 2 minutes. Then stir in the peas and the tarragon, and pour in the broth. Bring the soup to a simmer.

Reduce the heat to low and cook until the vegetables are tender, 10 to 15 minutes.

3. Transfer the soup, in batches, to a food processor, and puree it. Then return it to the pot and add the cream if you are using it. Return the soup to a simmer and serve it hot.

Kneadless Beer Bread

NEITHER TOM NOR I grew up eating home-baked bread. With so many kids, it was out of the question for both Mom and Bette. Although there are only two of them, my children are similarly deprived. I, and others like me who are honing our cooking avoidance skills, seldom (okay, never) bake bread. Why bother when there's a market nearby that sells fresh baguettes every day?

Who kneads it? Not I. Way too much trouble.

Okay, so maybe I would get Michelle Obama arms if I were willing to knead bread dough. That, I have to say, is a strong motivator, but apparently not strong enough: you don't see me rushing to the market to buy yeast.

But when someone told me about this unyeasted bread, I made notes. In this recipe there's no kneading, and the resulting loaf is dilly and beery, great with soup, and makes your house smell good.

✳ SERVES 6 TO 8

3 cups all-purpose flour

¼ cup chopped fresh dill

2 tablespoons baking powder

1 teaspoon salt

1 bottle (12 ounces) beer, at room temperature

4 tablespoons (½ stick) unsalted butter, melted, plus extra for the pan

1. Preheat the oven to 375°F. Generously butter a loaf pan and set it aside.

2. Mix the flour, dill, baking powder, and salt together in a large bowl. Pour in the beer and mix until everything is just combined.

3. Pour the dough into the prepared loaf pan. Drizzle the melted butter over the top of the dough, and bake until a knife stuck in the middle comes out clean, 35 to 40 minutes.

4. Turn the bread out onto a wire rack and let it rest for 5 minutes before serving. (It's best served warm or toasted.)

Picky Man's Gazpacho

MY HUSBAND LOVES TOMATOES. Raw tomatoes, that is. He will not eat them cooked. (It's the same with carrots. He loves 'em raw, hates 'em cooked.) His sister Julie, on the other hand, not only dislikes raw tomatoes, she finds them repulsive. She will not eat anything with seeds—even if they've been removed—including olives (which meant she was a child deprived of Bette's cream cheese and olive sandwiches). A pomegranate would give her a nervous breakdown.

Tom's other sister, Ellen, won't eat spaghetti sauce, hamburgers, meat loaf, cheese of any kind, jelly (hello?), peas, or lima beans. Like her father and Tom, she also dislikes onions and garlic, and, à la Julie, ix-nay the tomatoes and olives.

It's just another example of how kids are genetically designed to drive their parental menu-planners crazy.

Luckily for Bette, she also had a son named Johnny, who is an omnivore. I have never seen nor heard of Johnny saying no to a food. But, for that matter, Johnny is just not a "no" kind of guy: he's a "yes" kind, in every respect. Ask him if he will share his oysters: he will say yes. Ask him if he will change your tire while you check your Facebook page and he will say yes. Ask him if he'd like to ski down a slope clearly marked with a skull and crossbones and he will say yes, and he'll go first. A man on TV asked Johnny to buy an Ab-O-Ciser and he said yes. (His wife had issues with that one.)

So maybe it follows that, with his level of positivity, he'd eat anything that's set before him.

Due to the high level of pickiness in her family, when Bette started making gazpacho, she and Johnny were the only takers. Now I've invented a version that leaves out some of the ingredients that offended Tom (onions and red peppers). Julie and Ellen remain hopeless, with their hostility toward tomatoes, but at least now, when I ask, "Want some gazpacho?" it's not just Johnny who says, "Yes."

If Johnny were coming over for dinner, I'd serve this gazpacho with smoked salmon sandwiches (see page 44), although he and I would be the only ones eating them. Tom and the kids still place smoked salmon in the gefilte fish category. Maybe one day that will change, but meanwhile, all the more for me (and Johnny).

✳ SERVES 4 TO 6

2 pounds heirloom tomatoes (about 4 large tomatoes), coarsely chopped

1 hothouse (English) cucumber, halved and coarsely chopped

¼ cup olive oil

2 tablespoons red wine vinegar

4 cloves garlic, minced

½ teaspoon kosher salt

¼ teaspoon freshly ground black pepper

2 tablespoons chopped fresh parsley

2 tablespoons chopped fresh basil

1. Place the tomatoes in a food processor and pulse a few times until they are finely chopped. Transfer them to a large bowl. Place the cucumber in the processor and pulse until it is finely chopped; add it to the tomatoes in the bowl.

2. Add the olive oil, vinegar, garlic, salt, pepper, parsley, and basil to the tomato mixture and stir to combine everything well. Refrigerate the gazpacho for at least 1 hour, or overnight, before serving.

Smokin' Salmon Samwich

SMOKED SALMON IS ONE OF THOSE THINGS nobody ever told me about until I was grown up. I mean, I guess I heard about it, but it was food beyond my reach. It never appeared in our kitchen; in small-town Illinois, it seemed exotic.

Other things I didn't see much of included calves' liver and veal kidneys, but when I tasted them for the first time, I knew it would be the last. I had quite a different reaction to silky, seductive smoked salmon.

I've never been able to convince my children of the virtues of smoked salmon: they have thus far refused to taste it. If you have a more open-minded group at your house, try this sandwich—it's pretty great. ✳ SERVES 4

1 cup crème fraîche

1 tablespoon finely chopped fresh
     parsley

1 tablespoon finely chopped fresh dill

1 tablespoon fresh lemon juice,
     or to taste

Salt and freshly ground black pepper,
     to taste

8 slices dark pumpernickel or
     whole wheat bread

8 ounces smoked salmon, thinly sliced

2 plum tomatoes, seeded and diced

Red-leaf or other lettuce, or arugula

1. Mix the crème fraîche, parsley, dill, lemon juice, and salt and pepper in a bowl.

2. Smear one side of a slice of bread with some of the crème fraîche mixture. Cover it with about 2 ounces of the salmon, then a sprinkling of tomato, and then a lettuce leaf. Smear another slice of bread with the crème fraîche and put it on top to make a sandwich. Make 3 more sandwiches this way, cut them in half, and serve.

SCOTT AND THE PUPIK

CHICKEN NOODLE SOUP is the mother of all soups. On anybody's list of comfort foods, it's number one. Well, except Scott's.

My brother-in-law Scott finds chicken soup disgusting and a little scary. He has his reasons: it's because of the pupik, which his mother Gilda used to add to her homemade version.

Some people spell it *pupick,* but in any case it's a Yiddish word, the definition of which varies depending on whom you ask. Some say that it's the gizzards and other odd-looking bits that you find in or attached to a roaster chicken. Others say it is the chicken's navel. But Scott's friend Nancy told him that the pupik is the poor bird's testicles. As Nancy recently reiterated: "Some chickens are roosters. All roosters (as opposed to capons) have testicles. Therefore, some chickens have testicles."

Whether or not Nancy's logic is sound, when it was soup time at Scott's house and Gilda asked, "DO YOU WANT THE PUPIK, SCOTTY?" (Scott says Gilda speaks in capital letters), it was understandable that her son answered in the negative, adding a few gagging sounds for emphasis. But Gilda was stubborn. She'd re-ask five minutes later, her ladle teeming with steaming chicken's balls: "DO YOU WANT THE PUPIK, SCOTTY?" Scott would re-decline with increasing irritation, only to be met with the question several more times, until, by meal's end, he was speed-dialing his therapist.

Okay, so maybe chicken soup gives Scott the *schpilkes,* but he's an anomaly. For most of us, it's quite the opposite.

Liza's Sort-of-Homemade Chicken Soup

I REMEMBER ONCE, when I was five or six, faking a cough so I could stay home from school. I presented Mom with my Camille impression and she bought it, so I got back into my bed and waited for her soup delivery. In retrospect, I know this was not so much an act of school avoidance as one of stealing a few hours of quiet face time with my mother, over a bowl of chicken soup.

My daughter Elizabeth has been known to commit the same fakery. Sometimes she'd have a cold or a challenging moment, but occasionally it was just a random need for time with Mom. Elizabeth would turn to me with a doleful look and moo, "Soooooouuuuuup." My heartstrings would go *zing* and I'd be happy to oblige. Even crabby cooks know that the pleasure derived from comforting a child far outweighs the inconvenience of making soup.

The trouble is, we crabby cooks are unlikely to have vats of homemade chicken broth in the freezer, ready for emergency soup. In general, we seldom make food that is intended for future use; we cook on an as-needed basis, as in, it's 5:30 and we need to make dinner. So whipping up chicken noodle soup on the spur of the moment usually means canned broth, doctored to appear homemade.

Recently I have actually taken a step toward being broth-ready. I throw the remains of roast chickens in the freezer, where they reside until I haul them out to make broth. I admit, sometimes this takes a while. I currently have two chicken carcasses staring at me every time I open the freezer.

When I do get around to making broth, I just throw the carcass in a soup pot, add an onion studded with a few cloves, a few sprigs of parsley, a chopped carrot, a chopped celery rib, a bay leaf, a sprig of thyme, a parsnip if I have one, and 2 quarts of water. I bring it all to a simmer and cook till it's reduced by half. That's it.

You will note that I omit the pupik. (If you are asking yourself what a pupik is, then you either skipped—shame on you!—or have already forgotten the explanation on page 45.) ✳ SERVES 4 TO 6

3 tablespoons olive oil

½ onion, chopped

1 rib celery, diced

1 carrot, peeled and diced

1 quart low-sodium chicken broth (homemade if possible)

8 ounces linguine, broken into 2-inch pieces

1 to 2 cups chopped cooked chicken (1-inch pieces)

2 tablespoons finely chopped fresh parsley

2 tablespoons finely chopped fresh dill

1. Heat the olive oil in a soup pot over medium-low heat. Add the onion and cook until it's soft and translucent, about 10 minutes. Stir in the celery and the carrot, and cook for 2 minutes more.

2. Add the chicken broth, raise the heat to medium, and bring the soup to a simmer. Add the pasta and cook until it is tender, about 10 minutes.

3. Add the chicken and cook just until it's heated through, about 2 minutes. Stir in the parsley and dill, and serve the soup nice and hot.

A POSTSCRIPT

EVEN NOW, IF SHE'S HAVING A BAD DAY, Elizabeth sometimes phones me with a plaintive, "Soooooouuuuup!" I have the same response as always, that *zing* in my heart and a desire to care for her. It's tough, however, since she is two thousand miles away. I send her a care package of Cup-a-Noodles and Double Chocolate Milanos, but it seems like a weak substitute for cozy bedside caretaking.

But Elizabeth's calls are becoming less frequent. My daughter is a junior in college; she has found new, nonparental sources of comfort. It's a good thing that she's self-sufficient, but I can't say I don't miss being the soup deliverer. When I walk past her and her sister's empty rooms in the course of the day, I remember the times I'd prop them up in bed with a tray. *(Zing.)* It occurs to me how things have turned around: now I'm the one who could use a little face time.

Tom comes home from work and he, too, looks down their quiet hallway and sighs. Then we go into the kitchen for a little comforting chicken soup.

THREE

The Cycle of Seven

(Burgers, Casseroles, and Other Regulars)

F OR MANY YEARS, my mother cooked for eight people every night. We never went out for dinner, except for that time when we moved houses and the pots and pans were in boxes, so Mom got a night off. (If I were she, I'd have moved more often.)

Take-out food was not plentiful in our neighborhood either. None of the interesting purveyors of flavorful food chose to set up business in our small Illinois town. (Think about it: life without takeout. OMG.) I never got acquainted with Chinese food or pizza till I went to college.

To simplify her life, my mother established a cycle of seven basic meals. The cycle was meat-heavy, light on chicken and fish. Although I remember an occasional pork chop, meat in smaller units was served infrequently; a big old roast was the preferred format.

We'd start out the week with roast lamb, which would be recycled into a lamb-a-rama (lamb casserole) later in the week. I hated the lamb-a-rama, but one advantage of those large family dinners was that if you didn't care for your entree, the chaos provided ample cover for surreptitious food disposal.

Tuesdays we had my favorite: spaghetti and meat sauce, made with ground beef, a can each of tomato sauce and tomato paste, and a handful of grated cheddar. Nobody didn't like it.

In one obsessive phase of my cooking life, I developed a meat sauce recipe that I thought would be tastier and healthier, made with turkey, finely chopped vegetables, wine, milk, and tomatoes. It took hours to cook.

This folly was short-lived. In those days, when I asked the children if they were hungry, they'd respond by asking me what was for dinner, implying that they might be hungry if the menu spoke to them—or not if it didn't. When I told them it was pasta and meat sauce, their eyes would brighten, they'd push their math books aside, and they'd move to the next level of questioning: Was it their grandmother's sauce or my healthy kind? If I answered that it was Nanni's, they'd rocket to the dinner table. If it was mine, they'd sigh and turn back to the algebra.

So I ditched my fancy-pants meat sauce and made Mom's whenever meat sauce was called for (until recent years, when the kids left home and Tom and I noticed our cholesterol rising).

Other items in Mom's cycle of seven included burgers, another roast (usually pork or pot roast), some kind of chicken, and often something fishy on Friday, like tuna casserole or fish sticks, in honor of a certain Christian tradition of eating fish on that day.

On Sundays, Mom was exhausted, spent. That was the day she

served Campbell's vegetable soup and honey toast (whole wheat bread smeared with butter and honey and broiled till toasty). This was the cycle's only nod to vegetarianism. "Health food" was not a popular concept yet. Tofu was unheard of in Illinois circa 1960, and even yogurt was eaten only by suspicious people. I knew a perfectly nice lady named Mrs. Greeley who was the subject of gossip because she ate something called wheat germ.

When I grew up and became a crabby cook, I would sometimes fall to my knees (in my mind, anyway) in gratitude when I recalled how much time my mother spent cooking for me, a service that, sadly, will never come my way again.

This chapter contains recipes for my own family's cycle of favorite entrees. The list started out short, in the days when the girls ate only white food. But over the years I was able to add an herb or a spice, an odd vegetable or some ground turkey, so by the time the kids left home, my cycle had expanded a lot.

Tom's Burgers

ONE THING TOM DOES VERY WELL is grill burgers. In spite of his vast ignorance about food preparation, he has an unerring instinct for when a burger reaches that perfect point of doneness. So, once or twice a summer, usually when we're vacationing on Cape Cod with his extended family, Tom takes over. He arranges his nicely shaped patties on the grill and hovers over them like a scientist observing the nuances of changes in beef when subjected to heat. He's focused, intent, and confident, and when he's done he presents his platter of plenty with smoke in his hair and a triumphant smile.

While I love Tom's burgers, when I'm doing burger duty, I like to spice things up a little, adding some chili salt and fresh tomato salsa.

✳ SERVES 4

For the tomato salsa

1 pound good and ripe plum tomatoes

1 jalapeño pepper

2 tablespoons finely chopped sweet onion, or more, if you like

1 clove garlic, minced

¼ cup finely chopped fresh cilantro

1 tablespoon fresh lime juice

Kosher salt and freshly ground black pepper, to taste

For the burgers

1½ pounds ground chuck (about 15% fat content)

2 teaspoons coarse salt

2 teaspoons chili powder

1 teaspoon ground cumin

1 teaspoon sweet paprika

½ teaspoon freshly ground black pepper

¼ teaspoon cayenne pepper

Vegetable oil, for the grill

4 hamburger buns, lightly toasted on the grill

1. Prepare the salsa first: Seed the tomatoes and cut them into ¼-inch dice. Seed and finely chop the jalapeño pepper (you might want to wear rubber gloves for this). Combine the tomatoes, jalapeño, onion, garlic, cilantro, lime juice, and salt and pepper in a bowl and set it aside.

2. Heat your grill to high.

3. While the grill is heating, form the meat into 4 equal patties. In a small bowl, combine the salt, chili powder, cumin, paprika, and the black and cayenne peppers. Sprinkle this chili salt generously on both sides of each patty.

4. Pour some vegetable oil on a paper towel, and using tongs, rub the towel over the grates of the grill to oil them. Place the patties on the grill and cover the grill. Cook the patties for about 4 minutes per side for medium-rare.

5. Serve the burgers on the buns, with the tomato salsa on the side.

AH, MEN

ALTHOUGH IT'S GREAT to have your husband take over the cooking chores once in a while, there is a drawback. When they do cook something that turns out well, many men who are not Iron Chefs expect inordinate amounts of praise. For those of us who cook daily, this can be irritating. My friend Leslie told me that she makes scrambled eggs at least 250 times a year. Her husband made scrambled eggs once recently for their daughter, and as Leslie put it, "he expected a testimonial dinner." My sister-in-law Suzie tells me she'd rather not let her husband cook at all because of the work involved in praising his efforts to his satisfaction. It's easier just to cook the damn dinner herself.

In spite of this, I'm glad when my husband does his grill thing. Although I still have to do the many other tasks involved in putting a meal on the table, I'm relieved of providing the protein centerpiece. And when his family, stunned to see him wielding a spatula, applauds his efforts as if he'd just climbed Everest, it's okay with me. With this kind of encouragement, maybe he'll cook more. (I'm not holding my breath.)

Lamburgers

I AM ALWAYS LOOKING for a new kind of burger, since they make it so easy to put dinner on the table. Here's my latest favorite: You make it out of lamb and throw in a few bouncy flavors and your dining companions will think it's dazzlingly original instead of just a five-minute dinner cop-out. These burgers are excellent with Minty Cuke Salad (page 204), among many other things.

I like this so much that, on the rare occasion when I am alone at dinnertime and not too lazy to cook, I make a lamburger for myself, pop open a Corona, settle back with Oliver, and do some serious cable surfing. ✳ SERVES 4

1 pound ground lamb

¼ cup crumbled feta cheese

2 tablespoons finely chopped oil-packed sun-dried tomatoes

2 tablespoons finely chopped sweet onion

2 tablespoons finely chopped fresh oregano

Salt and freshly ground black pepper, to taste

1 tablespoon olive oil

4 hamburger buns, lightly toasted on the grill, or 4 pita breads, warmed in the oven

1. Combine the lamb, feta, sun-dried tomatoes, onion, and oregano in a bowl, and form the mixture into 4 equal patties. Sprinkle the patties on both sides with salt and pepper.

2. Heat a grill pan or skillet over medium heat. Brush it with the oil and place the patties in the pan. Cook until they are nicely browned and cooked through, about 5 minutes per side.

3. Serve the lamburgers on buns or in pita breads.

Eggplant Burgers

ANOTHER INTERESTING BURGER VARIATION is the eggplant burger, especially if you have a vegetarian showing up for dinner.

Although I love eggplant and have tried (unsuccessfully) to get my family to love it, it has recently come to my attention that there is such a thing as loving eggplant too much.

Get this: A flight from Dubai empties at the Melbourne airport, a man is randomly yanked by the Security folks from the wad of disembarking passengers, and for once, they've picked a winner.

(I myself have been pulled over many times, only to disappoint the friskers with no carry-on item more life-threatening than . . . well, once I was carrying a wrench. Long story.) The guy has, in his suitcase, an eggplant.

Okay, so far, not that interesting. But then they tell the guy to drop his pants, apparently a routine request when you're caught transporting an eggplant. (Thank God they don't have the same rule for people carrying wrenches.) He's wearing black tights under his pants (always a red flag), and they tell him to drop the tights, too. There, wrapped in padded envelopes and strapped to his legs, are two pigeons.

The question that has not yet been publicly answered is, Why does a guy subject himself to a ten-hour plane flight with pigeons strapped to his calves? Isn't air travel punishing enough already? Maybe there's a shortage of pigeons in Australia, so they fetch big bucks. Or maybe this was some kind of fraternity hazing stunt. Or maybe it was actually the pigeons who were smuggling the man. . . .

Whatever the explanation, I know one thing: In the future, I will never knowingly carry an eggplant in my suitcase. And just in case they come up with some other goofy reason to make you drop your pants, I am definitely going to upgrade my travel underwear. ✳ SERVES 6

1 large eggplant
Kosher salt
2 tablespoons olive oil
1 large tomato, sliced
8 ounces fresh mozzarella,
 cut into 6 slices
6 hamburger buns, toasted,
 or 6 slices ciabatta (optional),
 warmed in the oven

1. Peel the eggplant and cut it into ¾-inch-thick rounds (you should have 6 slices). Sprinkle the slices lightly with salt, place them in a colander, and set them aside for about 20 minutes.

2. Meanwhile, position a rack about 6 inches from the heat source and preheat the broiler.

3. Rinse the eggplant slices, squeeze out the excess moisture, and pat them dry with paper towels.

4. Brush both sides of the eggplant slices with the olive oil, and place them on a baking sheet. Broil, turning them once, until they are lightly browned and tender, about 2 minutes per side.

5. Remove the baking sheet from the broiler and place a tomato slice on top of each eggplant slice, and a slice of mozzarella on top of that. Return the baking sheet to the broiler and continue broiling until the mozzarella has melted, about 2 minutes.

6. Serve as is, on a bun, or on a slice of ciabatta.

VARIATIONS If you serve the eggplant burgers on bread or buns, try spreading a schmear of basil pesto or sun-dried tomato pesto over the bread first.

Not-for-Scott Turkey Burgers

MY BROTHER-IN-LAW SCOTT claims that he will not eat turkey in any format other than roasted, Thanksgiving-style. He thinks ground turkey is peculiar and unappetizing.

If you have a relative as annoying as this, or if by any chance Scott is coming to your house for dinner, you will want to skip this turkey burger recipe. For that matter, don't bother with the recipes for turkey chili and burritos that follow either, unless you substitute beef for the turkey. For some reason Scott is okay with ground beef, but picky people like him often have such irritating quirks. As you already know from the previous chapter's pupik story (see page 45), Scott has negative feelings about chicken soup. In a recent development, he swore off panini, of all things. He sent his friends vicious anti-panini e-mails, the details of which I was spared, thanks to my handy "delete" button. Now the word on the street is that, since his recent business trip to Mumbai, Scott has gone vegan, sending his wife, Julie (who is a fabulous cook and an avid carnivore), into a tailspin. Just when she thought she had established a cycle of acceptable menus for her picky family, Scott threw her the vegan curveball and screwed everything up.

Scott is coming to visit in a few weeks. While I love my brother-in-law and would be happy to cook for him, I'm thinking that, rather than try to anticipate his food preferences *du jour,* we'll just go out for dinner (avoiding, of course, restaurants like the International House of Panini). ✳ SERVES 6

2 tablespoons olive oil, plus extra for the pan

1 small onion, chopped fine

3 cloves garlic, minced

1½ pounds ground turkey, half dark, half white meat

2 slices whole wheat bread

⅓ cup finely chopped fresh parsley

¼ cup low-sodium chicken broth

1 egg, lightly beaten

1 tablespoon fresh thyme leaves

1 teaspoon kosher salt

½ teaspoon freshly ground black pepper

Whole wheat buns, lightly toasted

Lettuce, sliced tomatoes, and mayo (see Note) for serving

1. Heat the 2 tablespoons of olive oil in a medium-size skillet over medium-low heat. Add the onion and cook until it is soft and translucent, about 10 minutes. Add the garlic and cook for 1 minute more. Transfer the onion mixture to a large mixing bowl and add the ground turkey.

2. Tear the bread slices into 1-inch pieces and place them in a food processor. Process briefly, until you have large crumbs. Add the bread crumbs to the turkey in the bowl. Add the parsley, broth, egg, thyme, salt, and pepper and mix well. Shape the mixture into 6 patties.

3. Wipe out the skillet. Heat about 1 tablespoon of oil in the skillet over medium heat. Add the burgers and cook until they are nicely browned and cooked through, about 5 minutes on each side. You may need to do this in two batches. Tent the first batch with aluminum foil to keep them warm while you cook the second batch.

4. Serve the burgers on whole wheat buns with lettuce and tomatoes and mayo.

NOTE I like to pump up that mayo like this: Mix ¾ cup mayo, ¼ cup crème fraîche, 1 tablespoon Dijon mustard, and a little freshly ground black pepper to taste.

★ Gobble-It-Up Turkey Chili

I KNOW. LIKE PAIN-IN-THE-ASS MINESTRONE (page 25), this recipe has a slightly daunting ingredient list. You're probably already getting irritable, imagining yourself chopping five vegetables while the rest of your family happily watches *Dancing with the Stars* and eats popcorn.

However, also like the minestrone, this chili is a Miracle Food: everyone will eat it. Not only that, they will love it, request it often, and devour it noisily, which makes it worth the aggravation. Plus, this chili has the added advantage of providing your group with all kinds of healthy vegetables cleverly disguised as something delicious.

I go light on the spices here because my husband is anti-spice. Tom is also fiercely opposed to onions, garlic, and red peppers (and about eighty other vegetables). If you live with such a person, do as I do and cook this chili when he or she is not in the vicinity of your kitchen. Ignorance will be bliss; they will eat it right up in happy oblivion.

If you find yourself with extra patience on the day you make this (which seldom happens to me), make a double batch and throw one in the freezer. You will be *so* glad you did, say, next Thursday when Margie invites you to go bowling but you need to do a family pre-feed before you go. ✳ SERVES 8 TO 10

¼ cup olive oil

1 medium onion, chopped

6 cloves garlic, minced

2 carrots, peeled and chopped

2 ribs celery, chopped

1 red bell pepper, stemmed, seeded, and diced

2 pounds ground turkey

2 teaspoons chili powder

1 teaspoon dried thyme

1 teaspoon ground coriander

1 teaspoon ground cumin

1 teaspoon salt

1 teaspoon freshly ground black pepper

½ teaspoon cayenne pepper (optional)

1 can (15 ounces) pinto beans, drained and rinsed

1 can (15 ounces) black beans, drained and rinsed

1 can (15 ounces) small white beans, drained and rinsed

2 cups tomato juice

2 cups low-sodium chicken broth

1 can (14 ounces) chopped tomatoes, with their juices

2 tablespoons tomato paste

Optional garnishes

Chopped fresh cilantro

Chopped onions

Sour cream

Grated cheddar cheese

1. Heat the oil in a large, heavy pot or Dutch oven over medium-low heat. Add the onion and cook until it's soft and translucent, about 10 minutes. Add the garlic and cook for 1 minute. Add the carrots, celery, and bell pepper, and cook, stirring occasionally, until the vegetables begin to soften, about 4 minutes.

2. Add the turkey, chili powder, thyme, coriander, cumin, salt, black pepper, and cayenne if you're using it. Cook, breaking the turkey up with a fork, until the meat is browned and well combined with the vegetables, about 5 minutes.

3. Add the beans, tomato juice, broth, tomatoes with their juices, and tomato paste, and stir to combine. Bring the chili to a simmer. Lower the heat and simmer, partially covered, stirring occasionally, until it's slightly reduced and the flavors are concentrated, about 45 minutes.

4. Serve the chili hot, with the optional garnishes on the side.

NOTE If you have any energy left after all this, make a salad and a skillet of cornbread and you've got yourself a dinner! Now go bowling with Margie and try to forget the whole ordeal.

VARIATIONS You can use just one kind of bean, if your family is confused by variety.

You also might want to adjust the spices. My family will eat nothing spicy, so I use less (or no) cayenne pepper. And if you don't happen to have coriander on hand, don't go rushing to the market, cursing this recipe and your life—just ditch the coriander. You can also add more chili powder if your family is more adventurous than mine.

P.S.: If you're like me, by the time you're done with this you may be in no mood to chop cilantro. Forget the Garnish Guilt: that stuff is optional. Just offer a little cheese or sour cream, unless your dinner guests include, say, Nancy Pelosi or Jay Leno, in which case you might want to pull out all the stops.

Burritos Your Way

OUR GOLDEN RETRIEVER, OLIVER, is turning three soon, and I've been thinking that the dog has matured beautifully. It's not just his body, which is no longer gangly but sleek and muscular. It's his behavior.

Oliver is much calmer these days, demanding to play at 4 A.M. only twice a week, tops. And he's more sophisticated in his choice of playthings, forgoing the duck-on-a-rope in favor of a taupe Dolce & Gabbana sandal.

Oliver's choosing more adult activities: He's taken up tennis. He prefers to do this when we're not home, but I see the evidence: tennis equipment is lovingly arranged in the yard. (The saliva wipes right off Tom's racquet.) And he's become more helpful around the house. When I returned from the market yesterday, that exuberant body block really accelerated the process of emptying my grocery bags.

He's also more social than he was a year ago. For instance, he initiates lively conversations with the mailman. It's lovely to see this new interest in interaction. Sadly, the mailman always seems to be in a hurry, rushing off before Oliver can complete a sentence.

In his new, less self-centered maturity, Oliver has shown an increased interest in other animals. When I take him for an on-leash stroll, the sight of a squirrel thrills him. (FYI: ice works really well on a dislocated shoulder.) Also, he very kindly helps gophers establish residence in our backyard with a little communal digging.

I will admit that Oliver needs a little polishing in the manners department. For instance, last night he should have asked politely before he ate Tom's burrito. But hey, details. Oliver has become one heck of a pooch.

✳ SERVES 4

8 large flour tortillas (10-inch size)

3 tablespoons fresh lime juice

1 tablespoon mayonnaise

1 clove garlic, minced

½ teaspoon ground cumin

¼ teaspoon salt

¼ teaspoon freshly ground black pepper

½ cup plus 2 tablespoons olive oil

1 pound ground turkey or beef

¼ cup taco seasoning, or to taste

1 can (15 ounces) pinto beans, drained and rinsed

4 cups romaine lettuce, cut crosswise into thin strips

1 cup grated cheddar cheese, or a combination of cheddar and Monterey Jack

3 plum tomatoes, seeded and chopped

4 scallions (white and light green parts), thinly sliced

1 avocado, pitted, peeled, and thinly sliced

8 sprigs fresh cilantro

1. Preheat the oven to 300°F.

2. Stack the tortillas, wrap them in aluminum foil, and place them in the oven to warm up.

3. Whisk the lime juice with the mayonnaise, garlic, cumin, salt, and pepper together in a small bowl.

Slowly add the ½ cup olive oil, whisking until the mixture thickens slightly. Set the dressing aside.

4. Heat the remaining 2 tablespoons of olive oil in a large skillet over medium heat. Add the turkey and the taco seasoning. Cook, breaking the turkey up with a fork, until it is no longer pink, about 5 minutes. Stir in the beans, lower the heat, and cook for 2 minutes. Then cover the mixture and set it aside.

5. Place the lettuce in a salad bowl. Toss the lettuce with just enough dressing to coat all the leaves. Set the salad bowl aside.

6. Place the cheese, tomatoes, scallions, avocado, and cilantro in separate small bowls.

7. Place a tortilla on each plate. Spoon about ½ cup of the turkey mixture onto the center of each tortilla, and then let each person add some lettuce and whatever other ingredients they want. To finish the burrito, fold up the bottom third of the tortilla, and then roll it up from left to right to make a tasty hand-held treat.

Skirt (or Pants) Steak Tacos

WHEN PEOPLE DISCUSS SKIRT STEAK (admittedly not a common occurrence), it makes me think of cows in tutus.

I don't know why someone would name a cut of beef after a girly garment. It seems almost oxymoronic.

The other problem with skirt steak is that if you serve it to your boy child, you may be asking for trouble. In this age of picky eaters, you are setting yourself up for a meal rejection, or at least a heated dinner debate about gender equality.

I suggest that, if you do have a son, you just call it pants steak.

Of course, if you have children of both genders, you will need to respond carefully when they ask what they are being fed. You could tell them to mind their own beeswax or just go with the less hostile, generic "It's steak." That way, you will have a relaxed dinner. That is, until they notice there are green beans on their plates. ✳ SERVES 4

1 pound skirt steak

3 tablespoons olive oil

1 tablespoon fresh lime juice

½ teaspoon chili powder

½ teaspoon ground cumin

½ teaspoon paprika

¾ teaspoon kosher salt

½ teaspoon freshly ground black pepper

2 tablespoons unsalted butter

2 large onions, halved and sliced

2 red or green jalapeño peppers, seeded and cut into small dice

1 teaspoon minced garlic

4 flour tortillas (8-inch size)

1 avocado, pitted, peeled, and cut lengthwise into 8 slices

2 tomatoes, seeded and thinly sliced

1. Lay the steak out on a plate or baking sheet. In a small bowl, mix 2 tablespoons of the olive oil with the lime juice, chili powder, cumin, paprika, ½ teaspoon of the salt, and ¼ teaspoon of the pepper. Pour the mixture over the steak, cover it, and set it aside to marinate at room temperature for about 30 minutes.

2. While the steak is marinating, melt the butter in the remaining 1 tablespoon olive oil in a large skillet over low heat. When the butter has melted, add the onions, jalapeño peppers, remaining ¼ teaspoon salt, and remaining ¼ teaspoon pepper. Cook until the onions are very tender and beginning to brown slightly, about 20 minutes. Add the garlic and cook for 1 minute. Set the mixture aside.

3. Meanwhile, preheat the oven to 300°F.

4. Stack the tortillas, wrap them in aluminum foil, and place them in the oven to warm up.

5. Heat a grill pan over medium heat, or heat an outdoor grill to medium.

6. Remove the steak from the marinade and grill it for about 4 minutes on each side for medium-rare. Let the steak rest for 5 minutes; then cut it into thin slices.

7. Remove the tortillas from the oven. To assemble the tacos, place some steak slices on the center of each tortilla. Add one fourth of the onion mixture, 2 slices of avocado, and 2 slices of tomato. Fold up the bottom third of the tortilla, then roll it from left to right to finish the taco, and serve them up.

NOTE Skirt steak cooked this way also makes a great addition to a salad.

What's Your Hurry Turkey

JUST AS MOM USED TO DO WITH LAMB (a roast one day, leftovers in a lamb-a-rama casserole the next), once in every recipe cycle I have a turkey festival. I cook a turkey breast in the slow cooker the first day, which is the easiest thing on earth, and then I use the leftovers for turkey pot pie the next day, which is not exactly the second easiest

thing on earth, but since the day
before was so easy, it balances out.

I love using a slow cooker. I just
throw in some ingredients, go to a
Zumba class or attend a Springsteen
concert, and dinner's waiting when
I get home. I can almost pretend someone else in my family cooked
it in my absence, a thing that will never happen outside of the realm
of my imagination.

This turkey is moist and comforting, great with Mashed New
Potatoes and Peas (page 138) and Cranberry Sauce (page 149).

✳ SERVES 6 TO 8

¼ cup low-sodium chicken broth

1 rib celery, coarsely chopped

1 carrot, peeled and cut into 1-inch pieces

2 sprigs fresh parsley

2 sprigs fresh thyme

1 clove garlic

1 turkey breast (4 to 5 pounds)

1 tablespoon olive oil

½ teaspoon salt

Freshly ground black pepper, to taste

1. Pour the broth into your slow
cooker. Add the celery, carrot, parsley,
and thyme. Lightly crush the garlic
clove and add it to the cooker.

2. Rinse the turkey breast and pat it
dry with paper towels. Rub it with
the olive oil, and sprinkle with the
salt and pepper. Place the turkey
breast on top of the vegetables.
Cover the cooker, turn the heat to
high, and cook for 1 hour.

3. Reduce the heat to low and cook
for 3 more hours.

4. Remove the turkey from the
cooker, tent it with aluminum foil,
and allow it to rest for 10 minutes.
Then slice and serve it with the pan
juices and the vegetables.

Richard Gere's Pot Pie

I WISH RICHARD GERE would give me another chance.

Once, many years ago, he came to dinner. Okay, I know what you're saying: "Excuse me? Why, pray tell, were *you* feeding Richard *Gere*?" Good question. Not only that, he was with the oh-so-gorgeous Cindy Crawford. *"Excuse me?"* Okay, just shut up and let me explain.

See, as I mentioned in the introduction, I was an actress for thirty years. One of my gigs was co-starring in a play with Richard (way back before he was, you know, *Richard Gere*). Also, Tom was, in a former life, an entertainment lawyer, and represented Richard. So, that's how we knew R.G. and C.C. and why they were in our house, meeting our then newborn daughter Elizabeth and partaking of a dubious turkey pot pie.

It seemed like a good idea at the time—a nice homey pot pie—although I'd never made one before. Later that night, I made a note-to-self, in bold font: **If R.G. is coming for dinner, make something you know, you stupid cow!**

Due to recipe mismanagement, I guess I omitted or mis-measured a few key crust ingredients. The insides of the pie were all right, but, although R.G. and C.C. were perfectly gracious about it, the crust tasted like tarragon-scented Play-Doh. Luckily, our colicky daughter commanded enough attention that nobody was too focused on the food, but it was a low point in my cooking life.

Since then, I have learned to use biscuits instead of a crust for pot pies: I'm just too crust-challenged. And if I'm too crabby to make biscuits, I have no compunction about calling on my friend Mr. Pillsbury to do it for me. These days, the market stocks a few varieties of very acceptable ready-to-bake biscuits, saving me the aggravation of making them.

So now I've got this pot pie thing down. Richard, if you are reading this, come on over. Let me exonerate myself for the Play-Doh pot pie of '89. ✳ SERVES 6

5 tablespoons unsalted butter

1 onion, chopped

2 medium carrots, peeled and sliced into ¼-inch-thick rounds

1 medium zucchini, trimmed, cut in half lengthwise, then into ¼-inch-thick slices

2 cups low-sodium chicken broth

1 cup milk

5 tablespoons all-purpose flour

4 cups coarsely chopped cooked turkey (bite-size chunks)

1 cup frozen corn kernels, thawed

1 cup frozen peas, thawed

¼ cup chopped fresh flat-leaf parsley

2 tablespoons chopped fresh dill or basil

1 package (16 ounces) frozen ready-to-bake biscuits, such as Pillsbury Grands

1. Preheat the oven to 425°F.

2. Melt the butter in a large saucepan over medium-low heat. Add the onion and cook it until it's soft and translucent, about 10 minutes.

3. Meanwhile, bring lightly salted water to a boil in a small saucepan, add the carrots, and cook them for 2 minutes. Add the zucchini and cook for another 2 minutes. Then drain the vegetables and set them aside.

4. Pour the broth and milk into the same saucepan and set it over low heat to warm the mixture.

5. Add the flour to the onions and cook, stirring, just to cook the flour a little, about 3 minutes. Gradually whisk in the warmed broth mixture. Cook, stirring occasionally, until the sauce thickens, about 5 minutes.

6. Add the reserved carrots and zucchini, the turkey, and the corn, peas, parsley, and dill to the sauce and mix well. Reduce the heat to low and let the stew simmer while you bake the biscuits.

7. Bake the biscuits according to the directions on the package.

8. Scoop the stew into individual soup or chili bowls, top each with a hot biscuit, and serve.

Crabby Cook Casserole

I'M USUALLY DUBIOUS of forwarded e-mails; typically they are useless time-sucks. But my sister Lindsay recently forwarded me an internet tidbit that intrigued me. It explained how and why my kitchen is actually a day spa.

First of all, apparently Cool Whip and mayonnaise can double as excellent hair conditioners, and for that final rinse, Lipton tea or Budweiser beer adds extra shine. Also, for a self-inflicted manicure, Pam cooking spray will dry those painted nails in seconds.

Another tip is that Jell-O can be used to freshen up smelly feet (okay, I have a little trouble getting my mind around that one); and if you go to your "everything" drawer and grab some Elmer's glue, you've got the makings of a facial. You just smear it on, let it dry, and peel it off. (I used to do that as a kid, to make believe I was hideously sunburned.)

These are all excellent ideas and much more wallet-friendly than similar services in the Hills (the Beverly ones). I'm tempted to try this stuff; finding a new use for my kitchen might make me like it more. The only thing is, I know what would happen. I'd be in mid-treatment and the doorbell would ring.

I'd have to open the door; the UPS guy would need my signature. I'd see the thought bubble above his head: "WTF?" There I'd be with mayo in my hair, Elmer's on my face, Jell-O in my shoes, Pam in one hand, Budweiser in the other. I'd put the Bud down to sign for the package. His thought bubble would change: "Obvious party animal."

"Oh, ha ha," I'd protest, "it's not what you think, ha ha! I'm just going to pour that on my head!"

Then I would be straitjacketed, the advantage of which would be that I wouldn't be able to cook dinner. But I also wouldn't be able to go to my Zumba lesson, so I think I'll skip the kitchen spa and just, you know, head for the Hills.

The next e-mail Lindsay forwarded to me was much more useful than its predecessor. She and I were e-bitching back and forth about having to make dinner for the five thousandth time. She forwarded me this recipe, which some equally crabby friend had forwarded to her. It's very tasty, and I especially like the fact that you can hurl in some green vegetables without precooking them. ✳ SERVES 4 TO 6

1 cup low-sodium chicken broth

1 cup milk

4 tablespoons (½ stick) unsalted butter

1 onion, chopped

1 tablespoon curry powder

¼ cup all-purpose flour

Kosher salt and freshly ground black pepper, to taste

1 store-bought rotisserie chicken, meat cut into bite-size pieces (about 4 cups)

12 ounces broccoli, cut into bite-size pieces (about 2 cups)

1 cup sliced almonds

Cooked rice or pasta, for serving

1. Preheat the oven 350°F.

2. Combine the broth and milk in a small saucepan, and heat over low heat just until the liquid is hot.

3. In a medium-size saucepan, melt the butter over low heat. Add the onion and cook until it's soft and translucent, about 10 minutes.

Sprinkle the onion with the curry powder and cook for 1 minute. Then gradually add the flour and cook, stirring, for 2 minutes, just to cook the flour a little.

4. Gradually add the hot broth mixture, stirring constantly. Simmer, stirring occasionally, until the sauce thickens, about 5 minutes. Taste the sauce and add salt and pepper, if needed. Then add the chicken, stir well, and set it aside.

5. Cover the bottom of a casserole dish with the broccoli pieces. Pour the chicken mixture over the broccoli. Sprinkle the almonds on top. Cover the casserole, put it in the oven, and bake for 40 minutes.

6. Remove the cover and bake for 5 more minutes, or until the almonds are toasty and the casserole is bubbly.

7. Serve with rice or pasta.

Abby's Casserole

I RECENTLY PRETENDED to be a Food Network chef. I'd seen a few episodes of Ina, Paula, Giada, and Rachael, and their cooking lives seemed so much more pleasant than my own, I thought I should try, at least for a day, to emulate those ladies, to curb my crabbiness and muster their level of enthusiasm. (Well, not Rachael's level. That would give me a hernia.) I started by selecting a recipe that would sort of fit snugly into that F.N. half-hour format. Check out the recipe—then read further to see how my "episode" went down. . . . ✳ SERVES 4 TO 6

2 tablespoons olive oil

1 onion, chopped

1 jalapeño pepper, seeded and minced (optional)

1 teaspoon minced garlic

1 pound ground beef

1 teaspoon chili powder

1 teaspoon ground cumin

1 teaspoon dried oregano

1 teaspoon paprika

½ teaspoon kosher salt

¼ teaspoon freshly ground black pepper

1½ cups tomato sauce

1 can (14 ounces) black beans, drained and rinsed

1 cup frozen corn kernels, thawed

6 corn tortillas (8-inch size)

2 cups grated cheddar or Monterey Jack cheese, or a blend

1. Preheat the oven to 375°F.

2. Heat the oil in a large skillet over medium-low heat. Add the onion, and the jalapeño if you're using it, and cook until they are tender, about 10 minutes. Add the garlic and cook for 1 minute more.

3. Add the beef to the skillet, raise the heat to medium, and cook, breaking it up with a fork, until it has just lost all its pink color, about 5 minutes. Stir in the chili powder, cumin, oregano, paprika, salt, and pepper, and cook until well mixed, 2 minutes or so. Add the tomato sauce, reduce the heat to low, and simmer the mixture to blend the flavors, about 10 minutes. Then add the black beans and the corn, mix well, and set the mixture aside.

4. Place a tortilla in a 10-inch, straight-sided casserole dish, and spread it with about ⅔ cup of the beef mixture. Sprinkle with ⅓ cup of the cheese. Repeat these layers five times, ending with cheese. Cover, and bake for 30 minutes.

5. Remove the cover and continue baking for 10 minutes, until the casserole is bubbly. Serve hot.

VARIATION Once I was halfway through making this and realized I had no tortillas. I used tortilla chips instead, and my daughters actually liked it better.

WHAT HAPPENED NEXT

ONCE I'D CHOSEN THE RECIPE for my "episode," the next thing I did was clean the bejeezus out of the kitchen, removing all personal items, like the fridge photos, the takeout menus, and the tennis shoes that were waiting for dog poop removal.

Once I had what looked like a Food Network kitchen, I did what all those fabulous TV chefs do to prep: I got my nails done, in a color called "Miami." Then I blew out my hair and put on a push-up bra and a low-cut t-shirt, forgoing the apron. (Have you ever seen Giada in one? I don't think so.) I gave myself kudos for getting an early start because, so far, making dinner had taken me four hours.

I read the ingredient list all the way through, pulling items from the cupboards and lining them up in order of use. It was then that I discovered I had no cumin. If I were not channeling Rachael, I'd have skipped it. Instead, I went to the market to get some, which took a while because the lady ahead of me at the checkout was buying so many lottery tickets.

When I got home, I chopped the onion and garlic and placed them and each spice in their own little ramekin. I lovingly arranged my parsley in a vase by the cutting board (*so* Ina), snipping off a few dead sprigs with kitchen shears that took me a while to find, because I had not used them since receiving them as a hostess gift from someone who did not know me very well.

Finally, I was ready. I stopped for a moment to freshen my lipstick and survey the beauty of my preparation. At this point, Tom came home from work. (It was 8 P.M.) He eyed the photo-free fridge and the conga line of spice ramekins. "Dinner's in the works," I assured him, in such a cheerful tone that he gave me a startled look before shuffling off to watch ESPN.

I found it challenging to keep the kitchen spotless and cook at the same time, the way Giada does. I went through a lot of paper towels. I also changed my t-shirt a couple of times, and stopped for a nail fix when the chopping knife sliced off a little fingernail *avec* "Miami." I was pretty beat when I got dinner on the table at 10:30. Tom was not very hungry because he had long since microwaved a macaroni and cheese.

I don't know how those gals do it. What took me most of the day appears to take them only a half an hour. I guess that's why they get the big bucks.

FOUR

A Toast to the Roast

WHEN I WAS A CHILD, my family spent many major holidays tearing up my grandfather's house. Between our visits, Papa seemed to forget what a hellishly big and noisy family we were. As we pulled up to his gray colonial house with its tidy white shutters, he'd wave cheerfully from the door. His white hair impeccably arranged, he'd be wearing his usual smoking jacket and suede slippers. He'd smile in happy anticipation, as if he were expecting Winston Churchill or Elizabeth Taylor. But when we piled out of the car, like that clown act in the circus (how many people can you fit in a green Ford?), his smile would fade and he'd retreat to the shadows of the foyer. We'd be left to exchange awkward greetings with the lady of the house.

My real grandmother died before my birth, and when I was seven, I witnessed Papa's marriage to a woman named Martha. I found this experience mind-bending, an odd twist in the normal order of things. But aside from her irregular entry into the family ranks, I was suspicious of Martha on many levels. My siblings and

I considered the indicators and concluded that Martha was a fake grandmother.

For one thing, she was divorced, which at that time seemed like a condition that only existed on the dark side, involving people who were really messed up, like criminals or Judy Garland. We knew of no other divorced grandmothers.

Also, Martha did not look like a normal grandmother. She was young and slim and way too athletic; she skied a lot, played tennis, and rode horses. I once saw a photo of her roping a steer, which I found disturbing; I felt strongly that grandmothers and cattle should lead separate lives.

Another of Martha's un-Nana-ish qualities was that she didn't like us. Now, everyone knows that proper grandmothers adore their grandchild's every thought and gesture, no matter how irritating they may be to others. But Martha had little patience for the darling offspring of her husband's son. This became abundantly clear one particular Easter Sunday, when she blew her top.

Admittedly, she was not unprovoked. Within an hour of our arrival, we'd spilled cranberry juice on two separate throw rugs and broken an antique vase. But it was my brother Billy who really sent her over the edge, when he shot Martha in the butt with an arrow (which, luckily, was rubber-tipped). This final straw led to a "lively discussion" between Martha and Papa about the pros and cons of entertaining relatives. This exchange took place behind closed doors, against which six ears were firmly pressed. We kids came away from our eavesdropping certain that Martha was not on our side, and was unlikely to cross over.

Later, at dinner, she came to like us even less.

Martha was not a gifted cook, but she tried, and she expected us to eat the food she labored over. On this occasion, she thrashed around in the kitchen for ages, cursing Julia Child, while we were happily occupied destroying the other rooms of her home and hunting for Easter eggs.

My father had prepped the hunt, scattering huge quantities of garish plastic eggs around Papa's substantial property. I did not search aggressively; I was too cowed by my competitors, who played about as gently as, say, the Green Bay Packers. But the eggs were easy to spot in the stark March landscape, so all six of us ended up with enough candy-filled eggs to kill off our appetite for Martha's cooking.

By the time we assembled at the dinner table, we were experiencing the biggest sugar rush since Halloween.

Martha emerged from the kitchen with a platter full of some kind of woodsy animal (think pheasant or deer) that had been roasted to within an inch of incineration. She tore off her apron and plopped into her chair while Papa, wielding an electric knife the size of his forearm, cut the poor beast into ten blackened parts.

I think she must've made him sign a prenuptial agreement waiving his rights to side dishes; the only other thing I recall being served was a sweet potato casserole. The potatoes were mashed, just stringy enough to make you gag, and baked with marshmallows on top.

Sugar-crazed and nauseated, we children rocked in our chairs, humming and rattling our forks, wishing the food before us could magically vanish. Only Billy's wish came true; he artfully scraped chunks of charred meat into a drawer that was positioned directly beneath his placemat. The rest of us were left to push the food around on our plates, thinking maybe we'd get lucky and it would just evaporate. We took turns getting up and going to the bathroom, and we adjusted our napkins frequently and passed the butter a lot, the theory being that if you looked busy, people would mistake your actions for eating.

But Martha was no fool, and when the food made its fifth circuit around our plates, she grew dangerously testy. By meal's end her irritation had escalated, leading to another "lively discussion" with Papa in the kitchen that ended in the f-word and a shattered dish.

To give her some credit, I don't think Martha fully realized, when she signed up for the job of grandmother, just how many grandchildren were involved; I'm not sure there was full disclosure. She could not have known how much cooking would be required on major holidays. If she had, she might have chucked the ring.

Being a crabby cook myself, I am empathetic in retrospect. On an Easter Sunday (or any holiday), it's hard enough to get up and cook for ten people, but when six of them are a crew of noise-loving, home-wrecking food rejecters, it's cause for serious irritation.

Martha is no longer alive and cooking (may she rest in peace). This chapter's full of easy recipes for family-size roasts, for holidays or any time, that would've made her life easier if she'd had them, starting with a big old Easter ham.

Ham I Am

WHEN EASTER ROLLS AROUND, the marketplace is flooded with images of cute animals—lamby-kins and chickies and duckies and bunnies. We home cooks are expected to come up with an Easter menu that includes a slaughtered, roasted version of one of those little cute-niks, but it's hard to get your mind around it. Just try going through the supermarket checkout with a leg of lamb in your cart while there's a stuffed fleecy-white relative of that leg's former owner staring down at you from atop the cash register.

Ham is less guilt-inducing because the piggy is not regularly featured in the crush of Easter creature-cuteness. Plus it's called ham, not piggy, so you can mentally disassociate it from the darling pink animal whose butt it once was.

I also like to serve ham because it's so easy to make, which leaves you energy to hide Easter eggs, and because you can easily work it so you have a lot of leftovers. (You know how I love two meals for the aggravation of one.) For Easter lunch, I go for the Creamy Dreamy Sweet Potatoes (page 140), in honor of the marshmallow-topped sweet potato casserole that my fake grandmother always served on that holiday. Add some Hot Slaw (page 147) or Bunny's Carrots 'n Snaps (page 136), and you're good to go. Serve leftovers with The Old Uncle's Rice Salad (page 205) and Kool Slaw (page 208) or Spud Salad (page 199). Golden Delicious Applesauce (page 148) is also great with this. ✳ SERVES 15 TO 20

½ cup apricot preserves

¼ cup (packed) dark brown sugar

2 tablespoons Dijon mustard

1 tablespoon balsamic vinegar

1 clove garlic, minced

¼ teaspoon ground cinnamon

¼ teaspoon freshly ground black pepper

1 bone-in ham (10 to 12 pounds), fully cooked and spiral cut, at room temperature

1. Preheat the oven to 350°F.

2. Combine the preserves, brown sugar, mustard, vinegar, garlic, cinnamon, and pepper in a food processor, and process until the mixture is a smooth glaze.

3. Place the ham in a roasting pan and brush it generously with the glaze. Bake until the ham is heated through and the glaze has browned nicely, about 1 hour.

4. Serve warm or at room temperature.

Mini-Thanksgiving Roast Turkey

THANKSGIVING IS A HOLIDAY I associate with disaster; my memory bank is loaded with images of Thanksgiving mishaps. I'm not quite sure why these bad things always seemed to happen, but maybe it was because people got so carried away with emotions triggered by the presence of all that family that they lost their balance or forgot how to carry platters of food.

One year my grandfather, seated at my parents' long dining table, temporarily forgot that he was sitting on a backless bench, rather than a proper chair. He was reminded of this fact when, leaning back to sip a last drop of wine, he crashed to the floor. (Luckily, grandfathers seldom sue for injuries sustained due to bad furniture.)

Sometimes, when we had a large number of guests, Mom hired some help for the occasion. One year, the help arrived having had a few too many Crantinis. While the woman did fine when she climbed the kitchen stairs to change, she descended those stairs in a tumble, as my father would say, "ass over teakettle." She was, luckily, unhurt, and even unfazed by the fact that her wig had arrived at the bottom of the stairs before she did.

Another year, a "helper" tripped while presenting the turkey, sending it skidding across the dining room into the jaws of an ecstatic dog. There was also the Thanksgiving in Baltimore, when Tom's sister Julie dropped a massive plate of sauerkraut on the floor, although this may have been engineered by certain members of my family who were thus relieved of the responsibility of eating the stuff.

Although it's an accident-prone holiday in our family, Thanksgiving has a fabulous menu, if you can manage to get the food to the table. However, the menu is so strongly associated with the holiday that serving it at other times of the year seems awkward. Plus, it's a lot of food to prepare if you don't have the holiday spirit to power you through all that cooking.

Nonetheless, I've resolved to do a mini-Thanksgiving now and then. I'll roast just a breast of turkey (my husband won't eat dark meat anyway), mash a few spuds, maybe buy some canned cranberry sauce, and, okay, I'm too crabby to make stuffing, but we're in the Thanksgiving ball park. Then I can use the leftover turkey for another meal the next day.

So try this recipe and have yourself a Thanksgiving dinner in February or May. With any luck, you will get through the meal without injuries or broken crockery. ✳ SERVES 6 TO 8, OR 4 WITH LEFTOVERS

1 bone-in turkey breast (4 to 5 pounds)
½ teaspoon paprika
½ teaspoon salt
Freshly ground black pepper, to taste
1 tablespoon unsalted butter, at room temperature
6 cloves garlic, lightly crushed
½ large onion, chopped
1 large carrot, peeled and chopped
1 bay leaf
1 sprig fresh parsley
½ teaspoon dried thyme
1 cup low-sodium chicken broth
½ cup dry white wine

1. Preheat the oven to 425°F.

2. Rinse the turkey and pat it dry. Place it in a 9 x 13-inch baking pan and sprinkle it with the paprika, salt, and pepper. Rub the butter all over the breast. Place the garlic, onion, carrot, bay leaf, parsley, and thyme in the pan. Pour the broth and wine into the pan, cover it tightly with aluminum foil, and roast for 30 minutes.

3. Discard the foil, baste the turkey, and reduce the oven temperature to 375°F. Continue roasting, basting occasionally, until the turkey is nicely browned, about 45 minutes.

4. Remove the turkey from the oven and let it rest for 10 to 15 minutes before serving.

5. Serve the turkey with the pan juices and vegetables, if anyone will eat them. (At my house, I eat *all* of them.)

PRIME TIME

TOM AND I ARE USUALLY ANTI-SOCIAL on New Year's Eve, but once in a while we celebrate by doing something more than TiVo-ing the ball dropping in Times Square. On one such occasion a few years ago, my brother Sam and his family came over, and since they'd just returned from Thailand, I thought it fitting to ring in the New Year with Party Pork Tenderloin, which is tasty enough to be celebratory but lean enough to accommodate the usual New Year's resolutions regarding weight loss.

At dinner, Sam informed us that the Thai prime minister had just been thrown out. I feared we were headed for dull conversation, but things livened up when Sam revealed the juicy details of Samak Sundaravej's ouster.

It seems that Samak hosted a cooking show before he rose to power. (I know, odd career path, right?) Apparently he was unable to resist returning to the show as a paid guest host on several occasions during his run as P.M., even though slumming in the commercial world is against the constitutional rules for political big shots. So they axed him.

I mean, what would drive a guy to give up all that power just to cook publicly? I get irritated just cooking privately in a home where my ouster is unlikely. But later, when I Googled him, I came to think of Samak as a kindred spirit; the title of his show was roughly translated as "Tasting and Grumbling." This thrills me; it sounds like a reality show about my life. They could just come over and perch a camera in my kitchen, right up atop the fridge, and come back once a week to collect their episode.

I never cook Thai food because (a) there are a lot of great takeout Thai restaurants in Los Angeles (why make it when you can take it?) and (b) my picky family won't eat it. But I was curious to know what recipes Samak gave up his career for, so I checked them out. My favorite is the one for pigs' legs in Coca-Cola.

Samak's recipe is a little vague and kind of short on precise measurements, but it could not be more intriguing.

First, you find 5 pig legs. (Ask your butcher. Be prepared for derisive laughter in response.) Then you're supposed to put them in a large (ya think?) pot and add 4 bottles of Coca-Cola. (My guess is you don't want to go with the Diet Coke.) Bring this to a boil.

Add a coriander root (do I know?), some garlic (he doesn't say how much—I say the more the merrier), 3 tablespoons of salt, some pepper, a bunch of fish sauce, 4 cinnamon sticks, a few shiitake mushroom stems, and some "pongapalo" (if I knew, I would tell you). Add enough water to the pot to cover all the charming ingredients and return it to a boil.

Boil for at least 3 hours. (A couple of weeks maybe.)

Samak then says to make a sweet sauce with "see-uan." (I have no idea. Stop asking me questions.)

This recipe serves about sixty, would be my guess, although I don't know where you're going to find even three people willing to eat this dish. Serve it anyway; your reputation as a cook will spread far and wide and nobody will ever come over for dinner again, which will save you a lot of trouble.

Party Pork Tenderloin

IF YOUR BUTCHER DOES NOT CARRY PIGS' LEGS, try this dish instead of the prime minister's (see page 80).

You can throw the meat in the marinade in the morning if you want, then put it in the oven at dinnertime. I for one can't face raw pork when the rooster is still crowing, so I just start marinating when I remember it needs to be done, which is often mere minutes before the dinner bell.

You can also make this for company, as I did for a festive New Year's Eve dinner a few years back (see page 80). If anyone declines it, claiming that their New Year's resolutions include giving up red meat, try to control your irritation. It's New Year's Eve, after all.

✳ SERVES 4

¼ cup soy sauce
¼ cup (packed) dark brown sugar
¼ cup fresh lemon juice
2 cloves garlic, minced
1 tablespoon grated fresh ginger,
    or 1 teaspoon ground ginger
1 tablespoon Dijon mustard
1 teaspoon dried oregano
2 pork tenderloins
    (about 1 pound each)
¾ cup fresh orange juice
2 tablespoons unsalted butter

1. Combine the soy sauce, brown sugar, lemon juice, garlic, ginger, mustard, and oregano in a bowl and mix well. Place the pork in a one-gallon plastic freezer bag and pour the marinade over it. Seal the bag and refrigerate the pork all day or for at least 3 hours, if you can.

2. About an hour before you want to serve the pork, preheat the oven to 375°F.

3. Place the pork in a roasting pan, reserving the marinade. Roast the pork until an instant-read thermometer inserted in the middle reads 150°F, 35 to 40 minutes. Tent the pork with aluminum foil and set it aside.

4. While the meat rests, combine the marinade, any pan juices, and the orange juice in a small saucepan over medium heat, and simmer until the sauce is reduced by half, 3 to 4 minutes. Stir in the butter until it melts.

5. Carve the pork into slices and top each serving with a spoonful of sauce.

NOTE This pork is great with Hot Slaw (page 147) and Golden Delicious Applesauce (page 148), or with Bunny's Carrots 'n Snaps (page 136) or Spinachy Rice (page 141).

VARIATIONS There are none. If they don't like it, tell them to go to IHOP.

Unca Sam's Grilled Leg of Lamb

THE SUMMER ALLOWS THE MALE FAMILY MEMBERS to get in touch with their inner chefs: there's a whole lot of grilling going on. My husband gets to make his perfect burgers, Uncle Johnny his perfect steaks. Even my nephew, Noah, has taken up the spatula in recent years. (Uncle Scott is an exception. He just makes martinis.)

Grilling is mandatory on the Fourth of July, and that's when my younger brother, Sam (who likes the kids to call him "Unca" as an homage to Donald Duck, whose nephews called him that), wins the "It Takes a Grillage" prize for his grilled butterflied leg of lamb. (I guess he inherited the I-love-lamb gene from Mom, who roasts a leg about fifty times a year.)

Sam has committed the recipe to memory and destroyed all hard copies of it because he's afraid the other male relatives will steal it and he will lose his standing as superior grill-master. So I had to twist his arm to get this, and for all I know he gave me an adjusted version, a fake. But it tastes great, and maybe it'll inspire a male in your life to get in touch with *his* inner chef. ✳ SERVES 8, OR 4 WITH LEFTOVERS FOR MOM'S LITTLE LOST LAMBWICHES (PAGE 21)

1 leg of lamb, trimmed of fat, boned and butterflied (About 5 pounds after boning. I wouldn't *dream* of suggesting you crabby cooks do all that nasty prep. Get the butcher to do it.)

¼ cup Dijon mustard

¼ cup olive oil

2 tablespoons balsamic vinegar

2 tablespoons fresh lemon juice

2 cloves garlic, minced

1 tablespoon chopped fresh rosemary

1 tablespoon chopped fresh oregano

2 tablespoons chopped fresh parsley

1 teaspoon kosher or other coarse salt

½ teaspoon freshly ground black pepper

1. Place the butterflied lamb, lying flat and open (like a book), on a large rimmed plate or in a baking dish. Combine all the remaining ingredients in a bowl, stir well, and pour the marinade over the lamb. Rub the marinade into the lamb; turn to coat on all sides, then cover and refrigerate it for at least 2 and as long as 8 hours.

2. When you are ready to cook the lamb, preheat your grill to medium.

3. Remove the lamb from the marinade, place it on the grill, and cook until the meat is nicely browned and an instant-read thermometer inserted in the thickest part reads 125°F for medium-rare, about 15 minutes per side. (You can cook it 4 to 5 minutes longer, to 140°F, if you like your meat closer to medium.)

4. Allow the lamb to rest for 5 to 10 minutes before you carve and serve it.

NOTE This lamb is good with many things. I like to serve it with a couple of salads, like Minty Cuke Salad (page 204) and The Old Uncle's Rice Salad (page 205) or Dog-Proof Caprese Salad (page 207).

Jessie's Roast Beef Tenderloin

I CAN'T HELP IT. Every year, shortly before Halloween, I start anticipating Christmas. In L.A. it's usually 90 degrees in October; there are none of the traditional indicators—like frost and people wearing sweaters—that December is around the corner. Nonetheless, I go into a holiday spin.

My mind starts to fill with burning questions like, Should I send Uncle Jinky the chocolate-covered graham crackers? Does Tom's assistant look good in yellow?

Would the girls wear reindeer underpants? Unlike my husband, who, perhaps wisely, does the bulk of his shopping after 6 P.M. on Christmas Eve, I'm obsessing and making lists and buying and returning and buying again and wrapping and shipping for weeks before C-day.

During this process, I tend to buy Christmas gifts for myself as well as for my giftees. My thinking goes, "Lindsay would love these socks, but then so would I." I get the socks, Lindsay gets a lovely turtleneck. This may not be a perfect display of Christmas spirit, but it keeps *my* spirits up.

One gift I always give myself at Christmas is a beef tenderloin. I know that not many of you would put this item high on your Santa list, but to me, it's right on top. This is because, on Christmas day, after all the weeks of nutty prep and all the day's activities, such as ripping off wrapping, making pancakes, determining where I can exchange the scarf from Aunt Jenny, making omelets, and trying on the girls' rejected reindeer underpants, I like to keep Christmas dinner simple, but special, which is just what B.T. is. Make extra for Boxing Day sandwiches and that beef is the gift that keeps on giving. ✳ SERVES 6 TO 8

1 beef tenderloin (3 to 4 pounds)
Salt and freshly ground black pepper, to taste
2 tablespoons olive oil

1. Preheat the oven to 425°F.

2. Rub the beef all over with salt and pepper. Heat the oil in a roasting pan (one that can go from stovetop to oven) over medium heat. Brown the meat on all sides in the hot oil, about 10 minutes total.

3. Place the pan in the oven and roast for 25 to 30 minutes for rare (125°F on an instant-read thermometer) or 35 to 40 minutes for medium (140°F).

4. Tent the roast with aluminum foil and let it rest for 10 minutes. Then carve it and serve.

VARIATIONS This is great cold, with a salad and a baguette.

The Stringy Meat Group

ONE OF MY FAVORITE THINGS IS WHAT, as kids, we used to call
"stringy meat." This sub-group of entrees includes things like short
ribs, pot roast, and stew, which are cooked for ages until they become
fork-tender, pull-apart, and deliciously stringy. The best thing my
mother-in-law ever made was brisket, her stringy meat specialty.

Bette's Brisket

BETTE GREW UP IN A RELIGIOUS HOUSEHOLD, but she rejected many
of the traditions of Judaism when she grew up. There were no bar or
bat mitzvahs for her kids, and she (and Donald) put up a Christmas
tree every year and welcomed the Easter bunny when he showed up.
A woman with an abundance of positive energy, Bette believed in
celebrating all holidays, regardless of their origin.

While she did not often set foot in a temple, Bette did honor
the Jewish holidays (and sometimes Christmas or New Year's) by
making a nice brisket. Brisket suits Bette's (and my) distracted
cooking style: you can put it in the oven and go out to buy a bathing
suit, and the brisket won't suffer if you return later than expected
having spent 45 minutes wandering the mall's parking structure
trying to remember where you parked your car.

It was Bette who first introduced me to brisket, and since then,
I've collected a few more Jewish mothers' recipes from friends.
Jeffrey's mom's is the most interesting: Taking a cue from the

prime minister's pigs' legs (see page 80), she braises the brisket in Coca-Cola and a package of dried Lipton onion soup mix. Susan's mom makes hers smothered in mounds of onions, while Carol's mom throws in dried apricots and prunes. All good variations, but the truth is, while I'm willing to stray, my family will have no other brisket than Bette's. ✳ SERVES 4 TO 6

1 tablespoon paprika, or more if needed
1 tablespoon kosher salt
Freshly ground black pepper, to taste
1 first-cut beef brisket
 (2½ to 3 pounds)
1 tablespoon olive oil
2 tablespoons unsalted butter
1 onion, minced
1 red bell pepper, stemmed, seeded,
 and coarsely chopped
1 teaspoon minced garlic
1 tomato, seeded and coarsely chopped
1½ cups low-sodium chicken broth

1. Preheat the oven to 325°F.

2. Rub the paprika, salt, and pepper into the brisket. Heat the oil in a Dutch oven over medium heat. Add the brisket and cook until it is browned, about 5 minutes on each side. Remove the meat from the pan and set it aside.

3. Wipe out the Dutch oven, reduce the heat to low, and melt the butter in it. Add the onion and cook gently until it is translucent and soft, 10 to 15 minutes. Add the bell pepper and cook for 2 minutes. Add the garlic and tomato, and cook for 1 minute.

4. Return the brisket to the Dutch oven, and add the broth. Bring it to a simmer. Then cover the pan and place it in the oven. Cook until the brisket is very tender, 2½ to 3 hours. You'll need to flip the meat every 30 minutes or so, so don't go to the golf course or anything.

5. When the meat is done, remove it from the oven and let it rest for 10 minutes. Then slice it across the grain and serve it right away (or, if you're really ahead of the game, let it cool, refrigerate it, and reheat and serve it sometime in the next few days).

NOTE This brisket is great with noodles and a green salad.

Short Ribs of Beef

WHEN I WAS GROWING UP, my family did not celebrate the Jewish holidays, just the Episcopalian ones.

I learned something about Judaism at school, since half the students were Jewish. I can still sing the menorah song (although I have a better handle on "Onward Christian Soldiers"). But in my childhood home, we never ate apples baked in honey, matzoh balls, charoset, or bagels. Neither did we have brisket, although we did eat other versions of stringy meat. Mom liked recipes like short ribs and pot roast, although not because she was distracted like Bette (or me), but because she had so many children she didn't know what to do.

Mom would throw some short ribs in the oven and then get into the station wagon to assume her duties as director of transportation for the remainder of the day. The six of us had to be driven to a variety of music lessons (including, over the years, trumpet, piano, flute, clarinet, violin, voice, and drums) and to our choice of competitive sports (basketball, figure skating, ice hockey, soccer, football, field hockey, and gymnastics) plus miscellaneous other activities like doctors, dentists, knitting, skateboarding, driving lessons, sleepovers, playdates, and the younger twins' rehearsals for a rock band called "The What."

When Mom was finally released from the station wagon at day's end, she'd issue a directive to start our homework, cook up some noodles and peas, put the laundry in the dryer, vacuum the living room, set the table, and conjure up a salad, by which time the meat would be stringy perfection and Mom would require a glass of sherry.

Whether or not you are celebrating a holiday, religious or otherwise, you can always celebrate a recipe that is so accommodating. ✳ SERVES 6 TO 8, OR 4 PEOPLE WITH LEFTOVERS, WHICH MAKE GREAT SANDWICHES (SEE FACING PAGE)

8 short ribs of beef (about 4 pounds)
¼ cup olive oil
1 onion, chopped
1 carrot, peeled and chopped
2 ribs celery, chopped
3 cloves garlic, minced
2 cups dry red wine
1 can (28 ounces) whole Italian tomatoes
1 bay leaf
2 teaspoons herbes de Provence
1 teaspoon salt
½ teaspoon freshly ground black pepper
1½ to 2 cups low-sodium chicken broth, homemade if possible

1. Preheat the oven to 400°F.

2. Place the short ribs on a baking sheet and roast them in the oven, turning them once, until they are evenly browned, about 20 minutes. When they're done, set the meat aside and reduce the oven temperature to 300°F.

3. Heat the oil in a large Dutch oven over medium-low heat. Add the onion, carrot, and celery, and cook until the vegetables are tender, about 20 minutes. Add the garlic and cook for 1 minute. Add the wine, raise the heat to medium, and cook until the wine has reduced by half, about 8 minutes.

4. Meanwhile, coarsely chop the tomatoes, reserving the juices.

5. Add the tomatoes and their juices to the Dutch oven, along with the bay leaf, herbes de Provence, salt, and pepper. Place the short ribs in the pot and add enough broth to cover the meat. Cover the pot and place it in the oven. Cook until the short ribs are very tender, about 3 hours. (While this is happening, you can go out and do six errands.)

6. Serve with noodles, potatoes, or Mama Beans (page 144).

Leftovers: Short Ribs of Beef Sandwiches

THIS RECIPE WAS THE HAPPY OUTCOME of a crabby moment, one of those 5-P.M.-and-no-idea-what's-for-dinner kind of moments. (You crabby cooks know where I'm coming from.)

It took great effort to crank up the energy for creative use of whatever was in the refrigerator. Irritably searching in there for inspiration, tossing the wilted celery, growling at the smelly onion half and the furry feta, I found the leftover short ribs from two days before. Hmmmm . . . in the depths of my mental recipe file I recalled something about pot roast sandwiches. Well, if pot roast, why not short ribs? And I just happened to have a baguette in the freezer.

The results were so good that these days I make short ribs not so much for the short ribs as for the short ribs sandwiches. This is a rare find: Make enough short ribs, and not only do you get two meals, but the second one is arguably better than the first. ✳ SERVES 4

Leftover short ribs of beef or brisket (about 2 cups shredded meat), with some pan juices
½ cup mayonnaise
¼ cup sour cream
1 tablespoon Dijon mustard
4 ciabatta or other good-quality sandwich rolls, split horizontally and lightly toasted
2 cups arugula or lettuce

1. Place the shredded meat and the pan juices in a small saucepan and warm over low heat until it is heated through.

2. Meanwhile, combine the mayonnaise, sour cream, and mustard in a small bowl. Spread some of the mayonnaise mixture on both sides of the rolls.

3. Place about ½ cup of the warmed beef on the bottom half of each roll, top with some arugula, and then replace the top half of the roll to make a sandwich. Slice the sandwich in half. Make 3 more sandwiches this way, and serve.

Veal Appeal Stew

OF COURSE, one of the world's favorite stringy-meat meals is stew.

I'm going to be honest with you: I don't like making stew. I find the browning of all those cubes of meat one of the most annoying tasks there is.

I do, however, love *eating* stew, so I make it once in a while and just endure the pain of browning. I usually serve it on the rare occasions when I have to cook dinner for a group on a cold winter night (which in California means the temperature dips to 60 degrees); it's the coziest make-in-advance dish in town. You can make it a couple of days before the guests show up, saving your D-day energy for things like searching for matching napkins or whitening your teeth (or, if you can stand it, cooking a little rice or pasta to go with the stew). ✳ SERVES 6

2 leeks (white and light green parts), well rinsed and patted dry

2 tablespoons unsalted butter

4 tablespoons olive oil

Salt

8 ounces cremini mushrooms

½ cup all-purpose flour

¼ teaspoon freshly ground black pepper

2 pounds veal, cut into 2-inch chunks

¾ cup dry white wine

1 can (14 ounces) diced tomatoes, with their juices

½ cup low-sodium chicken broth

2 tablespoons chopped fresh thyme

1. Coarsely chop the leeks. Melt 1 tablespoon of the butter in 1 tablespoon of the olive oil in a large Dutch oven over medium-low heat. Add the leeks, sprinkle them with ¼ teaspoon salt, and cook until they are soft, 6 to 7 minutes.

2. Meanwhile, wipe the mushrooms clean with a damp paper towel and coarsely chop them.

3. When the leeks are done, place them in a large bowl and set it aside.

4. Raise the heat under the Dutch oven to medium. Melt the remaining 1 tablespoon butter in another 1 tablespoon olive oil in the Dutch oven. Add the mushrooms and cook until they are tender and lightly browned, 5 to 6 minutes. Add the mushrooms to the leeks in the bowl.

5. In another bowl, combine the flour with ½ teaspoon salt and ¼ teaspoon pepper. Dredge the veal chunks in the flour, shaking off the excess.

6. Add the remaining 2 tablespoons olive oil to the Dutch oven and raise the heat slightly. When it is hot, add a batch of the veal chunks and brown them on all sides, about 6 minutes. Place the browned meat in the bowl with the vegetables, and repeat with the remaining veal.

7. Add the wine to the Dutch oven and stir, scraping up the brown bits. Add the tomatoes and their juices, the broth, and the thyme. Return the veal and vegetables to the Dutch oven. Bring the stew to a simmer, cover, and reduce the heat to low. Cook until the veal is very tender, about 1 hour and 20 minutes.

8. Taste, and add salt and pepper as needed. Serve piping hot.

VARIATIONS If you want to simplify this, you can omit the leeks and/or the mushrooms.

You could also throw in some potato chunks for the last 30 minutes of cooking. And you can vary the herbs, using sage or rosemary instead of thyme.

A POSTSCRIPT

EVERY DAY MY DOG, OLIVER, brings me his tattered, deflated soccer ball precisely at 5:35 P.M., minutes after he's eaten dinner, sensibly suggesting that I help him burn off a few kibble calories with a brisk game of soccer. I always oblige; otherwise he will follow me around the house for the rest of the evening, sadly dropping the ball at my feet and looking at me like I'm a bad mother.

"Awright, awright," I say to him.

One day recently, before the evening kickoff, I needed to have a few words with the man who was trimming our trees, and to put a load of delicates in the washing machine, and to flip the brisket that was simmering in the oven. (I was making Bette's recipe for Hanukkah.) As the dog and I headed outside, I plugged the headset into the phone and grabbed my laptop, which I placed on the patio table so I could monitor e-mails while we played. I was therefore simultaneously doing landscape management and laundry, cooking dinner, exercising the dog, communicating with my book editor, and making phone calls. Even for me this was high-level multitasking.

I got my sister on the phone and kicked the ball across the yard. *Thunk.* Oliver rocketed after it.

"What are you doing?" my sister asked. Her suspicion that my attention was divided was triggered by the *thunk,* the *brzzzzz* of a tree being sawed, and the *ka-ching* of an incoming e-mail.

"I'm talking to you. Whattya think I'm doing?" I replied as I ran inside to flip the brisket, then back out to re-engage with Oliver. I knew Lindsay was most likely multitasking too, although she doesn't have a hyperactive dog to cope with—only a lazy, no-account cat.

Oliver has set unusual rules for his soccer game. What happens is, I kick the ball and Oliver retrieves it but refuses to relinquish it until I hurl a tennis ball in his direction. He feigns an interest in the tennis ball, thereby releasing the soccer ball, which I kick across the yard, which he retrieves, and the game begins again.

It's an idiotic game, but it keeps Oliver happy for a while and, as it involves only my feet, leaves me a couple of free appendages with which to perform other chores.

"I'll be right back," I said to Oliver as I headed indoors to check on the laundry.

"What?"

"No, not you, him."

"What? Him who?"

Then Lindsay heard the sounds of laundry moving from washing machine to dryer.

"Call me back when you're not doing six other things, okay?" She hung up.

Oliver entered the laundry room and dropped the ball at my feet.

The thing is, the dog is incapable of multitasking. Aside from the fact that he has no hands or any acquaintance with technology, he is a single-minded kind of guy. There are only a pawful of tasks Oliver performs: eating, sleeping, defecating, playing soccer, and walking. He accomplishes all of these things, one at a time, to his satisfaction, each and every day, and he's the happiest guy I know.

The dryer was doing its job, the brisket would cook for another hour or so, the tree man had beheaded a juniper and was descending his ladder. I snapped shut my laptop, took off my headset, and looked at Oliver's sad face.

"Awright, awright," I said. "Let's do it your way." *Thunk.*

Twenty minutes later, when the dog seemed willing to rest, the game ended. I can't say that I felt as happy as Oliver, but I did feel sort of calm. Life is ordinarily so hectic that doing only one thing has almost the same effect as meditation.

I think I will try it again tomorrow. At 5:35 I will do nothing but play soccer with Oliver for twenty minutes. I don't know if this will become a trend, but at least it will make my single-minded best friend very happy.

FIVE
Let 'Em Eat Pasta

ALTHOUGH MY DAUGHTERS are only eighteen months apart, they could not be more different. One is calm, the other bouncy. One plays soccer, the other likes ballet. One is small-boned, the other not so much. One loves music, the other the theater. It's all good; it's a beautiful thing; *vive la différence.*

In the lunch-bag years, however, while I celebrated and bragged about their differences, marveling at the mysteries of genetics, one thing always bugged me: Could they at least both like egg salad? While those genes were getting mixed up and distributed in utero, couldn't Somebody have intervened to make both kids have the same food preferences?

Throughout elementary school, Elizabeth would eat only egg salad or tuna sandwiches. Nora would eat neither. When she had not declared war on sandwiches altogether, she'd eat only grilled cheese, which made packing her lunch tricky because I couldn't fit the electric grill in her backpack. So I'd just send her in with peanut butter crackers, string cheese, a tangerine, yogurt, and a cookie. At the end of the day, when Nora forgot to hide the incriminating evidence, I'd notice that her lunch bag still contained all the items, with the exception of the cookie. Elizabeth ate her sandwiches all right, until she became self-conscious and banned smelly food. Ix-nay the una-tay, likewise eggs (and bananas). Luckily, I was able to talk her into eating turkey.

Dinner was another issue. When I eliminated the menu items that one child or the other wouldn't eat, I was left with a short list of white foods: potatoes, apples (sliced and peeled), milk, and poultry if it was untouched by any colorful ingredient that might impart flavor. Then (thank God) there was pasta, without which my children would certainly have perished from malnutrition.

On days when feeding my kids made me crabby in the extreme, I'd calm myself by thinking of friends who had it worse, like Lynn, a carnivore whose family included a vegan, a pescatarian, and a toddler who would eat nothing but white toast; or Denise, with a vegetarian husband and a kid with allergies to peanut butter, dairy, and onions; or Lena, whose son would eat no pasta while her daughter would eat nothing but.

Then I'd think of my mother, packing lunches and making dinner for six kids every day. Her policy on food preferences was Tell, Don't Ask: you got what you got without a discussion about who likes what. This seems like an excellent idea. Why didn't I remember to do that with my own kids? I have made a note-to-self to adopt this policy in my next life, unless I get really lucky in that life and marry Mario Batali.

This chapter offers several recipes for pasta, the life- and sanity-saving entree, starting with the one my girls would eat in the days of white food and progressing, as they did, to recipes that are a little red, or even a little green.

Tony's Rigatoni

THIS RECIPE WAS ESSENTIAL during the kids' white food years, and later, when, as teens, they and their friends experimented with vegetarianism.

I don't usually like to bend over backward for vegetarians. I tend to favor the carnivores when I cook, figuring other types can just pick their way through the side dishes. But it's different with teenage visitors: I have an irrational need to please them. It's as if, on some level, I fear that if I don't feed them properly they will resort to feral teenagerish behavior. They'll toilet-paper my house or criticize my pants.

So, here's the scene: Nora and her friends enter the house in a cluster, like a single being with eight denim-clad legs. They're talking and texting, moving in a chatty, clicking wad to the kitchen, where they seat themselves expectantly at the table.

As I flutter about the kitchen, I feel like a bird cooking for a cat: Unless I make something delicious, they will eat me alive.

When I present them with Tony's Rigatoni, the girls are rendered speechless with delight. Except for the sound of pasta being chewed, silence descends. I have a moment to pace the kitchen, only relaxing when I overhear someone say, "Whoa, this is *so* good."

When they've finished, the girls leap up in unison, saying things like, "Omigod, that was so delicious!" or "That was the best pasta I ever had!" or (my favorite) "You are amazing!"

The girls thank me and deposit their plates in the dishwasher before resuming their cluster formation and moving off to the TV room.

Their praise and impeccable manners have filled me with so much good will that I find myself willing to perform another cooking task: chocolate chip cookies. ✳ SERVES 4

1 pound rigatoni

3 tablespoons unsalted butter

1 cup heavy (whipping) cream

1½ cups freshly grated Parmigiano-
Reggiano cheese

Salt and freshly ground black pepper

Pinch of ground nutmeg

1. Bring a large pot of salted water to a boil, add the rigatoni, and cook until it is al dente (just tender), about 12 minutes.

2. Meanwhile, in a pot that's big enough to hold all the pasta, melt the butter over medium-low heat. Add the cream, raise the heat just a little, and bring it to a simmer. Let it cook until the mixture thickens, about 1 minute. Then remove the pot from the heat.

3. Drain the pasta and add it to the pot. Set the pot over medium-low heat and stir the pasta to coat it with the cream. Add ⅔ cup of the cheese, salt and pepper to taste, and the nutmeg, and keep stirring until the sauce gets thicker and coats all the rigatoni, about 2 minutes.

4. Serve immediately, with the remaining cheese on the side.

VARIATIONS You can throw in ½ cup cooked peas at the end. Other throw-ins for non-vegetarians would be ½ cup chopped prosciutto or smoked salmon. I wouldn't dare risk any variations on this recipe for teenagers, though. They might get annoyed and short-sheet your bed.

Sorta Mac and Cheese

THANK GOD FOR THE DEFAULT FOOD: macaroni and cheese. Whenever I was out of energy and out of dinner ideas for my hungry girls, I'd opt for M 'n C, telling myself it was okay if they ate it twice (uh, okay, full disclosure: sometimes thrice) a week. I wonder how much my children have consumed so far in their lives. Enough to fill a Dumpster? A swimming pool? The Grand Canyon?

We've tried all varieties: Amy's frozen (thumbs up), Annie's (thumbs down), and Kraft (I was frightened by the color).

When the kids got older and would tolerate pasta of different shapes, I gave them this homemade version, a nice change from the smile-shaped tubes we have eaten so darn much of. ✳ SERVES 4 TO 6

5 tablespoons unsalted butter, plus extra for the baking dish

3 cups milk

¼ cup all-purpose flour

2 cups grated Gruyère cheese

1½ cups grated sharp cheddar cheese

½ teaspoon salt

¼ teaspoon freshly ground black pepper

¼ teaspoon cayenne pepper

⅛ teaspoon ground nutmeg

12 ounces penne pasta

3 cups bite-size broccoli florets

4 slices good-quality white bread

1. Preheat the oven to 350°F. Butter a 3-quart casserole or other baking dish, and set it aside.

2. Heat the milk in a medium-size saucepan over medium heat just until it starts to steam.

3. Meanwhile, melt 3 tablespoons of the butter in a separate saucepan over medium-low heat. Add the flour and cook, stirring, just to cook the flour a little, about 2 minutes. Gradually whisk in the hot milk. Cook the sauce, whisking

occasionally, until it thickens and starts to bubble, about 5 minutes.

4. Add 1½ cups of the Gruyère and all the cheddar to the sauce, and stir until the cheese melts, about 2 minutes. Then stir in the salt, black and cayenne peppers, and the nutmeg. Set the sauce aside.

5. Bring a large pot of salted water to a boil, add the penne, and cook until it is not quite tender, about 8 minutes. In the last minute of cooking, add the broccoli.

6. Drain the penne and broccoli well, and return them to the pot. Add the cheese sauce and combine everything well.

7. Remove the crusts from the bread and tear it into 1-inch pieces. Place the bread in a food processor and process for just a few seconds, until you have large crumbs. Melt the remaining 2 tablespoons butter in a small saucepan, and toss the crumbs with the butter.

8. Pour the penne mixture into the buttered baking dish, and sprinkle the remaining ½ cup Gruyère on top. Sprinkle the breadcrumbs on top of the cheese. Bake until the mixture is bubbly and the top is golden brown, about 35 minutes.

9. Let the mac and cheese sit for about 10 minutes before you serve it.

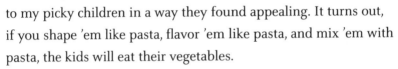

★ Dreamy Veggie Pasta

DURING THEIR WHITE FOOD YEARS, I researched and finally discovered how to present vegetables to my picky children in a way they found appealing. It turns out, if you shape 'em like pasta, flavor 'em like pasta, and mix 'em with pasta, the kids will eat their vegetables.

For this recipe revelation, I gave myself major points. I was suddenly able to feed the children previously forbidden foods like cabbage, onions, and zucchini, with their complete compliance. I got to gloat because of my nutritional triumph, and they got to gloat because their firm resistance to other vegetable recipes had paid off.

Now, some of you may be thinking, Excuse me, but would Ms. Genius like to explain why there are so many damn ingredients in this recipe? I hear you. But this is another Miracle Food: more than six ingredients, yes, and a fair amount of choppage, but it's worth it because the payoff is so big. It's a one-dish meal, everybody likes it, and it's nutrient-loaded.

So try it, and then call me. We'll get together for a group gloat.

✳ SERVES 4

2 medium-size zucchini

Kosher salt

2 carrots

½ head green cabbage,
   preferably Savoy

2 tablespoons unsalted butter

2 tablespoons olive oil

½ large onion, finely chopped

2 cloves garlic, minced

¾ cup low-sodium chicken broth

¼ cup heavy (whipping) cream

¼ cup chopped fresh flat-leaf parsley

¼ cup chopped fresh basil

Freshly ground black pepper, to taste

1 cup freshly grated Parmigiano-
   Reggiano cheese

12 ounces spaghetti or linguine,
   broken in half

1 cup pine nuts, toasted (see Note)

1. Trim the ends off the zucchini, cut the zucchini into 2-inch chunks, and then grate them in a food processor fitted with the shredding blade. Sprinkle the grated zucchini with ½ teaspoon kosher salt, place it in a colander, and set it aside.

2. Peel the carrots, cut them into chunks, and shred them in the food processor. Set the carrots aside.

3. Cut the cabbage into chunks, and then into strips, using the slicing blade in the food processor. Set the cabbage aside.

4. Melt the butter in the olive oil in a large skillet over medium-low heat. When the butter has melted, add the onion and cook until it is very soft, 10 to 15 minutes.

5. While the onion is cooking, set a large pot of salted water over high heat (for the pasta).

6. Add the garlic to the onion and cook for 1 minute. Add the cabbage and the carrots and cook, stirring occasionally, until the vegetables are tender, 5 minutes. Squeeze the zucchini to extract any liquid, add it to the skillet, and cook, stirring, for 2 minutes.

7. Add the broth, cover the skillet, and let the veggies cook for 5 minutes. Then add the cream and cook, stirring, until the sauce starts to thicken, about 2 minutes. Stir in the parsley and basil, ½ teaspoon kosher salt, and pepper to taste. Stir in ⅓ cup of the cheese, cover the skillet, and remove it from the heat.

8. Cook the spaghetti in the boiling water until it is al dente (just tender), about 10 minutes.

9. Drain the pasta and return it to the pasta pot. Add the vegetable mixture, combine well, and serve with the remaining grated cheese and the pine nuts on the side.

NOTE To toast pine nuts, place them on a baking sheet in a 350°F oven and toast them, stirring them once or twice, until they are golden and fragrant, about 10 minutes. Keep an eye on them, though. I literally always have to throw out the first batch because I've gotten distracted and forgot about them until I heard the smoke alarm.

VARIATIONS You can go a little wild with this, especially if your family is not veggiphobic. You can add green peas or shelled edamame, fresh corn kernels or chickpeas or sliced red peppers or mushrooms or . . . whatever vegetables your family tolerates. You can also add cooked chicken or shrimp, or a little chopped ham. I'm usually way too crabby to add more ingredients than are already listed, but if you're feeling exceptionally calm, or have had a martini, go for it.

Louie's Tomato Sauce

ONE DAY IN MID-CHILDHOOD, the girls relented and agreed to eat tomato sauce on their pasta, even though it was a garish color, not in keeping with their preference for the whiter-shade-of-pale foods. This was a great breakthrough, allowing me to liven up the weekly menus a little.

I developed my own recipe for tomato sauce, thanks to an encounter with a guy called Louie.

We met Louie because my husband has a thing about buying gas. It's sort of like asking for directions: he won't do it until the situation is dire. As you can imagine, this sometimes gets him in trouble, as it did when I was in labor, minutes away from giving birth to our second child. Luckily for Tom, I was in too much distress to hit him with a frying pan when he pulled into a gas station on the way to the hospital.

He got in trouble again on a family summer vacation when our big fat rental car conked out on Highway 95 just shy of our Connecticut destination. Tom coasted down an exit ramp, at the bottom of which the car just stopped, refusing to go one inch farther, stubborn as my husband.

A speedy guy in a pickup truck honked behind us. When Tom threw up his hands to indicate helplessness, Mr. Speedy screeched around us, yelling "Jackass!" at my husband, saving me the trouble.

Then we got lucky: Louie showed up. Louie was a middle-aged guy who looked and behaved like Clarence, the angel in *It's a Wonderful Life.* After he pushed our car to a shady off-road spot, he drove Tom to the gas station to fetch a couple of gallons.

Tom told me later that on their way, Louie had related the mini-series of his life: he was divorced and unemployed, had just had a fight with his girlfriend, and was on his way home to make tomato sauce.

Tomato sauce? In a lineup I'd never have picked Louie as the guy who makes tomato sauce. If I'd been in the car, hearing this directly, I'd have pressed him for details. Was cooking a form of post-spat therapy? Was he making a tomato sauce as a peace offering for the girlfriend or was he just, you know, hungry? If the former, then why tomato sauce? Why not chocolate cake? If the latter, then why not a simple peanut butter sandwich? Who taught him to make tomato sauce? The ex?

And then, of course, I'd have raised the most obvious question: "What's your *recipe* for tomato sauce?"

But it was my husband who had this conversation

with Louie, and for him, the recipe question is one that, of all the questions in the entire universe, he would be least likely to utter. The question "Can you tell me how to get to the Boston Hotel, since it's 2 A.M. and I am completely lost and my wife will shortly hit me with a frying pan?" is right up there in the realm of never-to-be-spoken, but asking for a recipe is in a whole other league. Tom would not even know how to put the words together.

So, he was riding shotgun with a man who had a recipe to share and the opportunity zipped right by. I was left to imagine how Louie would have made tomato sauce.

Here is a recipe that I feel is Louie-ish, if not exactly his. I include it here with gratitude for the kindness of a stranger who got our big fat rental up and running before I had time to locate a frying pan.

✳ MAKES ABOUT 4 CUPS

2 tablespoons unsalted butter
2 tablespoons olive oil
1 large red onion, chopped
2 pounds good-quality, very ripe
    tomatoes, coarsely chopped
1 teaspoon kosher salt

1. Melt the butter in the oil in a heavy saucepan over medium-low heat until the butter melts. Add the onion and cook until it is soft, about 10 minutes. Add the tomatoes and the salt, and raise the heat slightly to bring the mixture to a simmer. Cook until the tomato liquid thickens and the tomatoes are very tender, about 20 minutes.

2. Pour the tomatoes into the bowl of a food processor and pulse several times, until the sauce is almost smooth but still a little chunky.

3. Serve the sauce on a pasta of your choice, or freeze it and save it for a winter day.

Tomatoey Spaghetti

AFTER THE GIRLS GOT INTO LOUIE'S SAUCE, it was a short leap to
this pasta with uncooked tomatoes, a recipe that is a true friend
to the crabby cook.

One of the things that always annoyed me a lot was when I'd call
my family to come to dinner and they wouldn't show up for several
minutes. I couldn't leave the kitchen to round them up in a civilized
way, or else my counter-surfing dog would eat the dinner before we
did. So I'd have to yell, body-blocking Oliver as he leapt up to sample
the food that, after all my efforts, was sitting there, getting cold.

This recipe is perfect for avoiding the irritation caused by straggling
diners: it can be served at room temperature. On those occasions when
it takes your family twenty minutes to respond to the dinner bell, just
relax. It'll give you time to freshen your cocktail. ✳ SERVES 4 TO 6

8 plum tomatoes, seeded and coarsely
  chopped
⅔ cup extra-virgin olive oil
½ cup chopped fresh basil
1 teaspoon minced garlic
2 teaspoons red wine vinegar
Kosher salt and freshly ground black
  pepper
1 pound spaghetti
1 cup freshly grated Parmigiano-
  Reggiano cheese

1. Mix the tomatoes, olive oil, basil,
garlic, and vinegar in a large bowl.
Season with salt and pepper to taste,
cover the bowl, and let it sit at room
temperature for 1 hour.

2. About 20 minutes before you are
ready to serve the dish, bring a large
pot of salted water to a boil. Add the
spaghetti and cook until it's al dente
(just tender), about 10 minutes.

3. Drain the pasta, add it to the
tomato mixture, and mix well.

4. Serve hot or at room temperature,
with the cheese on the side.

Pesto Presto

GENERALLY SPEAKING, one does not want one's child to make life choices based on peer pressure. But when a peer pressured my kids into eating a new food, thereby expanding my menu options, I was all for it.

My children first sampled pasta with pesto because of peer pressure. For years they'd refused to try it because of its color. As I've said, pasta was one of their favorite foods, but only if it came in white. Eventually they accepted red sauce, but green was completely out of the question. It was way too suggestive of the odious world of vegetables.

But it was often the case that, during their growing years, the girls would go to a playdate or birthday party where they'd have to eat what the other kids ate or face social extinction. It was thanks to one of those occasions that they first tasted pesto, and they never looked back. These days, green is the new white. ✳ MAKES 2½ CUPS

3 cups fresh basil leaves

2 cloves garlic

⅔ cup chopped walnuts

⅓ cup pine nuts

1 cup olive oil

⅔ cup freshly grated Parmigiano-Reggiano cheese

⅓ cup freshly grated Pecorino Romano cheese

3 tablespoons mascarpone cheese, at room temperature

¼ teaspoon salt

¼ teaspoon freshly ground black pepper

1. Combine the basil, garlic, walnuts, and pine nuts in a food processor. Turn the processor on and add the olive oil in a slow stream, processing until the mixture is a thick paste.

2. Pour the pesto into a bowl and mix in the cheeses, salt, and pepper. You will have about 2½ cups. You'll need about a cup of pesto sauce for a pound of pasta. Freeze the rest for later.

VARIATIONS You can adjust the quantities of nuts and cheeses to your taste. You can try different herbs (parsley, mint, cilantro), or add a little grated lemon zest. And if you can't find mascarpone cheese, use cream cheese.

Shrimpini

AFTER ALL THE YEARS OF COOKING for my picky children, I am relieved to see that at college they've learned to eat formerly "icky" things like asparagus and scallops. However, while they and their peers have been busy embracing new foods, it seems that adults have been doing the opposite. In a stunning reversal, grownups have become pickier eaters than children.

This first came to my attention a few years ago at my friend Lynn's annual Bastille Day party, at which she traditionally serves moussaka. For years, people gobbled it up, without even a query as to why a Greek food on a French holiday. But on this particular July 14, two people had gone vegan, a third brought with her a frozen Jenny Craig entree, and another was on a raw food diet. So Lynn's family and dogs (and I) were the only well-fed guests that evening.

Now, I've had my food phases. Once, many years ago (before marriage, kids, and irritability), I vowed to eat only sweet potatoes and nuts for two weeks. This was part of a body-cleansing plan designed by a guy with a goatee who worked as a grain sorter at the nearby health food store. He promised that the results of my discipline would be enhanced energy, weight loss, and a better personality, plus an interest in having sex with him.

After about four days, I wearied of the diet. Nuts start to taste like wood after a while, and my skin was turning a disconcerting shade of orange.

Also, the grain sorter had been fired for being overly attentive to underage female customers.

But throughout this and other wacky phases, if I was invited to someone's home for dinner, I always ate whatever was served, as did everyone else. Now people have found all kinds of new and interesting reasons to reject food, and cooks, including myself, have found new causes to be crabby.

In my own house, Tom has recently emerged as the pickiest eater in the family. For years I didn't notice how many foods he wouldn't eat because I was catering to the girls, whose list of acceptable foods was even shorter than Tom's. Now that the kids are grown and adventurous eaters, they've left Tom way behind. He's finally been exposed.

When Elizabeth and Nora are home, I cook what *they* like: cooking according to Tom's preferences is just too boring. (How much chicken can a person eat?) They love this Shrimpini, although Tom does not. (He loves shrimp cold but not hot—I know, WTF, right?) We'll eat the pasta while he eats leftovers, and he does not complain. When Tom is surrounded by his daughters, you could feed him a braised tennis shoe and he'd still be in heaven. ✳ SERVES 4

1 pound linguine	4 tablespoons (½ stick) unsalted butter
2 pounds (about 24) large shrimp (I know, oxymoron), shelled and deveined	6 cloves garlic, minced
	½ cup dry white wine
	⅓ cup fresh lemon juice
5 tablespoons olive oil	¼ cup chopped fresh dill
Kosher salt and freshly ground black pepper	¼ cup chopped fresh parsley

1. Preheat the oven to 400°F. Line a baking sheet with aluminum foil.

2. Bring a large pot of salted water to a boil, add the linguine, and cook until it is al dente (just tender), about 10 minutes.

3. Meanwhile, place the shrimp on the baking sheet and drizzle about 2 tablespoons of the oil over them. Use your hands to rub the oil on the shrimp, distributing it evenly. Sprinkle the shrimp lightly with salt and pepper, and roast them in the oven until they are pink and just cooked through, 5 to 6 minutes. Tent the shrimp with foil to keep them warm.

4. Melt the butter with the remaining 3 tablespoons olive oil in a medium skillet over medium heat. Add the garlic and cook for 1 minute. Add the wine, 1 teaspoon kosher salt, and about 8 twists of the pepper mill, and cook until the wine has reduced by half, 3 to 4 minutes. Stir in the lemon juice and the herbs, and remove the sauce from the heat.

5. Drain the linguine, return it to the pot, and stir in the lemon-wine sauce. Serve the pasta immediately in individual pasta bowls, with the shrimp arranged on top.

Quirky Turkey Pasta

SPEAKING OF PICKY ADULTS, one of my crabbiest days as a cook was the day Mrs. Kerry came to dinner, which was also the day I discovered the hell of lasagna.

I'd invited this family to dinner, and I figured, what better food to prepare for a family than lasagna? It seemed like the no-brainer, please-one-please-'em-all, make-in-advance-while-the-kids-are-napping party food.

Well, are you familiar with the Spanish Steps in Rome? It turns out there are more steps in a lasagna recipe.

What with the meat sauce, vegetable choppage, béchamel sauce, noodle boiling, pan greasing, and ricotta schmearing, it took me about five hours from start to finish, and my kitchen looked like it did after the Northridge earthquake.

When I'd cleaned up and collapsed in the Barcalounger to reflect on my efforts, I thought, "This is not a recipe—it's a religious experience, and in a bad way."

So, I advise against making lasagna. Nor should you invite Mrs. Kerry to dinner.

I don't mean the wife of John Kerry, the political figure, just Mrs. Kerry from Sherman Oaks. The Kerry family were the lasagna guests, but Mr. Kerry's bad back was flaring up so only Mrs. Kerry and her ten-year-old daughter named Poopsie showed up. (Her actual name was, of course, not Poopsie. I tend to substitute the names of picky people with derisive alternatives.)

As we sat down to the steaming plates of lasagna, my family tucked right in. (The girls had not yet discovered their aversion to ricotta and oregano, and Tom was a couple of years away from swearing off red meat and pasta.)

But Mrs. Kerry used her fork to destroy, rather than eat. She pulled a noodle to the west wing of the plate, shoved a meat globule to the east, and rubbed ricotta around the southern tip, while telling us, in great detail, about her mother's trip to New Zealand, apparently to distract me from the fact that she was not eating her dinner.

Poopsie watched and imitated her every move.

When I offered a lovely dressed salad, Mrs. Kerry announced she didn't "do" salad dressing, and Poopsie seconded that emotion.

Now, as savvy cooks know, it is tough to undress a dressed salad. Starting over is pretty much your only option. Neither

Mrs. Kerry nor Poopsie protested when I got out fresh lettuce and started washing and spinning. My evil imagination had my dinner guests, in miniature, in the spinner with the greens, clinging desperately to the watercress and iceberg, screaming to be rescued. I spun with such ferocity that I lost the spinner to centrifugal force. It leapt from the counter, sending lettuce (and the mini-Kerrys) to all corners of the linoleum.

As I went for the broom, I made a promise to myself, which I broke several years later: I actually did have Mrs. Kerry to dinner again. But this time I did it smart: I made Quirky Turkey Pasta, a much simpler dish than lasagna. ✳ SERVES 4

3 tablespoons olive oil

½ onion, finely chopped

3 cloves garlic, minced

1 pound ground turkey (I like a mixture of half white and half dark meat)

1 teaspoon kosher salt

2 plum tomatoes, seeded and chopped

1 can (16 ounces) tomato sauce (see Note)

¼ cup low-sodium chicken broth

½ teaspoon dried basil

½ teaspoon ground cumin

Freshly ground black pepper, to taste

12 ounces fusilli

Freshly grated Parmigiano-Reggiano cheese, for serving

1. Bring a large pot of salted water to a boil.

2. Meanwhile, heat 2 tablespoons of the olive oil in a large, heavy saucepan or Dutch oven over medium-low heat. Add the onion and cook it until it's soft and translucent, about 10 minutes. Add the garlic and cook for 1 minute. Add the turkey and the salt, and cook, breaking the turkey up with a fork, just until it loses its pink color, about 5 minutes.

3. Add the tomatoes, tomato sauce, broth, basil, cumin, and pepper, and bring the sauce to a simmer. Let it simmer while you cook the pasta.

4. Add the fusilli to the boiling water and cook until it is al dente (just tender), about 10 minutes.

5. Drain the pasta and return it to the pasta pot. Add the turkey sauce to the pasta and mix well. Serve the pasta immediately, with the grated cheese on the side.

NOTE It would be great if we could have homemade tomato sauce on hand all the time. But let's face it, if you are a crabby cook, this just won't be happening. Preparing food that you are not going to eat immediately is not something crabby cooks are inclined to do. We barely get the necessities of the day taken care of, let alone dinner for next Thursday. Once in a while (like that time my neighbor gave me a crate of heirloom tomatoes), I get it together to make tomato sauce and put some in the freezer for later— but not often. So see if you can find a store-bought tomato sauce that isn't too, you know, store-bought. Muir makes a decent organic canned sauce, and Scarpetta, a brand that I found at Whole Foods, seems almost fresh but lives on the shelf.

But if you get inspired and it's tomato season, try making Louie's Tomato Sauce (page 104).

WHAT HAPPENED NEXT

O N THE NIGHT of the Quirky Turkey Kerry dinner, Poopsie had gone to college but Mr. K showed up.

Mr. K's back went out in the middle of the salad course (yes, it was dressed, to the nines), so he spent most of the evening flat on the floor with our dog, Oliver, licking his face. Even horizontal and in close proximity to a pooch, he managed to eat more than Mrs. Kerry, who, once again, danced with her dinner and went home hungry.

But I could laugh merrily all the way to the dog's dish: at least I hadn't spent all day preparing her rejected food.

So, if you are having dinner guests, heed my Recipe Red Alert and don't make lasagna. Stick to simple (and don't invite Mrs. Kerry).

SIX

Go, Fish!

I T WASN'T JUST THAT MY FAMILY were picky eaters. It was also that the children liked to eat dinner at 6:30 and my husband was not home until 8:30 most nights, so for a while I found myself making two different dinners at two different times, a situation that led to what was undoubtedly the crabbiest phase of my cooking life.

I resolved to make a change; I sought professional help. Not a therapist—I already had one—but a chef. Not a chef who would stink up my house all day cooking onions and monkfish, but someone who would just come over with dinner (as opposed to come over *for* dinner).

I found salvation (or so I thought) in the form of a tiny sixty-ish woman with spiky gray hair that stuck out around black-framed eyeglasses. Twice a week, in ugly chef pants and a badly stained apron, she delivered dinner to our house. (Cue: Hallelujah Chorus.)

From day one, Tom referred to her as The Lady, so her real name never fully lodged itself in my memory. I even had her in my address book as *Lady, The.*

The Lady was French and very crabby, and I thought these qualities made her a good bet: the French supposedly know how to cook and her crabbiness made her a kindred spirit. Also, she favored seafood, which I thought would be healthy for us. She'd show up daily, kicking Oliver out of her way as she entered the kitchen in those gross pants. She'd plunk steaming pots of fishy food down on the counter, snatch her check, and leave. My command of French was insufficient to grasp most of what she muttered as she exited, but the word *merde* rang a bell.

Yet I forgave her behavior. Of course she was crabby: she cooked all day, and then she had to schlep the food to us and other lazy-ass people for a fee that was only modest. The reason her fee was modest was that since each of her portions was the size of a Prius, one dinner would feed both me and my husband. What a bargain, I thought: two feedings for the price of one! And she'd bring it to the house! I could just throw the kids a pizza (Frisbee-style) and then all I had to do to prepare for dinner *avec mon mari* was chill the wineglasses!

Suddenly, *la vie* was looking *très belle!*

In honor of The Lady I bought placemats that read *le chien dans le jardin* with a picture of an Oliver look-alike leaping over a flower. (Real-life Oliver would be more likely to eat the flower than to leap over it.) I took to wearing an apron my sister had sent me for Christmas that had the Eiffel Tower on it. On Tuesdays and Thursdays, as the sun set in *l'ouest,* I'd light candles and present Tom with The Lady's offering of the day.

"*Voilà!*"

There was one problem with The Lady.

Now, you already know that I am not a picky eater, but I am picky in one respect: If I pay for prepared food, I prefer that it be edible. What The Lady brought was not edible food unless you happened to be, say, Oliver.

For a few nights, I was so thrilled that The Lady, not I, was cooking dinner for me and Tom that I chose to ignore how disgusting the food actually was.

"How very Mediterranean!" I'd exclaim over salmon that required an electric utensil to carve.

"Well . . . it's kind of . . . exotic!" I said in defense of a sea bass that tasted like a roasted soccer shoe.

Tom tried hard to embrace my new dinner plan. He wanted to alleviate my kitchen woes, to cut the ropes that tied me to the food processor. Still, the signs of his displeasure with The Lady's cuisine grew more obvious with each deep-fried sea urchin.

"Is this The Lady?" he'd ask, eyeing the unsightly mass on his plate with ill-concealed dread.

"Mais oui!" I'd say. Tom would sigh, take a few bites, and then summon Oliver.

This went on for several days, and I reveled in my new freedom. On The Lady nights, instead of chopping leeks and pounding veal, I went to Zumba classes.

Then The Lady made the fish soup.

She showed up with a vat of it, her sense of proportion even more whacked than usual.

It should have been a red flag when, as The Lady did her usual kick-'n-curse food drop, Oliver followed her to the door and sank his teeth into the hem of her pants. Although he released her immediately, the pants were a little ripped (as, I suspect, was The Lady). She let forth such a string of expletives and moans, you'd have thought she'd been mauled by a grizzly. When I apologized, wrote her a check to cover the cost of new pants, and promised to send Oliver to the Dog Whisperer, she was somewhat mollified.

The Lady exited, with one last, fierce *"Merde!"*

I gave Oliver a high five.

Her revenge was cooling on the kitchen counter.

I peeled back the Tupperware lid to inspect the soup. It was brown and viscous and smelled the way our bathroom did that time we had sewer gas. I poked around in it, looking for a friendly scallop, a cheery chunk of halibut, maybe a leek or a tomato. But the only identifiables I could find were okra, cabbage, and a few weary shrimp.

Finally slipping out of denial, I had to admit that this soup was hideous, offensive, the worst meal I'd been witness to since my brother poached a rabbit.

Just to be sure, I did the Canine Response Test. After carefully removing the shrimp shells, I gave a cup of the soup to Oliver. He sniffed it, looked at me sadly, and crossed the floor to sleep in a ventilated area.

Who was I kidding? The Lady's food sucked. I hated it, Tom hated it, even Oliver approached it with caution. My days as a delusional *Maîtresse du Café* needed to end; I needed to *renvoyer* the lady. I made the phone call, which (predictably) ended in the *m*-word.

Over the next several post-Lady weeks, I did some serious research, found a handful of good takeout places, and established a decent balance between home-cooked and outsourced meals, so my cooking duties became much less irritating. But "The Lady" became the generic term in our house for any food that was not cooked by me. Even the kids would ask, when presented with takeout food, regardless of its origin, "Is this The Lady?"

"Yes," I'd say, and then, merrily grabbing the car keys, "Oops, gotta go! I'm late for Zumba!"

This chapter offers many easy recipes for fish. If The Lady had had access to them, she might have been slightly less crabby and maybe would not have used the *m*-word quite so much.

Fish Soup The Lady Should Have Made

HERE'S A RECIPE FOR A FISH SOUP (or if you're feeling French, call it *Soupe de la Mer*) that The Lady could have made instead of that nasty *Soupe de la Merde* she brought us that caused Oliver to shred her pants.

Although the ingredient list is a tad long by my standards, you get a lot of bang for your buck: The stew is healthy, lean, and the kids like it. Also, you can make the base a couple of days in advance (or even freeze it) and, just before you're ready to eat, bring it to a simmer and throw in the seafood. ✳ SERVES 4 TO 6

3 tablespoons olive oil

1 onion, chopped

1 carrot, peeled and chopped

1 rib celery, chopped

½ teaspoon dried basil

½ teaspoon dried oregano

1 teaspoon kosher salt

Freshly ground black pepper, to taste

1 can (28 ounces) whole Italian plum tomatoes, drained and coarsely chopped

2 cups fish stock (many supermarkets carry frozen pints of good fish stock)

2 cups dry white wine

1 pound halibut, flounder, or other white fish, cut into bite-size chunks

8 large shrimp, shelled and deveined

8 sea scallops

1. Heat the olive oil in a heavy soup pot over medium-low heat. Add the onion and cook until it is soft and translucent, about 10 minutes.

2. Add the carrot, celery, basil, oregano, salt, and pepper, and cook, stirring occasionally, until the vegetables are tender, about 5 minutes. Add the tomatoes, stock, and wine, and bring the soup to a boil. Lower the heat and simmer, partially covered, for 30 minutes.

3. Five minutes before serving, add the halibut. Two minutes before serving, add the shrimp and the scallops. Serve immediately.

VARIATIONS Although I never do this because of my picky family, you can add mussels or clams to your stew: After you've made the base, add the shellfish and cook until the shells open; then remove the shellfish and set it aside. Cook the fish, shrimp, and scallops, then return the shellfish to the stew.

Pescatarian Salmon

I JUST HEARD THAT THE WORD *PESCATARIAN* has finally been entered into the pages of the Merriam-Webster's dictionary. You may wonder why I care about this word's new status, and I don't, not deeply, but it caught my attention because of Quentin.

We knew Quentin in the early years of our marriage because he was Tom's cousin Sarah's soon-to-be-ex-husband. They came over a few times for dinner, but then Sarah dumped Quentin and he vanished from our lives.

Six foot five, Quentin reminded me of a super-size Sherlock Holmes: he wore tweed, smoked a pipe, and spoke with a slight English accent, unusual for someone raised in the San Fernando Valley.

The most irksome thing about Quentin was the way he used words that were way bigger than the situation required. He once told five-year-old Elizabeth, when she resisted cleaning up her Legos, "Procrastination is the precursor of chaos." (Elizabeth was not impressed.)

Shortly before their separation, Quentin and Sarah came to dinner and Quentin rejected my lovely but labor-intensive beef stew, announcing that, due to "a quest to, sort of, reinvigorate and cleanse myself, I've become a pescatarian." I was already crabby thanks to browning fifty cubes of beef, making a separate meal for our children (who were in their White Food Phase), and spilling red wine on my pink suede shoes. I did not know what new form of pickiness pescatarianism was, but I was in no mood to request a definition. I shoved a plate in Quentin's hands: "Fine. Eat salad, big guy."

Later, when I had calmed down, I cracked open my Merriam-Webster's to look up "pescatarian," but it was not in there, leaving me to hope Sarah would get the divorce going so I would not have to bother figuring out Quentin's food preferences.

Now that the word has finally been admitted to the dictionary's pages, all the world knows its meaning. It's defined as a pesky person who eats only fish and fails to alert you to that irritating fact until you set a plate of beef stew in front of him. ✳ SERVES 6

6 pieces salmon fillet (about 6 ounces each)

6 tablespoons soy sauce

1. Preheat the broiler. Line a rimmed baking sheet with aluminum foil.

2. Place the salmon fillets, skin side down, on the prepared baking sheet, and brush 1 tablespoon of the soy sauce over each fillet. Broil until the fish is opaque all the way through and crispy on top, about 12 minutes.

3. Serve immediately.

Mellow Merlot Salmon

IF YOU THOUGHT PESCATARIAN SALMON was too easy and you would like something more challenging, you should have your head examined. If, after therapy, you still want a more complex salmon recipe, here's one that should satisfy your masochistic streak.

Although I am usually too lazy to make this, when I do, it's good enough that it makes me feel like an accomplished, talented chef instead of just a crabby cook staggering around the kitchen, cursing at a spatula. ✳ SERVES 4

1½ cups Merlot wine

2 shallots, finely chopped

7 tablespoons unsalted butter

4 pieces salmon fillet
(about 6 ounces each)

1 tablespoon olive oil

Kosher salt and freshly ground black
pepper, to taste

1. Put the Merlot and the shallots in a saucepan and bring to a simmer. Continue to simmer until the wine has reduced to about 3 tablespoons. (This will take a while, 15 to 20 minutes. File your nails.)

2. Meanwhile, preheat the oven to 500°F.

3. Swirl the butter, 1 tablespoon at a time, into the reduced wine mixture, stirring after each addition until it melts. Set the sauce aside.

4. Line a rimmed baking sheet with aluminum foil and place it in the oven to heat up for 5 minutes.

5. Rub the salmon fillets with the olive oil, and sprinkle them lightly with salt and pepper. Place the fillets, skin side down, on the hot baking sheet and reduce the oven temperature to 300°F. Roast the salmon for 10 to 12 minutes for medium-rare, or a little longer if you prefer. (My finicky husband likes his salmon *very* well done.)

6. Warm the wine sauce slightly if necessary. Pour some of it on each plate and place the salmon on top. Serve immediately.

Fish Stix

FISH WAS SELDOM ON THE MENU when I was growing up. In the suburbs of Chicago in the 1950s and '60s, it was hard to find anything truly fresh without conducting a serious search, for which my mother had neither the time nor the patience. Also, she thought of cooking fish for eight people as both daunting and smelly. It was so much easier to roast a steer.

However, once in a while my mother would be inspired to acquaint us with some form of seafood other than canned tuna, and she'd cook up some frozen fish sticks. She would serve them infrequently, allowing enough time between servings for us to forget how nasty they were. Even with a ketchup/stick ratio of 2 to 1, they were tough to choke down.

I think it was my father who hated them most. I once caught him spitting out a piece of fish stick with a ferocity equaled only by my daughter Elizabeth that time she took a bite of a soy hot dog.

But this fresh version of the stick was a breakthrough dish for my fish-resistant children. When they were young, they mistook them for something you'd get at McDonald's and ate them happily, with almost as much ketchup as I'd dumped on my stick dinner in the olden days. More recently, we've gone over to eating them with a tasty dip, which is only slightly more irritating to provide than the red stuff. ✳ SERVES 4

For the dip
½ cup mayonnaise
2 tablespoons crème fraîche or
  sour cream
2 tablespoons fresh lemon juice
2 tablespoons chopped fresh dill,
  or 1 teaspoon dried
1 clove garlic, minced
¼ teaspoon freshly ground black
  pepper

For the fish sticks
1 pound tilapia or other white fish
1 egg
1 cup panko (Japanese bread crumbs)
½ teaspoon paprika
½ teaspoon salt

Freshly ground black pepper, to taste
2 tablespoons vegetable oil

1. Prepare the dip: Combine all the dip ingredients in a small bowl, and mix well. Set the dip aside.

2. Rinse the fish and pat it dry with paper towels. Cut it into approximately 2 x 1-inch rectangles.

3. Beat the egg in a small bowl. Mix the panko, paprika, salt, and pepper together on a pie plate. Dip each fish piece into the egg and then into the panko mixture, coating it completely.

4. Heat the oil in a large nonstick skillet over medium heat. Place the fish pieces in the skillet and fry until they are golden, 2 to 3 minutes on each side.

5. Drain the fish on paper towels and serve immediately, with the dip on the side.

Under the Sea Scallops

AS I WAS COOKING THESE SCALLOPS the other day, the song "Under the Sea" came to mind, and it stuck there for hours. It's one of the genius songs from the movie *The Little Mermaid.* I must have watched it a thousand times. Well, actually I didn't watch it— I listened to it from the kitchen, when I used that video to keep the kids occupied in the adjoining room while I cooked their dinner.

I got to know a lot of movie soundtracks when I was cooking for young children; those videos were my weapons of mass distraction. Luckily, the girls' favorites were good stuff; it was the era of *Beauty and the Beast* and *Aladdin,* shows with entirely listener-friendly music that could take the edge off crabby cooking. I'd even catch myself dancing while draining the fusilli.

"Under the Sea" must have come to mind on scallop night because of the obvious seafood connection, although I don't think scallops actually appeared in the film. But then, I'm not sure what scallops look like in their original form, pre-shelling. For all I know there was a whole chorus line of them in the movie that I mistook for other fishy things, singing in brilliant unison:

When you serve scallops, every kid gallops
Right to the table, fast as they're able.
Nobody's bitchin' in Mama's kitchen
When dinner comes from down in the deep, from
Under the sea!

(Or something like that.) ✳ SERVES 4

1 cup fresh orange juice
½ cup dry white wine
1 large shallot, finely chopped
8 tablespoons (1 stick) unsalted butter
2 tablespoons fresh lime juice
2 tablespoons finely chopped fresh
  mint
20 to 24 sea scallops
Coarse salt and freshly ground black
  pepper, to taste
1 tablespoon vegetable oil

1. Pour the orange juice and the wine into a small saucepan, and add the shallot. Bring the mixture to a simmer over medium heat, and cook it until it is reduced to about ¼ cup, 12 to 15 minutes. Remove the pan from the heat and stir in the butter, 1 tablespoon at a time, stirring each addition until it melts. Stir in the lime juice and the mint, cover the pan, and set it aside.

2. Sprinkle the scallops lightly on both sides with salt and pepper. Heat the oil in a large nonstick skillet over medium heat. When the pan is hot, add the scallops and cook until they are golden on both sides, about 2 minutes per side.

3. Pour the sauce onto four plates, place the scallops on top, and serve.

Shrimpesto

I'M FEELING REALLY OUT OF STEP with the world. While browsing through *Real Simple* magazine, I stumbled upon the results of a survey of 2,600 women that revealed their top five wishes: (1) a spouse who makes more money than the current spouse, (2) plastic surgery, (3) to tell her boss exactly how she feels, (4) more kids, and (5) separate bathrooms.

As for number 1, it sounds like they want to swap the current spouse for a richer one. I *so* do not want this. Finding a new spouse would be way too time-consuming and would involve going on dates to places like Hooters. Besides, I like my spouse, although I hate the word "spouse," which makes him sound rodent-like.

As for number 2, I once saw a terrifying documentary of a face-lift that totally put me off—way too much gore—plus it's barbaric and anti-feminist and also I'd be afraid I'd end up looking like the pilot of a plane that's going way too fast.

Number 3 is irrelevant because I am my own boss and I tell myself exactly how I feel 24/7, which is sort of irritating, but most likely I will not fire myself as jobs are hard to get these days.

And 4? Nope. Had 'em, love 'em, done.

Number 5 is another story. On this one I'm finally in synch with the women surveyed. I believe that it's in the best interest of romantic partners to avoid seeing each other doing things involving floss, shower caps, bandages, ointment, razors, and . . . all that other stuff. The bathroom should be like Vegas: what happens in there stays in there, out of a spouse's line of vision. The best way to achieve that is with a his/ hers setup.

But I'd give up the separate bathrooms in a heartbeat if someone would grant me my fondest wish (and I'm stunned it's not number 1 on the *R.S.* list): I wish my spouse could cook.

This shrimp recipe is so simple that anybody's spouse could prepare it, even mine. (And I wish he would, so I'd have more time to look into building that second bathroom.) While he's at it, it wouldn't kill him to make a little rice to go with it. ✳ SERVES 4

For the pesto
1 clove garlic
½ cup chopped walnuts
1 cup (packed) fresh basil leaves
½ cup olive oil
2 teaspoons finely grated lemon zest
2 teaspoons fresh lemon juice
¼ teaspoon salt

For the shrimp
24 large shrimp, shelled and deveined
3 tablespoons olive oil
Kosher salt and freshly ground black pepper, to taste

1. Prepare the pesto: Place the garlic in a food processor and pulse until it is finely chopped. Add the walnuts and pulse briefly. Add the basil leaves, and with the motor running, add the oil in a thin stream, processing until the mixture forms a thick paste. Add the lemon zest and juice and the salt, and pulse briefly to combine. Set the pesto aside.

2. Place the shrimp in a bowl. Add 2 tablespoons of the olive oil, sprinkle with salt and pepper to taste, and toss to cover the shrimp evenly with the oil and seasonings.

3. Heat the remaining 1 tablespoon olive oil in a large skillet over medium heat. Add the shrimp and cook until they are pink, 2 to 3 minutes per side. Add the pesto to the skillet and remove it from the heat. Swirl the shrimp in the sauce to coat them.

4. Divide the shrimp among four plates and serve immediately.

NOTE These days you can find excellent frozen shelled, deveined shrimp to keep in the freezer for days when buying fresh shrimp is one errand too many.

Crumby John Dory

THERE'S WAY TMI THESE DAYS about which fish is endangered and which is hazardous to your health because of all the stuff we stupid humans dump in the water. I mean, I kind of want to know this stuff, but the warnings seem to change weekly, so it's hard to keep up, and I'm the lazy type who hates to research fish issues (a.k.a. fishues).

So I was grateful when my friend Carla told me that John Dory was one of the most healthful fish you can eat. I will admit that I sort of spaced out when she told me why that was the case, so don't ask me. I'm happy just to blithely take my friend's word for it and skip the research.

If you are lazy like me, then take *my* word for it and get yourself some J. Dory. If you can't find it, try this recipe with tilapia. I just heard someone on TV say that it has no fishues either, but I changed the channel before she explained why. (So sue me. *American Idol* was on.) ✳ SERVES 4

¼ cup whole almonds

1 clove garlic

2 tablespoons coarsely chopped fresh parsley

1 tablespoon fresh thyme leaves, or ½ teaspoon dried

2 thick slices country-style white bread

2 tablespoons unsalted butter, melted

½ teaspoon salt

¼ teaspoon freshly ground black pepper

4 fillets John Dory (6 to 8 ounces each)

1 tablespoon olive oil

Lemon wedges, for serving

1. Preheat the oven to 350°F. Line a rimmed baking sheet with aluminum foil.

2. Place the almonds in a food processor and process until they are finely chopped. Set the almonds aside.

3. Place the garlic, parsley, and thyme in the food processor and process until they are minced. Tear the bread into chunks, add them to the mixture in the processor, and process until they are reduced to large crumbs. Combine the bread mixture with the almonds, melted butter, salt, and pepper, and toss to mix well.

4. Spread the bread crumb mixture evenly in the prepared baking sheet, and bake until the crumbs are just golden and crispy, 12 to 15 minutes. Transfer the toasted crumbs to a bowl and raise the oven temperature to 425°F.

5. Lightly rub the fish fillets with the olive oil, and place them on the baking sheet. Cover them with the crumb mixture. Bake until the fish is flaky in the thickest part and the crumbs are nicely browned, 12 minutes or so.

6. Serve immediately, with lemon wedges alongside.

Swordfish (It Takes a Grillage)

THIS PAST MARCH, we had a Cuss Free Week in California. It looks like it's going to become a regular feature on the state calendar, seven gosh darn days during which we cussers must abstain.

While, as a crabby cook, I found the week challenging (especially around dinner time), I did pretty well, substituting words like "shoot" and "phooey" for my regular ones. I noticed, however, that others were not so compliant. For instance, that gas station attendant really let loose when I forgot to remove the gas pump/hose/thing from my vehicle before leaving his premises. Golly, he was mad. I tried to tell him about the significance of Cuss Free Week but I guess he didn't hear me, because he just told me to %@#%!! off.

Even my husband, Tom, who is normally a law-abiding citizen, broke the rules one night that week, when we lost power just as he snapped on the TV to chill with a little ESPN. In spite of my gentle reminder that California wasn't cussin', he uttered a few more naughty ones when forced to read the sports section by dim flashlight.

The good news was that I had just taken my gas grill out of hibernation, so I was able to grill some swordfish (one of Tom's favorites), which we ate by candlelight.

I will admit, however, that the next day, when Oliver vomited on the carpet just as I was leaving for the airport and then my flight was delayed three hours, I was glad when we were finally airborne, safely out of the state, so I could let fly with a little colorful language.

Anyway, try this swordfish. Whether or not your language is legally restricted, this recipe is so easy, there's no cussin' in the kitchen. ✳ SERVES 4

¼ cup olive oil, plus extra for the grill
¼ cup balsamic vinegar
1 tablespoon Dijon mustard
2 cloves garlic, minced
2 tablespoons chopped fresh rosemary
½ teaspoon coarse salt
Freshly ground black pepper, to taste
4 swordfish steaks (6 to 8 ounces each, 1-inch thick)

1. Mix the olive oil, vinegar, mustard, garlic, rosemary, salt, and pepper together in a small bowl. Place the swordfish steaks in a flat dish that can hold them in a single layer. Pour the marinade over the steaks, and turn them so both sides are well coated. Cover the dish with aluminum foil or plastic wrap, and let the fish marinate for an hour or so at room temperature.

2. Preheat your gas grill to medium, or prepare a charcoal grill.

3. When the grill is hot, brush the grate with oil to prevent the fish from sticking to it. Place the swordfish on the grill and cook for 5 to 7 minutes on each side, depending on the thickness of the fish. The fish is done when it is no longer pink in the middle and flakes easily.

4. Let the fish rest, tented with foil, for about 5 minutes before serving.

Bluefish, Whitefish

WHEN WE JOIN TOM'S EXTENDED FAMILY on Cape Cod for two weeks every summer, we are fifteen for dinner almost every night. There's a whole lot of cooking going on. (Are you familiar with the expression "a busman's holiday"?) But it's usually a group effort, so the pain is minimal—and the camaraderie is excellent.

One night, when I was new to the family—anxious to please but unacquainted with their food foibles—I bought a sack of bluefish to cook for dinner. When I displayed it for my sister-in-law Ellen, she informed me that bluefish was the one type of seafood that Grandpa Banky detested.

I had a rush of pre-prandial panic. It was too late for a re-shop, and my father-in-law always loved and counted on a nice dinner. I couldn't just irritably make him a PBJ while everyone else scarfed down fish, as I would with a kid. But while I was prepping the fish, imagining Banky's revulsion at the sight of it, and then at the sight of me, Ellen slipped me a recipe that she thought might be Banky-proof. Here it is. ✳ SERVES 4

2 pounds bluefish fillets
½ cup mayonnaise
2 tablespoons Dijon mustard
1 teaspoon minced garlic
Freshly ground black pepper
Lemon wedges, for serving

1. Preheat the broiler. Line a rimmed baking sheet with aluminum foil.

2. Place the fillets in the prepared baking sheet. Mix the mayonnaise, mustard, garlic, and pepper together in a small bowl, and schmear the mixture on the fish, covering it completely.

3. Broil the fish for 8 to 10 minutes, depending on the thickness. The fish is done when it flakes easily at the thickest part.

4. Serve the bluefish with lemon wedges.

WHAT HAPPENED NEXT

A S WE SAT DOWN TO DINNER, Banky-the-bluefish-hater asked what I was serving. I told a white lie.

"It's whitefish," I said. (Bluefish, whitefish—clearly I'd been reading too much Dr. Seuss.) My father-in-law ate every morsel. But I think he was on to me. Later, when we were drying the dishes, he was softly singing "Am I Blue?"

Sadly, Grandpa Banky (a.k.a. Donald) is no longer with us.

I always loved his *joie de vivre,* which included a rapturous appreciation of good food. Although I am a crabby cook, I am happy to have delivered a few meals to Banky (some in disguise) that he ate with great pleasure.

If there is a heaven, I'm sure he's there, and I'm sure they are feeding him well, serving no bluefish, I hope, unless it's "whitefish."

SEVEN

Beside Myself

THE TROUBLE WITH SIDE DISHES is that they're just side dishes. You have to cook them in addition to a whole lot of other stuff. In the years when I was cooking too much for picky people, I was usually too burned out at dinnertime to get my mind around side dishes.

If only family dinners could've been based on the model of those PTA potlucks I used to go to. PTA volunteers assembled for meetings in the evening and you'd get asked to bring *just* the salad, or *just* the carrots, and other people would provide the rest. I'd have been a less crabby cook if I could have cooked *just* the chicken, while my kids each brought a side dish and my husband contributed the brownies.

The only problem with the PTA potluck dinners was that you had to cook something for them and also cook dinner for your uninvited family. Two cooking events in one evening were one too many. (Well, actually, *two* too many, but who's counting?)

One PTA event I used to love, however, was their annual fair at the kids' elementary school, because they had a casserole fundraiser: people would donate casseroles for desperate housewives to buy and take home. I used to get up early on the day of the fair, not so much because I was an avid volunteer, willing to man (woman) a booth or monitor the silent auction, but because I wanted to get my hands on some frozen casseroles. You had to get there early because other desperados like me would get there even earlier and there'd be nothing left but that gnarly one with the sausage and okra.

I'd always go home with at least two casseroles, each the size of a Buick. I'd be thrilled that dinner was done for several days.

It was a nice school (not just because of the casseroles), but also a demanding one. They had a whole slew of events that required parental food donations. I'd do whatever I possibly could to avoid being responsible for the entree. That was the most odious job: cooking chicken for forty people. If I couldn't get the coveted assignment of bringing the bottled water, my next choice was dessert. I liked the idea of using it as an opportunity to bake things I found intriguing but would never make for my picky family, like date nut bars or lemon walnut cookies.

But crabby cooks tend to space out when it comes to cooking obligations. I invariably forgot the event, let alone my food task, until my child reminded me the morning of. So I'd tear down to the market, buy cookies, and throw them on a scenic platter so they'd look less like they were fresh from Costco.

One thing I used to do willingly was to provide sides for the monthly Teacher Appreciation Luncheons. I figured if I made something really delicious, I could curry favor with the teachers, so they'd look more favorably on my child and write her a strong college recommendation letter. Then I realized this was risky. In this new age of pickiness, they might not like what I brought. And if they found the sweet potatoes peculiar or the roasted asparagus too garlicky, they'd be subtly influenced. They'd find themselves rethinking the A– they were about to give my kid. Or what if they got ill and blamed it on my cooking? Forget applying to a fancy-pants East Coast university when the dean just vomited up your succotash.

So I backed off trying to impress the teachers, leaving my daughter to do so without my help.

Now that my girls are in college, I don't have any more school cooking obligations, thank goodness. This chapter is full of side dishes I might have brought to PTA events, and that we eat at my house if I'm not too crabby to make them.

Roasted Vegetables

HERE'S ONE SOLUTION TO THE PROBLEM of picky vegetable eaters. If you have a large baking sheet, you can cook a few different kinds of vegetables at once and let the picky people pick a pepper or whatever your picky people prefer to pick. ✳ SERVES 4

1 pound fingerling potatoes
3 tablespoons olive oil
1½ teaspoons minced garlic
¾ teaspoon salt
Freshly ground black pepper, to taste
4 carrots, peeled
1 pound asparagus
2 tablespoons chopped fresh parsley
2 tablespoons chopped fresh thyme
(optional)

1. Preheat the oven to 400°F.

2. Cut the potatoes in half lengthwise, and pat the cut sides dry with paper towels. Place the potatoes in a bowl and add 1 tablespoon of the oil, ½ teaspoon of the garlic, ¼ teaspoon of the salt, and a little pepper (a few twists of the mill). Toss everything together gently, and then arrange the potatoes in a single layer on a large baking sheet. Place it in the oven and roast for 5 minutes.

3. While the potatoes are cooking, cut the carrots into 1-inch slices. (If the carrots are very thick, make the slices thinner.) Place the carrots in the same bowl, and do as you did with the potatoes: add 1 tablespoon oil, ½ teaspoon garlic, ¼ teaspoon salt, and a little pepper. Mix well.

4. Remove the baking sheet from the oven, and arrange the carrots on it in a single layer. Return the baking sheet to the oven and roast for 10 minutes.

5. Meanwhile, trim off the ends of the asparagus, place the asparagus spears in the bowl, and toss them with 1 tablespoon oil, ½ teaspoon garlic, ¼ teaspoon salt, and a little pepper.

6. Remove the baking sheet from the oven, add the asparagus in a single layer, and continue roasting the vegetables until they are all tender, about 10 minutes.

7. Remove the baking sheet from the oven, sprinkle the vegetables with the parsley, and the thyme if you are using it, and serve.

VARIATIONS Infinite. You can add or substitute green beans (20 minutes), zucchini cut in half lengthwise (10 minutes), quartered onions (30 minutes), or whatever.

You can sprinkle the vegetables with grated Parmigiano-Reggiano cheese for the last few minutes of roasting. Or try other herbs or curry powder in place of the parsley and thyme.

And if you can't find fingerling potatoes, just use other small potatoes or cut larger potatoes into 1-inch chunks.

Bunny's Carrots 'n Snaps

FROM WHAT I UNDERSTAND, there's a new gizmo you can install in your phone that allows you to produce sounds that give you an excuse to end the call. So if you're in a conversation with a long-winded relative, you can press button #3 and it'll produce the sound of a baby crying ("Gotta hang up, it's diaper time!") or hit #2 for a dog whining ("Jeez, sorry, gotta feed the pup!").

One sound that's offered is of cows mooing. While this might work if you live on a dairy farm, anyone on the phone with me would be dubious if I excused myself to milk Daisy. My feeling is one should stick to sounds that don't defy credibility.

The crying baby would be tough for me to explain, as my children are grown. Likewise a runaway horse, say, or a nuclear explosion. Even the whining dog is a stretch; when Oliver is hungry, he doesn't complain. He just makes off with a roasted chicken or other countertop finds.

If I were to customize my sounds for maximum believability, I'd include one of a teenager yelling that she has no clean underwear. I'd alternate that choice with the sound of the neighbor honking at me to move my #@&%!! car, which my daughter has parked squarely in front of the neighbor's driveway. Another sound might be that of the postal worker threatening to sue because Oliver has shredded his pants.

A solidly credible sound for me would be that of the kitchen smoke alarm. Anyone familiar with my distracted cooking style would buy that completely ("Whoops, gotta run, kitchen's on fire!"). This past week I actually did have to hang up on someone because I was burning the vegetables (for the second time in a week).

What would be really useful would be a phone that would double as a fire extinguisher. Better yet, one that would actually cook the vegetables, allowing me more time to chat on the other line with long-winded relatives.

This is my new fave vegetable dish, all sweet and crunchy and minty, and so far I have never burnt it. ✳ SERVES 4 TO 6

2 tablespoons unsalted butter

4 large carrots, peeled and sliced into thin disks (I use the food processor for slicing)

1 clove garlic, minced

½ teaspoon coarse salt

Freshly ground black pepper to taste

8 ounces sugar snap peas, trimmed, strings removed

2 tablespoons finely chopped fresh mint

1 teaspoon finely grated lemon zest

1. Melt the butter in a large skillet over medium heat. Add the carrots, garlic, salt, and pepper, and cook, stirring, for 1 minute.

2. Add ¼ cup water, cover the skillet, reduce the heat to low, and cook, stirring occasionally, until the carrots are almost tender, 3 to 4 minutes.

3. Add the snap peas and cook until they are crisp-tender, 2 to 3 minutes.

4. Stir in the mint and the lemon zest, and serve.

Mashed New Potatoes and Peas

SOMEONE ONCE TOLD ME THAT NEW POTATOES are the healthiest kind of spud you can eat. This revelation occurred at a cocktail party, and although I can't remember her name, I have a clear image in my mind of the purveyor of this fascinating piece of information. She was extremely tall and slender, with bright red, wiry hair. Although she was very chic in a black sleeveless dress and harsh, black-rimmed glasses, she had a piece of spinach in her teeth, the residue of a tasty hors d'oeuvre that was making the rounds, which I'd avoided precisely because of the spinach-in-your-teeth factor.

I'm not sure why we were reduced to discussing root vegetables at a cocktail party, but I was so distracted by the spinach particle that I didn't absorb her lecture on the nutritional value of new potatoes (something about fiber ratios), so you'll have to Google that. But ever since that evening, when a potato is called for, I usually opt for the new (except when I'm baking potatoes, when I go for the Yukon Gold).

Anyway, there may be nutritional reasons for picking new potatoes, but I like this recipe mostly because there's no peeling involved, an activity that brings a curse to the lips of any crabby cook. You just chunk up the potatoes, boil 'em, and mash 'em.

Unsuspecting diners will think you're being original by showing a little skin, instead of what you really are being, which is just plain crabby. ✳ SERVES 4 TO 6

1 pound new red potatoes, cut in half
1 cup frozen peas, thawed
3 tablespoons unsalted butter
⅓ cup whole milk or half-and-half
½ teaspoon salt
Freshly ground black pepper, to taste

1. Bring a pot of lightly salted water to a boil. Add the potatoes, and cook until they are tender, about 15 minutes. Add the peas and cook for about 2 minutes more. Then drain the peas and potatoes and return them to the pot.

2. Add the butter, milk, salt, and pepper, and mash the potatoes and peas with a potato masher just until the potatoes are broken up and chunky—not entirely smooth.

3. Serve immediately.

VARIATIONS Add a sprinkle of chopped fresh parsley, dill, chives, and/or mint. And if you can't find new potatoes (which, the spinach-teeth-lady also informed me, are defined as any immature potato— I'd always assumed they were just the little red ones), you can just use larger red-skinned potatoes, cut into chunks.

Creamy Dreamy Sweet Potatoes

THIS DISH ALWAYS REMINDS ME of one my fake grandmother used to make: baked canned yams with marshmallows on top. The difference is that this recipe is sublime, while the F.G.'s always made me gag, due to my aversion to marshmallows.

I saw a video on YouTube of a study in which children, one after the other, are seated at a table with a marshmallow placed in front of them. A lady tells them they'll be left alone for a time, and that if they can resist eating the marshmallow, they'll get to eat two marshmallows upon her return. In the video, you see children exercising varying levels of restraint, from squirmy resistance to instant caving.

The researchers posited that the kids who were best able to postpone gratification were more likely to be successful later in life. But if I'd been one of the subjects, I'd have fooled all those smug, marshmallow-hugging scientists. I'd have been a model of restraint, breezing through to a double portion, but only because I don't *like* marshmallows. If they'd put a Junior Mint on the plate, I'd have been toast.

Based on what they assumed was my mature behavior, they'd have had me pegged as the next Ruth Bader Ginsburg or Beyoncé. (My husband would've preferred the latter.) Instead, of course, I grew up to be a crabby marshmallow-hater.

Anyway, try this dish out on your family. They will not be able to resist eating it, but this does not mean that they are losers—just that the spuds are dreamy. ✳ SERVES 5 OR 6

1 tablespoon unsalted butter

2 pounds (about 3 medium) sweet potatoes or yams

Kosher salt and freshly ground black pepper, to taste

2 tablespoons chopped fresh thyme leaves

1 cup heavy (whipping) cream

1. Preheat the oven to 425°F. Butter a casserole or gratin dish with the 1 tablespoon butter.

2. Peel the sweet potatoes and cut them into ¼-inch-thick slices. Arrange the potato slices in the prepared casserole dish in layers, sprinkling each layer lightly with salt, pepper, and a teaspoon or so of thyme. Pour the cream over the potatoes, making sure to coat the ones on top.

3. Cover the dish tightly, place it in the oven, and cook until the cream is almost absorbed and the potatoes almost tender, about 45 minutes. Then remove the cover, return the dish to the oven, and cook until the potatoes are very tender and the top is lightly browned, about 15 minutes.

4. Serve hot.

VARIATIONS You can change the seasoning: omit the thyme and sprinkle some curry powder on each layer, or try a mix of grated fresh ginger and grated orange zest. You can also throw in ½ cup chopped pecans or hazelnuts to make things more interesting. But please, no marshmallows.

Spinachy Rice

A FRIEND RECENTLY INFORMED ME that if you drop your cell phone in the toilet, you can retrieve it and place it in a jar of rice, and it will come chirping back to life. Supposedly the rice wicks away the offending toilet moisture. It's the same science that applies when you put rice in your salt shaker to keep the salt from getting clumpy. (I have never been organized enough to actually do this; I live with clumpy salt.)

If you are like me, you seldom venture into the bathroom with your cell phone. But my daughters have more intimate relations with their phones, and they have each had toilet/phone mishaps. On one such occasion, we tested the rice theory, burying Elizabeth's Nokia in a pile of Uncle Ben's and leaving it there for several hours. When we checked it for a pulse after all that rice immersion, it sputtered for a second, then resumed the death attitude and would not be resuscitated. We ended up having to throw out both the phone and a large quantity of what used to be perfectly good rice.

If you find yourself retrieving your cell phone from the jaws of your john, don't waste your time or your rice. Both can be put to better use making this delicious dish. It's so good that, if you can find a dry phone, you should invite some people over to share it. ✳ SERVES 4 TO 6

1 tablespoon unsalted butter

1 tablespoon olive oil

½ large onion, chopped

1 clove garlic, minced

4 cups cooked white or brown rice (see Note)

1 tablespoon soy sauce

½ cup grated Gruyère cheese

½ cup freshly grated cheddar cheese

3 to 4 cups baby spinach leaves

¼ teaspoon coarse salt

Freshly ground black pepper (about 6 twists of the mill)

1. Melt the butter in the olive oil in a wok, large skillet, or Dutch oven over medium-low heat. Add the onion and cook until it is soft and translucent, about 10 minutes. Add the garlic and cook for 1 minute.

2. Add the rice and soy sauce, and mix well with the onion and garlic. Add the cheeses and stir to mix them with the rice. Add the spinach, salt, and pepper, and gently combine all the ingredients.

3. Reduce the heat to its lowest setting, cover the wok, and cook, stirring occasionally, until the cheese has melted and the spinach has wilted, about 5 minutes.

4. Serve hot.

NOTE What? You don't happen to have 4 cups of leftover rice happily tucked away in your fridge? Then, all you have to do is bring 4 cups water to a boil in a large saucepan. Add 2 cups long-grain white or brown rice and a pinch or two of salt, stir, reduce the heat to a low simmer, cover the pot, and cook until tender, about 15 minutes for the white and 40 minutes for the brown. You can do this in the morning and then in the evening you'll feel positively un-crabby when it's time to make Spinachy Rice.

Cauliflower in Disguise

WHEN YOU SERVE THIS, your family will think you are giving them mashed potatoes, and this raises the question about full disclosure in cooking.

If a family member with highly refined taste buds gets suspicious and asks if he or she is eating mashed potatoes or some gnarly substitute, then it's up to you to decide which road to take. If you reply cheerfully and honestly that the vegetable in question is cauliflower, you may face irritating food rejection but you will sleep well that night, your conscience clear. Another option would be to jump from the table, pretending the lima beans are burning, thereby ducking the question. You could also do what I do: just lie. If sleep disturbance results, medicate. ✳ SERVES 4

1 head cauliflower, cored and broken into florets
¼ cup freshly grated Parmigiano-Reggiano cheese
3 tablespoons mascarpone cheese

½ teaspoon salt, or more if needed
Freshly ground black pepper, to taste
⅛ teaspoon ground nutmeg
2 tablespoons snipped fresh chives (optional)

1. Bring lightly salted water to a simmer in the bottom of a vegetable steamer. Place the cauliflower in the steamer basket, cover the steamer, and cook until the cauliflower is tender, about 15 minutes.

2. Transfer the cauliflower to a food processor, reserving the cooking water for the moment. Add the cheeses, salt, pepper, and nutmeg, and then puree. Taste, and add more salt, pepper, and/or nutmeg if needed. If the cauliflower seems a bit thick, stir in a spoonful or two of the cooking water.

3. Transfer the cauliflower to a serving bowl, sprinkle with the chives if you're using them, and serve.

Mama Beans

THESE BEANS MAKE A GOOD SIDE DISH, and they're also a fine main course on those nights when you completely forgot to buy food for dinner. You have no chicken, no beef, no pig products, and no patience, but you do have a few cans in the pantry. (My "pantry" is my garage, where I keep some emergency food supplies, supposedly reserved for earthquakes, stashed between the Christmas ornaments and the toolbox.) So you go to the pantry and retrieve some canned beans and tomatoes, and if you're lucky enough to have an onion lying around, you're good to go. Whip up some Mama Beans and rice, throw on some grated cheddar, and it's a meal all by itself. This happens often enough at my house, this last-minute pantry scramble, that the kids named the dish after me.

I like to add some jalapeño if I've got it, and a little zucchini, chopped small so my children won't suspect the presence of a green vegetable. And I always serve these beans with rice, or with riso or orzo pasta. ✳ SERVES 6 TO 8

2 tablespoons olive oil

1 medium onion, finely chopped

1 jalapeño pepper, seeded and finely chopped (optional)

2 cloves garlic, minced

2 cups canned crushed San Marzano tomatoes

1 medium zucchini, cut into ¼-inch dice

2 tablespoons chopped fresh oregano, or 1 teaspoon dried

½ teaspoon salt

Freshly ground black pepper, to taste

2 cans (15 ounces each) pinto beans or small white beans, rinsed and drained

Cooked rice or pasta, for serving

1 cup grated cheddar cheese

1. Heat the olive oil in a large skillet over medium-low heat. Add the onion, and the jalapeño if you're using it, and cook until the onion is soft and translucent, about 10 minutes. Add the garlic and cook for 1 minute.

2. Add the tomatoes, zucchini, oregano, salt, and pepper, and bring the mixture to a simmer. Cook until the zucchini is tender, about 3 minutes.

3. Add the beans and simmer until the sauce thickens a bit and the beans are heated through, 5 minutes. (Add a little water if you'd like the beans to be more "saucy.")

4. Serve hot, over rice or pasta, with the cheese sprinkled on top.

VARIATIONS You can use black beans instead of pinto beans, or a combination.

Zucchini Boats

I KNOW EXACTLY HOW THE HALF-CHEWED, desiccated disk of zucchini got into the linen closet; I can imagine the moment of its placement there.

It's dinnertime, and a kid has been told that vanilla pudding awaits those who finish their vegetables. She cheerfully pops that last piece of zucchini in her mouth, as if she's in full compliance. Then she excuses herself and goes to the bathroom, spitting the zucchini into her palm en route. Behind closed doors, she puts it in the closet under a striped beach towel. She's no dummy: it's winter and nobody will discover her deception until beach season. She washes her hands and goes merrily back to the table to receive her dessert.

I know this is what happened because I did the same thing so many times when I was a young vegetable-rejector. I had a different modus operandi, however. I flushed the offending food down the toilet, eliminating evidence. This was a popular method of disposal in my family. I can remember once spitting a gnarly string bean into the toilet, noting that someone had made a similar deposit ahead of me, but theirs was an exceptionally buoyant bean that had failed to flush.

When the flushing method was not possible, say when parents' suspicions were aroused by too much bathroom activity (or a flush failure), you'd have to get creative. My own children had it much harder as there are only two of them, so their actions were very exposed. But when I was growing up with five siblings, the chaos of our family dinners allowed for rolling peas to the floor, slipping a fistful of lima beans to whatever pet was under the table, or even whipping something out the window, as my brother once did with a broccoli spear.

Given how good we were at not eating green vegetables, it's amazing we didn't all get rickets or whatever you get when you are nutritionally deprived.

This kid-friendly zucchini dish is likely to be eaten, rather than disposed of. You can make the boats in advance and just pop 'em in the oven when dinner is upon you. And it presents well: it looks as though you went to much more trouble than you actually went to, so you will score points with those who give points for such achievements.

✳ SERVES 4

2 medium zucchini

1 tablespoon basil pesto, homemade (see page 127) or store-bought

Salt and freshly ground black pepper

2 tablespoons freshly grated Parmigiano-Reggiano cheese

1. Preheat the oven to 425°F.

2. Slice the zucchini in half lengthwise. Using a small spoon, scoop out the pulp of each zucchini half, leaving a shell that's about ¼-inch thick. Set the zucchini shells aside and place the pulp in a small bowl.

3. Chop the zucchini pulp. Add the pesto, ¼ teaspoon salt, and pepper to taste. Lightly salt the boats, and fill them with the zucchini/pesto mixture. Place the boats on a baking sheet and sprinkle them with the cheese.

4. Bake the zucchini boats until the cheese is bubbly and the zucchini is tender, about 20 minutes.

VARIATION Add ¼ cup toasted pine nuts to the zucchini/pesto mixture before you stuff your boats.

Hot Slaw

I LIKE TO THINK OF THIS DISH as the hot big brother of coleslaw— it's all cabbagey, healthy, and easy as pie.

But this raises the following question: Why do people say things are "easy as pie"? If they mean easy as *eating* pie, then I get it. But I think they usually mean easy as *making* a pie, which makes me wonder if the person who came up with the expression ever made a pie, because it is *so* not easy. And this reminds me that I actually once made a cabbage pie, which was quite terrible.

Anyway, this dish is a great side for most roasts, or for Chicken Nuggets (page 218) or for Fish Stix (page 122). ✳ SERVES 4 TO 6

½ head green cabbage (I prefer Savoy)
2 carrots, peeled
3 tablespoons unsalted butter
1 teaspoon salt
Freshly ground black pepper, to taste
¼ cup finely chopped fresh parsley
¼ cup finely chopped fresh dill
1 tablespoon grated lemon zest

1. Cut the cabbage half in half; then cut those halves in half. Place these large chunks of cabbage in a food processor fitted with the slicing disk, and slice them. Set the cabbage aside.

2. Grate the carrots in the food processor, using the grating disk. Set the carrots aside.

3. Melt the butter in a large skillet over medium heat. Add the cabbage, carrots, salt, and pepper. Cook, stirring occasionally, until the vegetables are tender, 10 minutes.

4. Stir in the parsley, dill, and lemon zest, and serve.

Golden Delicious Applesauce

THIS IS MY IDEA OF PERFECTION: a recipe with only one ingredient. I like to make it for that reason alone, just to revel in the fact that I have only one thing to mess with.

But it also happens to be really good with potato pancakes or roast pork, or topped with yogurt for breakfast. ✳ MAKES ABOUT 2 CUPS

4 Golden Delicious apples

1. Preheat the oven to 350°F.

2. Core the apples, using an apple corer or a knife. Cut the apples

in half vertically, and place the halves, cut side down (skin up), on a rimmed baking sheet. Place the baking sheet in the oven and cook until the apples are quite tender when pierced with a fork, 40 to 45 minutes. Remove the apples from the oven and let them cool.

3. When the apples are cool enough to handle, remove the skin and mash them with a potato masher, or place the fruit in a food processor and pulse five or six times, until you have a chunky sauce. Done!

Cranberry Sauce

ALTHOUGH I HAVE TO TELL YOU that Thanksgiving is one meal I really don't mind making (the holiday spirit propels me through the rough parts), there have been many years when I spent the holiday giving thanks that my sister-in-law was hosting, so all I had to do was bring a side dish.

I like to offer to make cranberry sauce, since this is the easiest task there is. Plus you can make it days in advance and just de-fridge it on the day, dump it into a scenic bowl, take it to Julie's house, and grab a Crantini (see page 160). This sauce is so good, the guests will actually think you lifted a finger.

Cranberry Sauce is also great with roasted or grilled chicken, or mixed with a little mayo as a sandwich spread. ✳ MAKES ABOUT 2½ CUPS

1 cup red wine (I like Merlot or Zinfandel), plus extra for drinking while you cook
1 cup (packed) light brown sugar
1 bag (12 ounces) fresh cranberries
½ cup sweetened dried cherries
Finely grated zest of 1 tangerine

1 cinnamon stick (about 3 inches)
1 sprig fresh rosemary
½ cup chopped walnuts (optional)

1. Combine the wine and brown sugar in a medium-size saucepan and bring to a boil over medium

heat. (Try not to drink too much of the extra wine yet, or you will screw this thing up.)

2. Add the cranberries, cherries, tangerine zest, cinnamon stick, rosemary, and walnuts. Reduce the heat to a simmer, partially cover the pan, and cook until the sauce thickens and the cranberries pop, 10 to 15 minutes. (At this point, you may drink a little of the extra wine because you are almost done.)

3. Dump the sauce into a scenic bowl, discarding the cinnamon stick and rosemary sprig, and refrigerate it until it's time to go to Julie's house, or wherever you are going. (Put the wine bottle away now and get a grip.)

L.A. Stuffing

IT'S DIFFICULT TO FEEL THANKSGIVING-Y IN L.A. because even in November, it looks like August outside. Mother Nature, in her recent whackedness, has been randomly eliminating the few seasonal changes we are supposed to have here. L.A. is just all hot and fire-scorched in the fall—relentlessly sunny.

I know many of you will have no patience with my whining about warm weather. But trust me, it gets old, and when you've grown up with Illinois Thanksgivings, all cold and smelling like wet leaves, L.A. in November just doesn't feel right.

I was in New York just before Thanksgiving recently, and it was 50 degrees and rainy, just *so* November. Everyone was complaining about the weather except me. I was all perky, even when my hair went into full frizz mode: "I am *so* happy to see rain! To wear a scarf!" I'd chirp, alienating all the damp New Yorkers within hearing distance.

BESIDE MYSELF | 151

I went back to L.A. determined that, even though Ms. Nature was continuing to work out her issues (it was up to 80 degrees on Turkey Day), I was going to make Thanksgiving feel like Thanksgiving. I began by making this stuffing. ✳ SERVES 6

1 package corn bread mix
4 tablespoons (½ stick) unsalted butter plus extra for the baking dish
1 large onion, finely chopped
1 teaspoon minced garlic
2 ribs celery, cut into small dice
1 large apple, cored and cut into ½-inch pieces
¼ cup finely chopped fresh parsley
1 teaspoon kosher salt
1 teaspoon crumbled dried sage
½ teaspoon dried marjoram
½ teaspoon dried thyme
¼ teaspoon freshly ground black pepper
⅛ teaspoon cayenne pepper
½ cup sweetened dried cranberries
½ cup pecan halves
1 egg, lightly beaten

1. The day before you plan to make the stuffing, cook the cornbread according to the directions on the package. When the cornbread is cool, cut it into ¾-inch cubes and set it aside on a plate at room temperature to dry out overnight.

2. Preheat the oven to 375°F. Butter a 3-quart casserole or other baking dish.

3. Melt the butter in a large skillet over medium-low heat. Add the onion and cook until it is soft, about 10 minutes. Add the garlic and cook for 1 minute.

4. Add the celery and apple and cook until they are soft, about 10 minutes. In the last 2 minutes or so of cooking, stir in the parsley, salt, sage, marjoram, thyme, and black and cayenne peppers.

5. In a large bowl, combine the cornbread cubes with the cranberries and pecans. Add the onion mixture and combine everything well. While you stir, crush some of the cornbread cubes into crumbs. Stir in the egg. Spoon the stuffing into the buttered baking dish and bake until the top is lightly browned, 30 to 35 minutes.

6. Serve hot.

What Happened Next

WHILE THE STUFFING ALONE could not mitigate the fact that the holiday was overheated, it helped. I also made a turkey, of course (which was a small disaster due to a malfunctioning meat thermometer, but nobody cared), and some cranberry sauce and mashed potatoes and gravy and so on. We ate after dark, lit a fire (and turned on the air conditioning), the gentlemen wore tweed, and it seemed almost November-ish.

I intend to keep making this stuffing, along with other seasonal foods, throughout our so-called winter months in an effort to sustain the cozy feeling of Thanksgiving. I just have to remember not to get confused and invite twelve members of my extended family to dinner.

EIGHT

Let Me (Not)

Entertain You

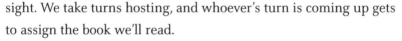

O NE REGULAR EVENT on my
entertaining calendar is the
night I host my book group.
There are eight of us, it's a lively and
diverse bunch, we've been meeting every six
weeks or so since 1997, and there's no end in
sight. We take turns hosting, and whoever's turn is coming up gets
to assign the book we'll read.

To be honest, our meetings are more like dinner parties than literary
discussions. Everybody's a good cook and can set a cute table. Usually
the hostess will make an effort to decorate and feed in a way that's
thematically consistent with the book she's selected. So, for example,
when Alyson chose *Memoirs of a Geisha,* she served sushi and put
mini-parasols in our cocktails. Mind you, if we're reading something like
Angela's Ashes, in which the characters often share a single potato for
dinner, the hostess will pump it up a little and serve, say, an Irish stew.

Even with my poor attitude about cooking, I enjoy hosting the
book group—but I'd like it more if I didn't suffer from Hostess Anxiety
Syndrome.

One of the symptoms of H.A.S. is menu panic: What do I serve?

This is somewhat mitigated on book group nights by the fact that I will have picked a book a month in advance (carefully considering the culinary ramifications of my choice), so at least I'll have zeroed in on a safe food theme. (I would never pick, say, *Six Days in Provence*—I'd have to cook a delicious five-course French meal!)

One trick I've learned is to scope out my takeout options first, and then pick the book that features that kind of cooking. The last time it was my turn, I'd just discovered an excellent falafel place close to home, so I picked a book that takes place in Egypt (*Midaq Alley*). I wasn't at all sure that falafel exists in Egypt, but it seemed Egypt-related, and I walked like an Egyptian when I served it, thereby reinforcing my theme (although possibly irritating my guests).

One book group issue that aggravates my H.A.S. is that my turn falls immediately after Julie's and often close to Christmas, a time of year when Julie goes all out. She and her family spend two full weeks decorating their home. They have a Christmas tree that's so big they need machinery to install it. They have two complete miniature villages, with electric trains and ice skaters zipping around. They've got wreaths on every door and elves in every corner who mutter holiday greetings when you pass.

The whole family cooks: the table is groaning. I'm groaning too: I'm next in line to host book group and Julie has set the bar sky-high.

My response is to slip into denial; I just don't think about my upcoming turn. When the day arrives, I wake up with a little gasp of realization and begin a frenzied preparation for the evening. After ordering the takeout, I invariably discover that I have only seven matching placemats, the napkins are wrinkly and stained, and my wineglasses are mismatched. This always takes me by surprise; I could swear I was better equipped. Sometimes I think Oliver must be partying when we're out, wreaking havoc with my dining accessories.

I fold the napkins creatively to avoid stain exposure, putting the worst one at my place, along with the most tarnished fork, the oddest wine glass, and the only red placemat. Then I rush to the garden and cut some bougainvillea to throw in the center, and the table becomes presentable, as long as nobody looks too closely.

My turn to host is coming right up and I'm feeling my H.A.S. kicking in. I'm thinking maybe I'll assign John Grisham's *Playing for Pizza*. Domino's is just minutes away.

Cocktails

I LIKE TO LISTEN TO THE RADIO when I'm cooking, N.P.R. to be specific. I try to time tedious kitchen tasks to the broadcast of my favorite show, *All Things Considered.* My husband refers to it as "All Things Boring," but I often find its random content so intriguing that I forget what I'm doing and burn the limas. (You may have noticed that I often say "burn the limas." I use this expression generically, referring to any kitchen mishap, although I did actually burn the limas recently, but that's another story.)

Anyway, on *All Things Considered/Boring* I recently heard a story that really caught my ear. It was about the pentail tree shrew, a critter that lives in the Malaysian jungle, resembles a mouse both in fur style and in stature, and is nocturnal.

Wait, it gets better.

What the tree shrew does on its nocturnal forays is to visit a certain kind of palm whose blossoms are dripping with nectar that is fermented, which is to say, alcoholic, beer-like. Mr. Shrew is out all night boozing, apparently consuming the human equivalent of nine glasses of wine a night.

If I drank that much, I'd be turning cartwheels on Mulholland Drive.

But what interests scientists is that tree shrews (the only mammals besides humans that are chronic boozers) still walk in a straight line after all that carousing; they show no signs of drunkenness. The theory is that these party animals have cranked-up metabolisms that burn the alcohol much faster than ours do.

It's too bad they can't bottle that, whatever it is that powers the tree shrew, and put it in a pill to hand out at parties to people who've had "a few tee many martoonis."

Basil Martooni

SPEAKING OF MARTOONIS, this is an amazing version, flavored with lime and basil. But although the tree shrew could suck down nine of these babies, I'd stick to one, unless you can get the tree shrew to drive you home. ✳ SERVES 2

1 ounce simple syrup (see Note on page 159)
3 or 4 fresh basil leaves, coarsely chopped
1 ounce (2 tablespoons) fresh lime juice
3 ounces vodka
Ice cubes

1. Place the simple syrup and the basil leaves in a cocktail shaker and muddle them gently to extract as much flavor and color from the basil as possible. (Muddled about muddling? See the recipe for mojitos on page 159.)

2. Add the lime juice, vodka, and a few ice cubes to the shaker, shake vigorously, and then strain into two martini glasses. (Or make like a tree shrew and drink it all yourself.)

Party Time Margarita

WHEN TOM AND I WERE FIRST MARRIED, we went to a small dinner party with a guest list that included a fancy-pants studio executive. When cocktail orders were taken, she said she drank only margaritas. The host, anxious to impress but clearly unprepared, conjured up a sad little packet of margarita mix. Ms. Fancy Pants watched disdainfully as he moistened the dreary powder with tequila.

Since then, I've always tried to be prepared, alcoholically speaking. Before party time, I stock up on margarita fixings (I like to make them with grapefruit juice), along with the ingredients for martinis, mojitos, and Bloody Lucys. But over the years, I sort of forgot about spirits that weren't requested much, which is why I came up short the night Jack Nicholson wanted Jack Daniels.

As I've said, with Tom now in the thick of the movie business, we sometimes cross paths with hefty dudes like Nicholson. On the night of the Jack Daniels, we were hosting a business party, and it was a starry night in every sense.

I'm not really sure why Jack was there, and it was clear that he wasn't so sure either. He looked like he does when the Lakers lose. When he asked Tom for some Jack Daniels, there was urgency in his voice. He followed Tom to the kitchen on a whiskey hunt. They searched the cupboards and then (to my mortification) the garage, where they found all the detritus of our lives, but no whiskey.

"How 'bout a lovely grapefruit margarita?" I chirped. Jack growled, went to grab his gorgeous young date, and left the premises.

The next morning I bought a bottle of Jack Daniels. It is still unopened in the cupboard (most people would rather have a margarita), but, hey, you never know. ✳ SERVES 1 OR 2

3 ounces fresh grapefruit juice

2 ounces tequila

1 ounce Grand Marnier

1 tablespoon fresh lime juice

Ice cubes

Lime wedges, for garnish

Combine all the ingredients except the lime wedges in a cocktail shaker, and shake for about 30 seconds. Strain the mixture into one large or two small margarita glasses. Add a lime wedge to each drink, and serve.

Lemon Drop

I RECENTLY READ that the Australian police, fed up with alcohol-related violence at car racing events, are cracking down. At the Bathurst 1000, a three-day race, they decided to set some fun-killing limits: only 24 cans of beer per person per day. I mean, for Pete's sake, we all know the fun doesn't start 'til 25, right?

Just when I was gonna cash in some mileage and head to Bratwurst, or whatever it's called, for some awesome party time, I have to ask, what's the point? I might as well stay here and go to a damn Rams game (or are we the Vikings? The L.A. Colts? I can never remember), where they have no such limits and better hot dogs.

Not to mention that the Aussies are limiting wine to 4 litres per person. I know, so what's a litre, right? Well, I Googled it: a litre is 33 ounces, roughly, so each person gets, uh, what's 33 times 4? Well you get the picture. It's downright Draconian. If I imposed those limits on my book group, they'd never come over.

Next time they come I'm planning on serving Lemon Drops, which are really tasty. Luckily we live in a free country, not in frickin' Australia, or I'd have to limit each guest to a couple dozen. ✳ SERVES 2 TO 3

2 ounces vodka

1 ounce (2 tablespoons) fresh
  lemon juice

½ ounce Cointreau

1 tablespoon simple syrup (see Note)

Crushed ice

Pour the vodka, lemon juice, Cointreau, and simple syrup into a cocktail shaker. Add ice, and shake until the drink is well chilled, about 30 seconds. Strain the mixture into shot glasses, and serve.

NOTE You can buy simple syrup, but it's easy enough to make. Combine 1 cup of water with 1 cup of sugar in a medium saucepan and bring the mixture to a simmer over medium heat. Cook until the sugar has dissolved. Cool, and use in your cocktails.

Mojo Mojito

I'VE JUST LEARNED WHAT A MUDDLER IS. Never having been savvy about bartending tools, I'd not heard of a muddler until my daughter's boyfriend told me about it. Once I recovered from the fact that my daughter was dating someone so knowledgeable about cocktail-related equipment, I got excited about purchasing a muddler.

While the dictionary does define the verb "muddle" as "to mix together an alcoholic potion" (or something like that), the definition I'm accustomed to is the one about being muddled, as in brain-challenged (due to sleep deprivation or too much cooking). I have used the word countless times in that latter context, and have had it tossed in my direction. But this muddle was a new one on me.

So, if you have a muddler, try it out on this refreshing mojito. Do not drink too many mojitos or you, too, will be muddled. ✳ SERVES 1

10 fresh mint leaves, plus 1 sprig for garnish

Juice of 1 lime

1 teaspoon confectioners' sugar

Crushed ice

1½ ounces light rum

Dash of Angostura bitters

2 ounces club soda

1. Place the mint leaves in a tall chilled glass. Add the lime juice and the confectioners' sugar. Gently muddle the mixture to release the flavor of the mint.

2. Add some ice, and then the rum and the bitters, and stir. Add the club soda and serve.

VARIATIONS For an extra kick, use Prosecco or champagne instead of the club soda. And if you don't own a muddler, do what I did before I discovered muddlers: use a fork.

Holiday Crantini

SO, IT'S THANKSGIVING, the turkey's in the oven, you are making the stuffing—omitting the chestnuts to accommodate Cousin Larry and leaving the pecans out of the cranberry relish because your daughter won't eat them and making the mashed potatoes with soy milk because a niece is lactose-intolerant—and you've just burned the green beans while everyone else is out playing touch football. You're getting a tad crabby.

If this Turkey Day scenario sounds vaguely familiar, I suggest that before you even start cooking on the day, you have a pre-emptive Holiday Crantini. Things will go much more smoothly. ✳ SERVES 1

Ice cubes

2 ounces vodka

2 ounces cranberry juice

1 ounce vermouth

A twist of lime zest

2 or 3 fresh cranberries

1. Place some ice in a cocktail shaker, then add the vodka, cranberry juice, and vermouth. Shake well (as if you were shaking Cousin Larry for whining about chestnuts in the stuffing).

2. Strain the mixture into a martini glass, add a nice lime twist, and float the cranberries on top.

3. Serve the cocktail, but only to those who offer to wash the dishes.

Bloody Lucy

I KNOW THIS DRINK IS SUPPOSED TO BE CALLED BLOODY MARY, but we renamed it because of an episode at our house involving Aunt Lucy, who guzzled down a few too many and had to surrender her car keys.

Given the picky universe we live in, I like to offer the basic mix and let my guests select which alcoholic beverage they will add. If they're in a Japanese mood, they can dump in a little sake, or aquavit if they're feeling Danish. (I, for one, seldom feel Danish.) So put the tomatoey stuff in a pitcher, leave the bottles of booze on the side, and see what happens. Hopefully your guests will be mature enough to exercise restraint, or you'll end up with a lot of car keys. ✳ SERVES 8

4 cups tomato juice
½ cup fresh lemon juice
1 tablespoon prepared horseradish
1 tablespoon Worcestershire sauce
8 dashes Tabasco sauce (or more if you're a spicy type)
Kosher salt and freshly ground black pepper, to taste
Celery sticks, for garnish

Bottles of whiskey, lemon-flavored vodka, aquavit, gin, and sake

1. Combine the tomato juice, lemon juice, horseradish, Worcestershire sauce, Tabasco, and salt and pepper in a large pitcher. Stir well.

2. Have bottles of booze at the ready. Per the request of each guest, pour 1½ ounces or so of their preferred spirit over ice cubes in a cocktail glass. Add about ½ cup of the tomato mixture and a celery stick to stir with. (If you are serving Lucy, go light on the spirits.)

VARIATIONS If it's a cool day, and/or you want to make sure nobody passes out in your living room and stays 'til Tuesday, simmer the tomato mixture in a pan with 1½ cups vodka for about 10 minutes and serve it warm, like soup, in a mug. All the alcohol will burn off but the flavor will be excellent.

New Year's Mimosa

I'M FASCINATED BY HOW VARIOUS CULTURES ring in the New Year.

I've heard that in Colombia, if you have an urge to travel in the New Year (yes ma'am, I do), you walk around the house with a suitcase at midnight on the 31st.

In Denmark, if you have a particular wish for the New Year, you make it while jumping off a chair. (If you've had too much aquavit or whatever it is Danes drink, this could get ugly.)

In Venezuela, you buy and wear new yellow underwear on New Year's Eve for good luck in the upcoming year.

Perhaps my favorite ritual is in Japan, where there's an Abusive Language Festival: you climb a hill to an ancient temple, screaming profanities at whoever caused you trouble in the old year. (When you get to the temple, you chill and get happy.) I think if I had to pick someone to curse at, it could be my cable guy, who thinks that when he says between 9 and 11 it includes 5:30.

Not to be greedy, but wouldn't one greatly increase one's chances of overall happiness in the New Year by combining these rituals? I was thinking I could put on yellow underpants and jump off a chair while holding a suitcase and cursing the cable guy. The trouble is, of course, my family would commit me to a mental hospital, and I'd be unable to reap the benefits of my actions. So instead, I think I'll stick to the American way of ringing in the New Year with a good old mimosa. ✳ SERVES 8 TO 10

1 cup fresh orange juice 1 cup orange-flavored vodka Ice cubes 1 bottle of champagne	Combine the orange juice and vodka in a large pitcher, and add some ice. Pour in the champagne, mix, and serve in champagne glasses.

DINNER WITH THE FAMOUS WIFE

ALTHOUGH MY HUSBAND'S WORK brings him within a stone's throw of lots of celebrities, it took me years to get comfortable with entertaining some of the flashy people he has done business with.

In the early years of our marriage, we had a house that was tiny and kid-messy. I had no confidence that it could gracefully accommodate stars, and less confidence in my ability to cook for them. So I was pretty crabby when I got roped into making dinner for The Famous Wife.

She is not a Famous Wife in the sense that she is married to a Famous Husband, like, say, one of the Mrs. Donald Trumps. Her husband is just your average lawyer, while she is *totally* famous.

One evening, my husband informed me that the couple were in town for only about thirty-six hours, so he'd invited them to come to dinner (in about twenty-four).

"You did *what?*" Tom fled the kitchen, skillfully ducking the sponge that I hurled in his direction.

I immediately went into Menu Obsession mode: what do you cook for a Famous Wife who undoubtedly dines at La Grenouille twice a week?

Then it clicked; it was a no-brainer.

"Hello, is this The Chili Shack? I'd like to order two quarts of number four, extra spicy, please."

Then I zipped over to Costco to pick up one of their awesome lemon cakes, and I was done, I was Menu Satisfied.

The following evening, I sent our wee daughters out with Deirdre, the babysitter, for a few hours so I could obsess about what to wear and have a pre-prandial glass of wine without interference.

After careful consideration, I chose a jaunty outfit for the evening: cropped leggings, leopard-print flats, and a striped French tee shirt. I was considering red lipstick when I heard a screech-'n-crash outside. From the bathroom window I could see that someone who sucked at parallel parking had backed a yellow Mercedes into our neighbor's trash can.

"Yikes, could that be them?" I said out loud. "They're ten minutes early!"

Trying to keep my irritation in check, I went to open the front door and slapped on a big smile.

A teenage girl popped out of the driver's seat, apparently unfazed by her recent encounter with a waste receptacle. She brushed something from the lap of her distressed jeans and then rapped impatiently on the car's roof.

"Come *on*. We're, like, here," she loudly informed the occupants of the back seat.

The lawyer and his Famous Wife emerged from the car. The lawyer was all corduroy and messy hair. He looked pale and uncertain, as if he were about to vomit. After steadying himself, he observed his surroundings as if he had been deposited on an unknown planet.

The Wife, on the other hand—oh, my.

First the legs appeared: long, lean, and tan, ending in formidable Manolos. The body followed, with that slow-mo kind of grace that suggests years of ballet. She wore an impeccable pale blue dinner suit—Armani would be my guess—and her blond hair was short and sleek, like feathers. It was tucked behind ears that were studded with something sparkly.

I rubbed sweaty palms on my leggings, my outfit confidence seriously shaken.

The teenager tossed back long black hair impatiently. "Could you possibly move a little slower?" she asked.

As the threesome marched up the little path toward our door, I realized I'd forgotten to do a scan of the garden after the kids' morning playdate. The F.W.'s eyes strayed to her left to behold, in the tangle of ivy, a cluster of naked Barbie dolls. Eyes right: an azalea bush decked out with a string of lights shaped like chili peppers.

I took the dishtowel off my shoulder and said, "Welcome!" loudly enough, I hoped, to distract The Famous Wife from the appalling details of my world.

Then I made a note-to-self to kill my husband later: he was conveniently in the bathroom for The Arrival. I knew his whereabouts because I heard, we all heard, a telltale flush.

"Come on in. How 'bout some sangria?" I said, simultaneously remembering that I'd forgotten to make the sangria.

Tom, unaware that the guests were in the house, emerged from the bathroom, still zipping.

"DAH!" This is what he always says when he's startled, usually startling others with the force of his exclamation.

Names were announced and hands shaken as we stood in the so-called foyer, which was actually three square feet of space by the front door dedicated to awkward introductions.

"And this is our daughter, Tina." Of course it was.

"I'd love some sangria," said Tina the teen.

"Pah, ha, ha," her mother fake-laughed. "Sangria is alcohol, darling. How 'bout a Sprite?"

"Oh, for crissakes, Mother, I'm, like, sixteen," Tina spat out. Her nails, I noticed, were painted a color called "Wicked." I know this because I used it on Halloween when I dressed as Evil Incarnate for my friend Lynn's costume party.

"Pah, ha, I know, darling. Just a few more years of Sprite for you. Pah, ha. . . ."

Tina growled.

"Well, let's *all* have Sprite!" said the lawyer, whose name I'd already forgotten in my fit of social anxiety.

"Sprite it is!" said my husband, leaping to the kitchen, a couple feet due south of the foyer.

"I'll just check on dinner," I said, trying to sound like Donna Reed. "Please sit down in the living room!" As I groped in the cupboard for the tequila, I heard The F.W.'s Manolos click toward the sofa.

Tom offered them their frosty glasses, careful to set aside for us the two that smelled like a Mexican honeymoon.

"So . . ." The Famous Wife offered up a tepid opener.

Her daughter jumped into the pause. "So, what?" she said, her hostility so steamy I feared it would stain the sofa.

The F.W. ignored her daughter and pressed on. "Something smells wonderful. What . . . ?"

"Chili!" I cried, and played invisible castanets. "Olé! Ha!" Okay, so sue me. I was just trying to crush the bad vibes with jocularity.

Tina liked me, I could tell. Teenagers smirk and roll their eyeballs when they like you.

"Is it really, really spicy?" she asked me. There was mischief in her question.

"Tina, please . . ." her mother began.

"Yes, ma'am, I don't mess with mild!" I'm sorry to say I may have repeated the castanet thing. Tina's laughter was loud and heavy, directed at Mom like cannonballs. The Famous Wife sank into her chair, wounded, beautiful, and helpless.

Her husband snapped to attention. "For Pete's sake, Tina, take it easy, willya?" Tina fell back into the sofa in a sullen slump.

"I've got an ulcer, I'm afraid," The F.W. said. "Spicy food is a little tricky for me . . .

"Oh, crap," I said out loud, although I'd only meant to think it. "I mean, I'm so sorry, jeez, bad menu choice."

"Oh, please, don't worry," The F.W. said.

"No, uh, I could whip up a sandwich. I think I have some leftover mac and cheese. . . ."

"Please, don't bother. It's fine. Happens all the time, I'm afraid. . . ."

I was stumped, wind out of my sails, castanets discarded. "Okay, let's eat, I guess." I smiled really hard as I got up and slipped Tom my empty glass with a meaningful look.

At dinner, Tina silently ate quite a lot. Tom and the lawyer talked about the movie business, a conversation I pretended to be engrossed in because I couldn't think of a thing to say to The F.W. She nibbled on a tortilla, also feigning an interest in the man talk. When she got up to help me clear the dishes, I thought it a perfect moment to behave in a mature way and try for a verbal exchange.

"So, aren't we glad we have dishwashers," I said cheerfully, jamming chili bowls into the KitchenAid.

"Oh, yes, I don't know what I'd do without Jerry," she said, chuckling.

"Who's Jerry?" I asked.

The F.W. looked at me. "Jerry . . ." she said, calmly. In the thought bubble above her head was the question, *Are you the stupidest person in the entire world?*

"OHHHhhh, ha-HA, you mean THAT Jerry," I said, suddenly remembering her husband's name. "Ha-HAH!"

Luckily, at that moment Deirdre returned with the girls, one of whom had taken a tumble on the path and was whimpering. Never was I so happy to see a bloody knee.

"Baby!" I leapt to Nora's (my) rescue. I picked her up and she folded her little body around my torso, all warm with emotion. Her cotton dress was stained with popsicle juice and she smelled like cotton candy. Her sister, Elizabeth, wrapped her arms around my thigh and the three of us lurched in the direction of the bathroom.

"We should get out of your hair," I heard The F.W. say as I clattered around the bathroom, pretending I couldn't locate the Hello Kitty Band-Aids. The Manolos clicked to the foyer.

"Aw, poor kid," Jerry sympathized, yanking open the door and pushing Tina into the night.

"Bye, huh, and, you know, thanks," the teen murmured.

I peeked out from the bathroom and waved. "Thanks for coming!" I shouted.

Tom walked the family to their car, or rather tried to keep up with them as they raced in its direction. It was several minutes before they took off. I imagined they were either having a squabble or deciding where to go to get a real dinner. When the application of six Band-Aids to Nora's knee finally calmed her, I heard them fire up the Mercedes and screech off into the night.

When Tom and I were cleaning up later, I made several notes-to-self:

1. Never invite anyone to dinner again.

2. Although you will never again have people for dinner, buy more tequila, just in case you do.

3. In the unlikely event that you should ever again have dinner guests, memorize their names before, not after, the dinner party. And make some appetizers, for Pete's sake!

There's an App(etizer) for That

GOT DINNER GUESTS? It's a good idea to have one or two apps (appetizers, that is) on hand, especially if there's a Famous Wife or some other notable personage on the premises.

The only trouble is preparing apps on top of cooking dinner, which can send a person into task overload. Here's a handful of app recipes that are easy and guaranteed to satisfy the appetite of anyone who, like The Famous Wife, won't eat their dinner.

No-Brainer Cheese Crisps

THIS IS MY FAVE, because it involves only one ingredient and also it's a little bit elegant. ✳ MAKES 12 CRISPS

1 cup freshly grated Parmigiano-Reggiano cheese

1. Preheat the oven to 350°F. Line a baking sheet with parchment paper.

2. Place heaping tablespoons of the cheese on the lined baking sheet, spacing them 2 inches apart. With the back of your spoon, gently press the top of each mound of cheese to spread it slightly.

3. Bake until the cheese has melted and is just starting to turn golden, about 5 minutes. Cool the crisps on the parchment for at least 10 minutes.

4. Serve them warm or at room temperature.

Scenic Cheese Platter

I HAD SOME LAST-MINUTE COCKTAIL VISITORS RECENTLY—cousins, to be exact. Luckily I had the makings of a scenic cheese platter handy, leftovers from a book group meeting.

Cousin Charles pointed out that it was Groundhog Day, a fact that would otherwise have gone right by me.

Groundhog Day comes and goes in L.A. and nobody notices. We can't afford such trivial ceremonies in this big, broke state, and also, since it's usually 70 degrees in February, discussion of seasonal changes here is a fatuous time-waster. You're better off talking about more relevant issues, like that rumor I heard about condos on the moon, or the most recent governor to walk the Appalachian Trail.

Groundhog Day, however, is a big deal in many other more with-it locations, like Canada. Although if it's February in Alberta, you don't need to hire a rodent to tell you there will be six more weeks of winter.

In Staten Island, it's a different story; you might actually see a crocus in New York before March. But the G-Day ceremony there one recent February, featuring a recalcitrant groundhog named Staten Island Chuck, turned into a mini-melee when the g-hog bit poor old Mayor Bloomberg. Apparently not ready for his close-up, Chuck refused to come out of his hole. Bloomberg tried to lure him with a corncob, which resulted in the attack. Luckily, the animal was pronounced rabies-free and the mayor resumed his less challenging duties later in the day.

Don't they vet these animals? You'd think they could find, in N.Y.'s vast pool of highly qualified g-hogs, one that wouldn't bite the hand that feeds him. I will say, however, in the animal's defense, that if the mayor were to offer me a corncob, I might bite his hand, too. Next time, if Bloomberg wants cooperation, he should be equipped with more upscale nibbles, like the classic rodent favorite: a nice piece of cheese. Complement it with some fruit, nuts, and bread to make a nice scenic cheese platter, and he'll have that groundhog eating out of his hand.

✳ SERVES 8, OR 1 GROUNDHOG

1 wedge (about 10 ounces) Brie cheese

2 pears (any kind), cored and thinly sliced lengthwise

2 cups Spicy Nuts (page 172)

1 baguette, cut into thin slices

1. Preheat the oven to 350°F.

2. Place the cheese on a baking sheet and bake until it just starts to melt, about 5 minutes.

3. Meanwhile, arrange the pear slices on a platter. Place the nuts in a bowl and add it to the platter. When the cheese is ready, place it on the platter, arrange the baguette slices around it, and serve immediately.

Spicy Nuts

THE BEST PART ABOUT THESE NUTS is that you can make them way in advance, like two weeks, so on party day, you just drag them out and add them to your cheese platter. The only problem with this strategy is that, since I'm brain-challenged (especially when it comes to entertaining), I am likely, in the two-week waiting period, to forget that I've made the nuts. So, in the hours just before my guests arrive, I'll go tearing around making them all over again. Try not to let this happen. Place a Post-it on your nut bin saying, "You've already made them, stupid." ✳ MAKES 2½ CUPS

1 egg white
1 bag (10 ounces) shelled pecans (about 2½ cups)
¼ cup sugar
2 teaspoons curry powder
1 teaspoon ground cumin
1 teaspoon kosher salt
¼ teaspoon freshly ground black pepper
¼ teaspoon cayenne pepper

1. Preheat the oven to 250°F. Line a baking sheet with parchment paper.

2. In a large bowl, whisk the egg white until it is foamy. Then add the pecans and toss gently to coat them evenly. In a separate bowl, combine the sugar, curry powder, cumin, salt, and black and cayenne peppers. Add this mixture to the nuts and toss to distribute the spices evenly.

3. Place the pecans in a single layer on the prepared baking sheet, and bake until they are fragrant and sizzling and the sugar has mostly melted, about 35 minutes. Let the nuts cool completely on the baking sheet.

4. Break up any nuts that are sticking together, and store the nuts in an airtight container for up to 2 weeks.

NOTE These nuts are also great on top of a salad (see Wolverine Salad, page 202) or crushed and sprinkled on a scoop of ginger ice cream.

VARIATIONS Use other kinds of nuts, such as walnuts, or a mixture of nuts.

Julie's Cheese Ball

MY IN-LAWS, SCOTT AND JULIE, were having a dinner party, which in their household means Julie is having a dinner party and Scott is showing up. Julie cooked for three days, butterflying lamb legs, baking her famous chocolate roll, and shortly before the guests' arrival, prepping a cheese ball appetizer. Just as she was artfully surrounding it with crackers, her hair loose and her apron soiled from her labors, Scott sauntered into the kitchen, having completed his dinner party chores. (He'd purchased the ice.) He eyed the cheese ball, and then he made a fatal error.

"Oh, no, the dreaded cheese ball!" he said in a stab at humor.

Julie snapped. She picked up the cheese ball and whipped it at her husband with a ferocity and accuracy of aim reminiscent of, say, Peyton Manning. Luckily, Scott is a dodgeball expert; he ducked just in time. The cheese ball sailed just over his head, so close it parted his hair. It hit the wall with a *smack,* stuck just long enough to create a stain to mark the occasion, and plopped to the floor. Scott, enraged at what he later referred to as a "frontal assault," stormed upstairs just as the doorbell rang.

Later, in an attempt at self-defense, Scott claimed that his "joke" was not unlike many lively cheese ball comments he had thrown Julie's way in previous fun-filled moments of pre-party banter. He said that "women have a way of changing the rules of engagement in the middle of the game."

Well, I love my brother-in-law, but guess whose side I'm on? Maybe it's just because I'm a crabby cook, but I think that anyone willing to take on a dinner party is entitled to all the mood swings she can muster. If the spouse chooses to breeze through the kitchen, fresh from the treadmill or from watching the Baltimore Orioles on television or from taking a refreshing nap, and makes a crack about the appetizer, he deserves what he gets.

One suggestion for Julie: next time, aim lower. ✳ SERVES 8

8 ounces cream cheese, at room
temperature
1 cup shredded cheddar cheese
½ cup crumbled blue cheese
½ cup finely chopped walnuts, pecans,
or pistachios

1. Combine the cheeses well and form them into a ball.

2. Place the nuts on a pie plate. Roll the cheese ball in the nuts until it's completely covered. Wrap the cheese ball and chill it for 2 hours or up to 2 days. Remove it from the refrigerator about 30 minutes before serving time.

3. Place the cheese ball on a platter and serve it with crackers. (Or throw it at your no-good husband.)

VARIATIONS Instead of nuts, roll the cheese ball in finely chopped herbs—for example, a mixture such as parsley, chives, and dill or basil.

Famous Hummus

WHEN NORA WAS IN HIGH SCHOOL, she told me that I had become famous among her friends for making tasty hummus. I was honored, although I'd never imagined or hoped I'd become well known for throwing chickpeas into the Cuisinart.

As I've told you, Nora was always such a picky eater that it was tough to come up with any kind of variety when I packed her lunches for school. In her last years in high school, we pretty much got down to turkey sandwiches (on a baguette only, NO lettuce) or hummus with pita. When it was a hummus day, she shared it with her friends, building my reputation as an expert bean-crusher.

This hummus is so likable that you can give it to anybody—vegans, vegetarians, pescatarians, libertarians, librarians—and they will eat it and you, too, will become famous. ✳ SERVES 8, DEPENDING ON HOW HUNGRY THEY ARE AND WHETHER YOU ARE ALSO SERVING A CHEESE BALL

2 cans (15 ounces each) chickpeas, drained and rinsed

¼ cup tahini (sesame paste)

¼ cup olive oil

Juice of 1 lemon

2 cloves garlic, minced

1 teaspoon ground cumin

½ teaspoon kosher salt, or to taste

¼ teaspoon freshly ground black pepper

1. Place all the ingredients in a food processor, add 3 tablespoons water, and process until smooth. If you prefer a thinner consistency, add a little more water.

2. Transfer the hummus to a bowl, cover it with plastic wrap, and refrigerate it for about 1 hour to let the flavors blend. Allow it to return to room temperature before serving.

3. Serve it with pita bread or chips.

My Big Fat Greek Platter

IF YOU REALLY WANT TO MAKE a big fat Greek statement with your apps, to take it up a notch, to become the envy of less-inspired, low-life cooks, try this Greek combo-plate, adding marinated olives and feta cheese to your hummus on a platter.

The good news is that you prepare it all way in advance, so on the day of your party, you are not in a big fat crabby mood.

My supermarket has an olive bar, with a few kinds of unpitted olives (which work best for this recipe). If your market does not have this, use canned or jarred imported olives, just making sure to rinse them well. ✳ SERVES 8 TO 12

For the olives

> 2 cups olives (not pitted, any kind or a mixture)
> ½ cup extra-virgin olive oil
> 2 cloves garlic, crushed
> 2 sprigs fresh rosemary
> 2 sprigs fresh thyme
> 1 bay leaf
> Freshly ground black pepper, to taste

For the cheese

> 8 ounces feta cheese
> 1 tablespoon chopped fresh oregano
> Freshly ground black pepper
> 1 cup extra-virgin olive oil

> 2 cups hummus (see page 174)
> 8 pita breads, each cut into 6 wedges

1. One to two days before serving, prepare the olives and the cheese: Rinse the olives and pat them dry. Combine the olives, olive oil, garlic, rosemary sprigs, thyme sprigs, bay leaf, and pepper in a bowl suitable for serving. Cover and refrigerate. Place the feta in a shallow bowl suitable for serving. Sprinkle it with the oregano and pepper (3 or 4 twists of the mill), and then pour the olive oil over it. Cover it with plastic wrap and refrigerate it.

2. At least 2 hours or up to 24 hours before serving, prepare the hummus.

3. Two hours before serving, remove the hummus, cheese, and olives from the refrigerator, and arrange them on your platter. (You can remove the garlic and herbs from the olives if you like, and discard them, but I like leaving them in the bowl.) Surround them with the pita wedges and serve, with small serving knives for spreading the cheese and hummus.

NOTE Make sure everybody dips their bread in the olive oil surrounding the feta before spreading on the cheese. Mmmm.

Super Bowl Bean Dip 'n Guac

I'M PROBABLY THE MOST IRRITATING PERSON at a Super Bowl gathering; I merrily show up and ask, "Okay, so who's playing?" I am completely clueless. As I'm writing this, I, a Chicago native, can't even remember the name of my birth city's football team. (Are they the Chargers? The Jazz? The Zebras? It'll come to me. . . .) I know they used to have a player whose nickname was The Refrigerator, which caught my attention.

But if I'm short on info, I'm long on enthusiasm. I'm even willing to cook for the Super Bowl, especially if we go to my brother's house and all I have to make is appetizers.

Bean Dip 'n Guac are perfect food choices for the occasion. Chips are involved, which are a mainstay of the S.B. cuisine, and the dip is served warm, which works well on a cold January day (which in L.A. means it's below 70 degrees). And nobody doesn't like a little guacamole.

Bean Dip

BESIDES SERVING IT ON SUPER BOWL SUNDAYS, I sometimes used to make this dip for the kids for an easy dinner, baked in individual ramekins instead of a baking dish. Served with bowls of vegetable soup, it made the girls very happy. ✳ SERVES 6 TO 8

¼ cup vegetable oil

1 cup finely chopped onion

2 cloves garlic, minced

2 teaspoons ground cumin

½ teaspoon salt, or to taste

2 cans (15 ounces each) pinto beans, drained and rinsed

½ cup sour cream

1 cup store-bought salsa

1 cup shredded cheddar cheese (or a mix of cheddar and Monterey Jack)

¼ cup chopped fresh cilantro (optional)

¼ cup chopped scallions, white and green parts (optional)

1. Preheat the oven to 375°F.

2. Heat the oil in a heavy-bottomed medium saucepan over medium-low heat. Add the onion and cook until it is soft and translucent, about 10 minutes. Add the garlic, cumin, and salt, and cook for 1 minute. Stir in the pinto beans and cook, mashing them with a potato masher, for 2 to 3 minutes. The mixture should be almost smooth but still somewhat chunky.

3. Spread the bean mixture in an 8-inch square baking dish. Spread the sour cream on top of the beans, and the salsa on top of the sour cream. Sprinkle the cheese evenly over the salsa.

4. Cover the pan with aluminum foil and bake for 20 minutes. Then remove the foil and continue baking until the cheese is melted and bubbly, another 10 minutes.

5. Sprinkle the bean dip with the cilantro and scallions if you like, and serve with tortilla or pita chips.

6. Now pray Chicago wins. (What *are* they called? The Playboys? The Jets? The Ruminators? It'll come to me. . . .)

Guac

IN CALIFORNIA, WITH OUR ABUNDANCE OF AVOCADOS, we eat this crowd-pleaser all year round, even if no sporting event is involved. It's also great to throw in a burrito or taco, or to plop on top of a salad. ✳ MAKES ABOUT 3 CUPS

4 avocados

2 plum tomatoes, seeded and cut into ½-inch dice

½ small onion, finely chopped

½ cup chopped fresh cilantro

1 to 2 jalapeño peppers (depending on your taste for spice), seeded and finely chopped

2 tablespoons fresh lime juice

2 cloves garlic, minced (or pressed)

1 teaspoon ground cumin

½ teaspoon kosher salt, or to taste

¼ teaspoon freshly ground black pepper

1. Cut the avocados in half, remove the pits, and set the pits aside. Peel the avocado halves, put them in a bowl, and coarsely chop them (or mash them with a potato masher).

Then mix in all the remaining ingredients.

2. Press the reserved pits down into the bowl of guacamole (I'm told this helps keep it from turning brown), cover the bowl with plastic wrap, and chill it until you're ready to serve, up to 2 hours.

3. Discard the pits and serve the guac with tortilla chips.

VARIATIONS My husband says cilantro tastes like soap. If you are serving someone like him, omit it, or substitute parsley or (per my niece Lily's suggestion) try mint. You can also make Shortcut Guac by chopping the avocados and just mixing in some of your supermarket's best freshly made salsa.

Sassy Sliders

I USED TO LOVE GOING TO A CERTAIN SKI LODGE, in part because they served delicious little sliders as an *après ski* treat with cocktails. But then this weird thing happened at that very same lodge.

It was all over the news: a man boarded a ski lift with the innocent intention of skiing with his child and ended up hanging from the lift for a solid fifteen minutes, upside down and pantless. No, not panting: I said pantless. Pant-free. *Sans pantalons.* As in the Full Monty. Frostbite in unusual places.

There was a long, confusing explanation as to how this happened, but it was unconvincing. The truth, I suspect, was that something that's never supposed to happen simply *did* happen to poor Peter Pants-off. It was like having a meteor land on your head, but much less likely. In fact, if it was any consolation to poor Robert Redbottom, the event was historically unique.

This story gave me a whole new reason to avoid downhill skiing, aside from the daunting task of finding a ski outfit that doesn't make me look like a horse's ass and my weepy panic attacks on the steeper slopes. As long as there's a possibility, no matter how remote, that I could end up hanging pantless from a lift, my skis will remain in the closet.

Meanwhile, I'll just make these sliders at home, in the safety of my securely belted blue jeans. ✳ MAKES 8 SLIDERS

1 pound ground beef

1½ tablespoons olive oil, plus extra for the skillet

1 teaspoon Dijon mustard

Kosher salt

Freshly ground black pepper

½ cup mayonnaise

2 teaspoons chipotle puree (see Note)

1 tablespoon fresh lime juice

1 teaspoon minced garlic

½ cup grated cheddar cheese, or a mix of cheddar and Monterey Jack

8 dinner rolls

1. Preheat the broiler.

2. Place the ground beef in a large bowl. Add the oil, mustard, ½ teaspoon salt, and ¼ teaspoon pepper and mix well. Divide the meat into 8 portions and form 8 small patties.

3. In a small bowl, mix together the mayonnaise, chipotle puree, lime juice, garlic, ¼ teaspoon salt, and ¼ teaspoon pepper.

4. Rub a large skillet lightly with a little olive oil, and set it over medium heat. When the skillet is hot, add the patties and cook until they are well browned on the bottom, about 3 minutes. Flip the patties over and sprinkle each one with a tablespoon of the grated cheese. Continue cooking until the cheese has melted and the sliders are well browned on the other side, about 3 minutes.

5. While the sliders are cooking, split the rolls horizontally, place them on a baking sheet, split side up, and toast them lightly under the broiler. Spread a little of the chipotle mayo on the toasted sides of each roll.

6. Sandwich each slider in a dinner roll, forming a mini-burger, and serve hot.

NOTE If your market doesn't carry chipotle puree, simply puree a small (7-ounce) can of chipotle peppers in adobo sauce in your food processor.

Veggies 'n Dip

THERE ARE FEW THINGS THAT MAKE ME AS CRABBY AS WHEN, just before a dinner party, just after I've vacuumed the dining room, set the table, concealed the dog vomit stain on the rug, broken off half of one candle so it matches the other one in height, made a pot of chili, chilled the wine, made sure there was toilet paper in the guest bathroom, dug the decaf out of the freezer, secured the hem of my skirt with duct tape, and smoothed my hair with "Secret Weapon" by John Frieda, just when I've done all that and I think I'm ready to be a swinging hostess, I remember that my appetizer choice is Veggies 'n Dip and I therefore have to chop and slice twelve vegetables. I have been known to come to this realization and to drive somewhere at high speed to buy cheese and crackers, abandoning my V 'n D plan, which seemed like such a good one when I thought of it. My point is, V 'n D is not the ideal appetizer if you are a crabby (and somewhat disorganized) cook. However, people, especially picky people (who, let's face it, are in the majority), like V 'n D because they can pick their veggies and the dip is optional.

There are a couple of slightly less painful ways to serve V 'n D if you must. The bottom line is, keep it simple. My supermarket has sugar snap peas that are pre-strung, so you can just throw them on a plate, maybe with some of those handy snack carrots. Steamed asparagus is a good way to go, too. I mean, you have to trim and steam it, but people like it and it looks dramatic on a platter. Plus you can count it as your first course and plunge right into the entree afterward.

Here are a couple of dip options. Make the dip the day before so you'll have one less thing to complain about on the day of.

Schmear a Spear

THIS SIMPLE, KID-FRIENDLY DIP won't offend anyone who might have issues with the next dip and all its wacky spices. I like it best with asparagus, but it'll go with any vegetable. ✳ SERVES 8 TO 10

¾ cup mayonnaise

¼ cup crème fraîche

2 tablespoons chopped fresh dill

2 tablespoons snipped fresh chives

2 tablespoons fresh lemon juice

1 clove garlic, crushed

¼ teaspoon coarse salt

¼ teaspoon freshly ground black pepper

2 pounds asparagus

1. Whisk all the ingredients, except the asparagus, together in a bowl. Cover and refrigerate for at least 1 hour or overnight.

2. At least 2 hours or up to a day before you will serve it, prepare the asparagus: Bring lightly salted water to a simmer in a vegetable steamer. Trim off the ends of the asparagus and place the spears in the steamer basket. Cover the steamer and cook until the asparagus is just tender, about 3 minutes. Transfer the asparagus to paper towels to dry and cool; then refrigerate it until you are ready to serve.

3. Place the asparagus on a platter with a bowl of the dip, and serve.

Too-Many-Ingredients Curry Dip

WHEN A FRIEND GAVE ME this ingredient-heavy recipe, it had even *more* ingredients than it has now. I was too crabby to cope with such a list (especially before entertaining), so I whittled it down to what I considered the bare essentials. The recipe still has sixteen items, so brace yourself. The payoff? It's delish. ✳ MAKES ABOUT 2 CUPS

1½ cups mayonnaise

¼ cup sour cream

¼ cup mango chutney

¼ cup finely chopped sweet onion

¼ cup diced red bell pepper

2 cloves garlic, pressed (or grated on a fine grater)

2 tablespoons curry powder

1 teaspoon sugar

1 teaspoon finely grated lemon zest

1 teaspoon ground turmeric

½ teaspoon ground cumin

¼ teaspoon ground ginger

¼ teaspoon ground cardamom

¼ teaspoon ground coriander

¼ teaspoon salt

Dash of Tabasco sauce (a drop or two)

1. Combine all the ingredients in a bowl, and mix well. Cover the bowl with plastic wrap and refrigerate the dip overnight.

2. Serve the dip with your choice of crudités: carrots, sugar snap peas, endive spears, bell pepper strips . . . whatever you have the patience to prepare.

Blunch: Perfect for Party Payback

THE THING ABOUT SUNDAY BLUNCH (which of course is more commonly known as brunch, but when she was three, Nora renamed it) is that if, like me, you cook all week until you're so crabby you scream at your husband to take you to a restaurant for a big fat change, you are probably of at least two minds (is it possible to be of three minds?) about cooking for guests on Sunday morning.

However, I would like to posit that it's actually one of the less painful ways to do Party Payback.

Party Payback is what you have to do when you've been entertained at someone else's home and you must reciprocate. As I write this, we are negotiating a dinner date at the Shermans' house and I'm already plotting the Party Payback. I'm thinking maybe I'll invite the Shermans to the blunch I'm having for visiting in-laws next week, killing a couple of birds with one stone. But will I get proper credit? Will they accept it as full Party Payback if it's only a blunch and if I feed them *before* we get to their house for dinner?

These questions and others like them are what spin my world.

Although it requires an early wake-up call, I find the cooking involved in blunch is relatively easy if you play your cards right. You can do a lot in advance, and people don't stay too long because who wants to be socializing on Sunday morning when they could be home reading the Sunday *Times* in their underpants? So they eat fast and get out of your house and you still have a few hours left in the day to do something meaningful, like yell at your teenager or take an iPad tutorial.

Another positive thing about blunch is that, as with any party involving food, it's a good way to get all those fabulous breakfast-y recipes out of your system that you would never otherwise make because everybody's in such a big fat hurry on regular mornings.

One piece of menu-planning advice: as my mother would say, ix-nay the acon-bay. The reality of bacon is that you go to the trouble to make enough for a crowd and then half of them will have just gone vegan or taken up a pork-free religion or whatever and you end up eating B.L.T.'s 'til Thursday.

Here are recipes for a bunch of blunch items that are so good you won't need acon-bay. I am not suggesting that you or I should serve *all* these dishes on one occasion. You just cook until you can see crabbiness on the horizon and then stop. I plan to make a few of these dishes for the in-laws and the Shermans, and save the rest for my next blunch, the next time Party Payback rears its ugly head.

Granola Your Way

MAKE HOMEMADE GRANOLA FOR BLUNCH and people will think you are the new Martha Stewart (*sans* jail). However, I suggest you make a very basic version and leave all the fruits and most of the nuts on the side. This is to accommodate eaters who have a fit if they see a date or a Brazil nut rubbing up against an oat. Keep the thrilling ingredients optional; otherwise all those picky adults will loudly complain and you will get irritated and require a Bloody Lucy (to be found, conveniently, on page 161).

Another fine idea for irritation prevention is to offer several kinds of dairy toppings for the granola. Providing not just regular milk, but low-fat, soy, and skim milk, as well as Lactaid or any other milk-of-the-moment, will preempt the bitching about milk preferences. The only trouble will be conjuring up all those tiny pitchers. ✳ MAKES 8 CUPS

For the granola

4 cups old-fashioned rolled oats

2 cups sweetened shredded coconut

2 cups finely chopped walnuts

¾ cup canola or safflower oil

½ cup honey

For the optional additions

1 cup raw sunflower seeds

1 cup sliced almonds

1 cup toasted cashews, hazelnuts,
   brazil nuts, or pine nuts

1 cup sweetened dried cranberries,
   cherries, or apricots

1 cup chopped dates

1 cup raisins

For serving

Many milk varieties (see headnote)

Vanilla yogurt (see Note)

1. Preheat the oven to 325°F.

2. Mix the oats, coconut, walnuts, oil, and honey together in a large bowl. Spread the granola on a large rimmed baking sheet and bake, stirring it once or twice, until it's golden brown, 35 to 40 minutes. (Keep an eye on it so it doesn't brown too much.)

3. Let the granola cool on the baking sheet, stirring it occasionally while it cools. Then store it in an airtight container.

4. Serve the granola with bowls of the optional additions, and with milk or vanilla yogurt.

NOTE Make your own vanilla yogurt to use as a topping for the granola. I like to do this even though it's a whole extra procedure, because it tastes better than commercial vanilla yogurt and is not so sweet. Just do this: stir 1½ teaspoons vanilla extract and ¼ cup honey into a quart of plain yogurt.

GRANOLA AS A HOSTESS GIFT

I LIKE TO GIVE GRANOLA as a hostess gift. I know what you're thinking: Why would a crabby cook add another cooking chore to her day? Why not just give the hostess a can opener? And you would be right, of course, but if I'm going to a dinner party and am therefore relieved of dinner duty myself, I don't mind using my limited cooking energy to make granola. I wrap it up in a scenic jar with a ribbon and present it to my hostess, who invariably appreciates the granola, as she already has several can openers.

When I do make a granola gift, I add a cup of dried cherries and a cup of sunflower seeds to the basic recipe, and nobody complains.

# Granola Bars

YOU CAN SERVE GRANOLA BARS INSTEAD OF GRANOLA, saving yourself from the irritating issues of milk varieties and bowl washing. Everybody likes these, making them a Miracle Food. ✳ MAKES 12 TO 16 BARS, DEPENDING ON HOW YOU CUT THEM

2 cups old-fashioned rolled oats

1 cup unsweetened shredded coconut

½ cup raw sunflower seeds

1 cup walnut halves

½ cup (packed) dark brown sugar

½ cup honey

3 tablespoons unsalted butter, plus extra for the baking dish

1 teaspoon vanilla extract

¼ teaspoon salt

½ cup sweetened dried cherries

¼ cup ground flaxseed

½ teaspoon ground cinnamon

½ cup white chocolate chips

1. Preheat the oven to 350°F. Butter a 9 x 13-inch baking dish, line it with parchment paper, and butter the parchment.

2. In a large bowl, combine the oats, coconut, and sunflower seeds. Crush the walnuts (I do this with the bottom of my measuring cup) to break them up. Add the walnuts to the oat mixture. Spread the mixture on a baking sheet and bake in the oven until the oats are slightly golden and fragrant, 10 to 12 minutes. Return the oat mixture to the bowl and reduce the oven temperature to 300°F.

3. Meanwhile, place the brown sugar, honey, butter, vanilla, and salt in a small saucepan. Cook over medium-low heat until the sugar has dissolved.

4. Add the cherries, flax seed, and cinnamon to the oat mixture and mix well. Pour the honey mixture over the oats and mix well. When the oat mixture has cooled slightly, mix in the white chocolate chips.

5. Pour the oat mixture into the prepared baking dish and press it down gently to make it compact. Bake until it is golden, 25 minutes.

6. Allow the pan to cool slightly, and then cut 12 granola bars (or more if you want them to be smaller)—but don't remove them from the pan. (They are harder to cut after cooling completely.) After cutting, allow the bars to cool completely in the pan.

7. Serve, or place the bars in an airtight container and store them for 3 to 4 days.

Easy Cheesy Thing

THIS IS A TASTY DISH, but you should avoid serving it to cardiac patients, and try to get in a little exercise yourself after you eat it. Better yet, since you assemble the dish the night before, use your pre-brunch morning to go on the treadmill, in a preemptive strike against calories.

The last time I served this, I worked off some of it by chasing my dog, Oliver, around the house, screaming and wielding a frying pan. I was highly motivated: the beast had polished off a good half of the Thing while my back was turned. ✳ SERVES 6 TO 8

7 tablespoons unsalted butter

1½ cups grated cheddar cheese

1 cup grated Gruyère cheese

8 small or 6 large croissants

7 large eggs

2 large egg whites

2 cups half-and-half (if this makes you faint, use milk)

½ teaspoon salt

Freshly ground black pepper, to taste

⅛ teaspoon cayenne pepper

1. Use 1 tablespoon of the butter to grease a 13 x 9-inch baking dish. Sprinkle ½ cup of the cheddar cheese over the bottom of the dish. Combine the remaining 1 cup cheddar and the Gruyère in a bowl and set it aside.

2. Cut the croissants in half lengthwise, then in half crosswise. Arrange the bottom pieces, cut side up, on top of the cheese in the baking dish. Sprinkle half of the combined cheeses on top. Arrange the top pieces of the croissants on top of the cheeses, cut side down. Sprinkle the remaining cheese on top of the croissants.

3. In a large bowl, beat the eggs, egg whites, half-and-half, salt, black pepper, and cayenne together. Pour the egg mixture over the croissants. Cover the dish with plastic wrap and refrigerate it overnight.

4. About 1 hour before you want to serve the casserole, preheat the oven to 350°F.

5. Melt the remaining 6 tablespoons butter in a small saucepan over low heat, and drizzle it over top of the egg mixture. Bake until it is bubbly and the top is golden, about 45 minutes. Serve hot.

VARIATIONS You can add a little diced ham to this dish, tucked in between the layers.

Green Eggs and (Optional) Ham

A FRITTATA IS A GREAT EGG DISH FOR BLUNCH (for a smaller group) because you can serve it at room temperature, so you're not frantically scrambling eggs while everyone else is in the other room laughing over their mimosas.

I once tried to trick my children into eating green food by offering them this dish while reading them Dr. Seuss's *Green Eggs and Ham*. Well, they loved the book, but no amount of high-minded literature would change their food-i-tude.

Now that they are grown and gone to college and I'm no longer in a position to monitor their vegetable intake, I've turned my attention to Tom, our family's pickiest eater. One thing he does like is asparagus, and this frittata, besides being blunch-friendly, is also a good quick dinner when it's just the two of us. (No Dr. Seuss required.) ✳ SERVES 6 TO 8

8 eggs

¾ cup grated Gruyère cheese

½ cup freshly grated Parmigiano-Reggiano cheese

½ cup diced ham (optional)

¼ cup chopped fresh herbs (parsley with dill or basil, and chives too, if you like)

¼ teaspoon freshly ground black pepper

3 tablespoons unsalted butter

2 leeks (white and light green parts only), well rinsed and chopped

1 pound asparagus

½ teaspoon salt

1. In a large bowl, beat the eggs together until blended. Then mix in ½ cup of the Gruyère, ¼ cup of the Parmigiano-Reggiano, the ham if you're using it, the herbs, and the pepper. Set the bowl aside.

2. Melt the butter in a 10-inch nonstick broiler-proof skillet over medium-low heat. Add the leeks and cook until they are soft and translucent, about 10 minutes.

3. Meanwhile, bring salted water to a simmer in a vegetable steamer.

Break off the tough ends of the asparagus and steam the spears in the vegetable steamer until just tender, 3 to 4 minutes. Set the asparagus aside to cool briefly; then cut it into 1½-inch-long pieces.

4. When the leeks are done, add the asparagus to the skillet. Add the salt and toss the vegetables together gently. Reduce the heat to as low as it will go.

5. Give the egg mixture a stir and pour it carefully into the skillet. Sprinkle the remaining cheeses on top. Allow the frittata to cook, without stirring, until it is set on the bottom but still quite moist on top, about 10 minutes.

6. Meanwhile, preheat the broiler.

7. Transfer the skillet to the broiler and cook the frittata until it is set on top and just turning golden brown, 2 to 3 minutes.

8. Remove the skillet from the oven, slide the frittata onto a platter, and cut it into wedges. (Sometimes it won't slide easily, in which case you can just slice it in the skillet and place the wedges on your platter.) Serve hot or at room temperature.

Baked French Toast (That's Actually from Illinois)

WHILE THIS DISH BEARS A STRIKING RESEMBLANCE to baked French toast, the recipe actually comes out of Chicago, not France. An accommodating restaurant owner there shared it with a friend of mine, who shared it with me.

I love things you can make the night before. You just wake up, throw this in the oven, and spend the next hour cursing at the Sunday crossword puzzle.

The only trouble with making this the night before is that you have to make it the night before. Having just cleaned up the kitchen after dinner, you have to haul out eggs and bread and start cooking again. If you are a crabby cook, you will be exponentially crabbier by the time you go to bed, maybe even cursing the blunch guests who caused you all this trouble. Luckily, such feelings usually subside while you sleep, and when, the next morning, you pop this sucker in the oven, you feel downright *smug.* ✳ SERVES 8

1 tablespoon unsalted butter, for the baking dish

1 loaf good-quality white bread (I prefer challah)

6 large eggs

3 cups milk

1½ teaspoons vanilla extract

1 teaspoon ground cinnamon

¼ teaspoon ground nutmeg

For the topping

¾ cup (packed) dark brown sugar

8 tablespoons (1 stick) unsalted butter, at room temperature

2 tablespoons maple syrup

¾ cup chopped pecans or walnuts (optional)

For serving

Maple syrup

Unsalted butter

1. Butter a 9 x 13-inch baking dish. If your bread has excess crust, as challah does, remove some of it; otherwise, leave the crust on. Cut the loaf into ¾-inch-thick slices. Arrange the slices in two layers in the baking dish, breaking them as needed to fill in the empty spaces.

2. Whisk the eggs, milk, vanilla, cinnamon, and nutmeg together in a bowl. Pour the mixture over the bread. Cover the dish with plastic wrap and refrigerate it overnight.

3. About 1¼ hours before you want to serve the French toast, preheat the oven to 350°F.

4. Prepare the topping: Combine the brown sugar, butter, and maple syrup in a bowl and mix well. Stir in the nuts, if you're using them. Spread the mixture evenly over the bread.

5. Bake the French toast, uncovered, until it is puffed, bubbly, and golden brown, about 1 hour. (You should be able to get through at least two sections of the Sunday *Times* before it's done.)

6. This dish looks fantastic right out of the oven, so serve it right away, with maple syrup and extra butter.

VARIATION Instead of reading the paper while the French toast bakes, you could jump on the treadmill in a preemptive strike against calories, but I personally am way too crabby to exercise before breakfast.

A POSTSCRIPT

IN AN EFFORT TO GET MYSELF INTERESTED in entertaining more, I thought I'd repaint my dining room. As I'd once heard an interior designer suggest on television, I wanted to "wrap that D.R. in a warm white." How hard could that be? You go to the paint store, buy a few gallons, and slap it on.

So I did that first part: I went to a paint store. But when I told the salesman I needed white paint, he pulled out that color chart that opens up like a fan to reveal 600 different shades of white and throws you into a full-on panic attack. (I've never responded well to a multitude of choices.)

"Can you narrow it down to, say, the warm ones?" I asked. The salesman licked his fingers and snapped shut maybe a third of the Panic Wheel, leaving me with only about 400 decisions to make. I grew pale (roughly the shade of #68—"Buttermilk") and moisture sprang from my armpits. Clearly this was too much for me.

I went home and launched a large-scale obsession. I asked friends and relatives for their thoughts on white paint. I visited my neighbor on the pretext of borrowing a can opener and secured the name of her paint color. I called a hotel where I'd once admired the bedroom walls. I asked the bookseller, the neurologist, the florist—anywhere I saw a good white, I asked someone what it was. I went online, did some social networking, picked the brains of people I did not know.

When I'd finally assembled a group of color candidates, the wall of my dining room became a patchwork of samples, which I checked on at different times of the day as the light shifted. In the evening, I cleverly hid the patchwork behind the portrait of my great-grandfather so Tom would not see it and have me committed.

I made a final decision and booked the painter. Then I panicked and unbooked him. I had thrown away the rejected samples, but in a frenzy of uncertainty, I rebought them for another look. Maybe "Clunch" would be better than "Matchstick." Or should I reconsider "Oatmeal?" Why had I rejected "Satin Slipper?"

I made a new final decision, and this time, I painted the room. I hated it. I repainted the room. I was still unsure but I had to commit because my mahjong group was coming for dinner in two days and I would have to switch from paint obsession to menu obsession.

If you, too, would like to wrap your D.R. in a warm white, try "Oatmeal." I tell you this to save you weeks of trial and error, time better spent mastering the tango, buying a new garden hose, or writing your congresswoman. If you do write her, please ask her what color she painted *her* dining room.

NINE
Salad Days

MY BROTHER-IN-LAW FRANK ONCE
SAID that whoever invented bagged
prewashed lettuce should win the Nobel Prize.
What crabby cook would not agree? Here's the new
recipe for salad: rip open bag, toss lettuce in bowl, hurl in
some dressing, and you're done.

I revisited the olden days of salad making recently when I
prepared a Saturday Salad for my mahjong group. We call ourselves
that because we originally intended to learn and play mahjong, but
we never got around to it. Someday maybe, but the group's current
agenda is to get out of the house and yack.

I like hosting the Mahjongs because (a) it's a small membership
(four, easy to feed) and (b) they are crabby cooks too, so thrilled to
have someone else give them dinner that they'd be happy with frozen
pizza (and maybe a little vodka).

On this particular occasion I decided that, since all we were eating
was salad, I'd live it up and go for the real thing: old times' salad for
old times' sake.

First, I shopped for lettuces, a thing I had not done in a while. I'd
forgotten that there are an awful lot of lettuce varieties these days,
all kinds of species and subspecies. When faced with a lot of choices,
my usual reaction is to get anxious, freeze, and then overbuy, like

the time I went home with four pairs of tennis shoes. So, although I was decisive enough to nix the radicchio, I bought butter lettuce, romaine, red-leaf, watercress, spinach, arugula, and endive.

I went home and spread the lovely lettuces across the kitchen counter. I chopped and fiddled and ripped and hurled them into the icy waters of my salad spinner, and then I spun the bejeezus out of them. However, my ancient spinner was defective; the lettuce was still damp in spite of its rigorous exercise, so I wrapped it all up in paper towels.

By now I'd used a thousand gallons of water and a couple trees' worth of paper towels, and I was beginning to feel the kind of irritation associated with T.M.A. recipes (Too Much Activity).

Finally, I got the lettuce dried. My kitchen was so full of greens, you'd have though I was catering a bunny convention.

Then I remembered that I still had to tear all those tender watercress leaves from their stems, which I did with a level of irritability I usually reserve for people who talk on cell phones in the doctor's waiting room. And that was just the tip of the iceberg lettuce. I still had to assemble the Saturday Salad, which meant steaming asparagus, ripping the flesh from a chicken carcass, and making a dressing.

My guests arrived while I was still ripping flesh, but since it was the Mahjongs, it was totally fine. They grabbed the martini shaker and went to town and we ate eventually.

But as I tossed the salad, I remembered Frank's words and I made a note-to-self to call the Nobel nominating committee. Meanwhile, this chapter offers lots of salad recipes, for which I suggest you go with prewashed lettuce, avoiding T.M.A.

Saturday Salad

THE SALAD THAT I MADE FOR THE MAHJONGS is a kindred spirit of
Bette's Saturday Soup (page 21), the concoction my mother-in-law,
Bette, used to throw together on weekends, using the week's leftovers.

As you know by now, I contrive to produce leftovers; I always
cook extra chicken or beef so I get two meals for the aggravation of
one. With this salad you can use the remains of your roasted or grilled
chicken or meat or whatever. Just throw it on top of some sturdy
greens, along with a few other scenic items.

If you have no leftovers, buy a rotisserie chicken at the market
and pretend you roasted it yourself so you get extra points from your
diners.

The other ingredients in the salad will vary, but by the end of
any given week I usually have a half a cucumber that needs eating, a
lonely cup of chickpeas or beans, and some sliced cheese that is close
to expiration, so I throw those in. I like to add asparagus because
it gives the salad a little *oomph.* This usually means I have to cook
it, since I rarely have leftover asparagus lying around, but you can
substitute any leftover green veggie, like string beans or whatever.
And don't hesitate to throw in those extra new potatoes you cooked
on Tuesday, or even some random handful of penne or fusilli that's
lurking in your fridge. Just don't go overboard, like Bette did once
with the soup, and add a tooth-marked hot dog.

Please note that the dressing for this salad is my own quirky thing:
it involves half an egg yolk. (Save the rest of the egg for breakfast.)
Although I'm told that the vinegar kills any possible bacteria in the
raw egg, you can omit the yolk if it makes you nervous. ✳ SERVES 4

1 pound asparagus, ends trimmed

1 tablespoon balsamic vinegar

1 tablespoon red wine vinegar

1 teaspoon Dijon mustard

½ egg yolk

½ cup extra-virgin olive oil

1 clove garlic, mashed or minced

¼ teaspoon salt

¼ teaspoon freshly ground black pepper

1 to 2 teaspoons fresh lemon juice, to taste

6 cups mixed salad greens (any kind your family likes), prewashed or rinsed and patted dry

¼ cup finely chopped fresh herbs (parsley and basil, thyme, or dill)

2 to 3 cups leftover meat or chicken, cut into bite-size pieces

8 ounces sliced Jarlsberg cheese, cut into thin strips

8 ounces sliced Colby cheese, cut into thin strips

½ hothouse (English) cucumber, thinly sliced

2 plum tomatoes, seeded and chopped

1 cup canned chickpeas, drained and rinsed

1. Bring lightly salted water to a simmer in a vegetable steamer. Place the asparagus in the steamer basket, cover the steamer, and cook until crisp-tender, 3 to 4 minutes. Remove the asparagus from the steamer and place it on paper towels to cool. When it's cool, cut it into 2-inch pieces and set it aside.

2. Prepare the dressing: Whisk the vinegars and mustard together in a bowl; then whisk in the egg yolk. Slowly add the olive oil, whisking until the dressing thickens. Whisk in the garlic, salt, and pepper. Add the lemon juice and set the dressing aside.

3. Place the salad greens and the herbs in a large salad bowl. Toss the salad, adding just enough dressing to coat the greens completely. Divide the greens among four plates. Arrange the asparagus, meat or chicken, cheeses, cucumber slices, tomatoes, and chickpeas on top of the greens and serve, with extra dressing on the side.

Spud Salad

I SELDOM ATE POTATO SALAD AS A CHILD. I think this was because, back in those days in Illinois, the basic midwestern recipe involved peeling a lot of those big old brown spuds. When my mother, who cooked for eight of us every day, selected the carbo portion of the daily menu, she balked at making anything that labor-intensive. It was so much easier just to bake the damn spuds and be done with it.

These days, with the introduction of umpteen potato varieties and a trend toward not peeling them, it's a whole new ball game. You can use those cute tiny blue ones, the adorable fingerlings, or, my family's favorite, wee pink new potatoes. Just steam them, skin intact, and you're done.

I like to throw some string beans into the salad; you've got carbs and greens covered and you just have to come up with a little protein. Whip up some Picnic Chicken (page 220) and you're ready for a great patio dinner. Spud Salad is also great with Chicken Nuggets (page 218) or Fish Stix (page 122). ✳ SERVES 4

1 pound red new potatoes, cut in half (or use large red potatoes, cut into 1-inch chunks)

8 ounces string beans, cut into 1½-inch pieces (try to find haricots verts, the tiny French kind)

¾ cup mayonnaise

¼ cup crème fraîche

2 tablespoons fresh lemon juice

1 teaspoon Dijon mustard

¼ cup snipped fresh chives

¼ cup finely chopped fresh parsley

¼ cup finely chopped fresh basil or dill

Salt and freshly ground black pepper, to taste

1. Bring a pot of lightly salted water to a boil. Add the potatoes, reduce the heat, and simmer until they are just about tender, about 15 minutes. Add the beans and cook until they are crisp-tender, about 3 minutes. Drain the vegetables and set them aside to cool.

2. Whisk the mayonnaise, crème fraîche, lemon juice, and mustard together in a bowl. Stir in the herbs, and season with salt and pepper.

3. Place the potatoes and beans in a large salad bowl, and toss them gently with enough dressing to coat the vegetables well. Taste, and add more salt and pepper if needed. Let the salad sit for an hour or so before serving.

NOTE If you trust the refrigerator raiders (you do?), you can make the salad ahead of time and store it, covered, in the fridge for up to 2 days. Bring it to room temperature before you serve it.

VARIATIONS There are a million ways to mess with potato salad. You can play with the herbs: try tarragon or thyme, for example. You can substitute some chopped scallions for the chives. You can add a couple of chopped hard-cooked eggs, some chopped cucumber, or some peas or edamame . . . it's endless. I keep it simple due to the pickiness factor in my family (I'm pushing it with the addition of beans), but you shouldn't hesitate to experiment.

The Girls' Favorite Salad

WHEN MY KIDS FINALLY AGREED TO EAT SALAD, I saw it as a harbinger of a new, open-minded approach to eating. Suddenly it seemed possible to imagine serving them artichokes and ratatouille, creamed spinach, and even portobello mushrooms.

As it turned out, my excitement was premature—to this day they will eat none of the aforementioned—but at least we were making headway.

It took a while to break down the kids' resistance to salad. I started by offering a simple crudités bowl. The girls would eat a couple of carrots but never the celery, bell pepper, or cucumber. So I gave up on that and launched the lettuce project, trying iceberg, butter lettuce, red-leaf, and watercress. No, no, no, and no. (I think the watercress even made one of them weep a little.) I switched focus, whipping up dressing after dressing, even resorting to a ketchup/mayo mix. Nix. I tried bacon bits, croutons, everything short of sprinkling the salad with Skittles. Nothing.

Then I hit on it. Or probably more accurately, my discovery of a perfect salad formula coincided with the girls' advancing open-mindedness. The combination of ingredients in The Girls' Favorite Salad sent my daughters sailing off into the land of salad acceptance, and they haven't looked back. ✳ SERVES 4 TO 6

2 tablespoons mayonnaise

2 tablespoons red wine vinegar

2 tablespoons fresh lemon juice

1 teaspoon Dijon mustard

¼ cup finely chopped fresh parsley

¼ cup finely chopped fresh basil (optional)

1 clove garlic, minced

¼ teaspoon salt

¼ teaspoon freshly ground black pepper

¾ cup canola or safflower oil

1 head romaine lettuce

¼ cup freshly grated Parmigiano-Reggiano cheese

1 cup halved grape tomatoes (optional)

1 cup croutons (optional)

1. Combine the mayonnaise, vinegar, lemon juice, mustard, parsley, basil if you're using it, garlic, salt, and pepper in a blender and blend for a few seconds to combine (or blend the ingredients by hand). With the blender running (or the whisk whisking), add the oil in a slow stream. Set the dressing aside.

2. Wash the lettuce, removing any damaged outer leaves, and pat it dry with paper towels. Cut it into bite-size pieces. Place the lettuce in a salad bowl, and toss it with enough dressing to coat all the leaves. Add the cheese and toss again. Place the tomatoes and croutons on top of the salad, if you're using them, and serve.

Wolverine Salad

MAYBE IT'S BECAUSE I'M GIVEN TO FLIGHTS OF CUCKOO FANTASY
when I'm performing tedious culinary tasks, or maybe I'm just,
you know, losing it. But when the salad hands I had ordered online
arrived, I became Wolverine. If you have never seen an *X-Men* movie,
you might not know who this is. Think Hugh Jackman, hairier and
half-naked. I know, perfect, right?

Well, Wolverine does have one unusual physical characteristic,
which is these scary metal claws he uses when he's messing up bad
people. And although the salad hands are cuter (white plastic with
bright green handles), when you hold them, you can't help but feel
like that iconic superhero. At least, I can't.

If only I could, along with the hands, acquire some of Wolverine's
special skills: (1) When wounded, he heals instantly. This would
have come in handy the other day when, with my usual kitchen
impatience, I sliced my finger instead of the carrot. (2) He never
ages. He's been rushing around for centuries, growling and stabbing
people, and he still looks like, well, Hugh Jackman.

It's not such a bad way to get through the dinner hour. Grab
those salad hands and flip your imagination switch: tossing a salad
becomes much more interesting. I just have to try not to growl at
people, which is a stretch for me even when I'm empty-handed.

This is one of my favorite salads, with or without the hands.

✳ SERVES 4 TO 6

For the dressing
2 tablespoons fresh lemon juice
1 tablespoon balsamic vinegar
1 teaspoon Dijon mustard
1 teaspoon Worcestershire sauce

1 garlic clove, minced
½ cup olive oil
¼ teaspoon salt
¼ teaspoon freshly ground black
  pepper

For the salad

> 6 cups mixed salad greens, rinsed and patted dry
>
> ¾ cup Spicy Nuts (page 172)
>
> ¾ cup dried sweetened cranberries
>
> About ½ cup crumbled ricotta salata

1. Prepare the dressing: Whisk the lemon juice, vinegar, mustard, Worcestershire sauce, and garlic together in a bowl. Slowly add the olive oil, whisking constantly until the dressing thickens. Whisk in the salt and pepper. Set the dressing aside.

2. Place the salad greens, Spicy Nuts, and dried cranberries in a salad bowl. Toss the salad gently, gradually adding just enough dressing to coat the greens completely.

3. Divide the salad among four to six salad plates, sprinkle each with a tablespoon or so of the cheese, and serve.

VARIATIONS This is another good salad to turn into a full meal by adding grilled chicken or, better yet, leftover butterflied leg of lamb.

You can substitute dried cherries for the cranberries, and if you can't face making Spicy Nuts, just use lightly toasted pecans.

Cherry Salad

THIS IS A COUSIN OF THE WOLVERINE SALAD, nutty and fruity. It makes a nice change from the usual, but it does involve a little labor. You've got to pit a whole bunch of cherries, which is not the kind of task crabby cooks are drawn to. But here's a tip: Until Apple makes an app that'll do the job for you, get yourself a cherry-pitter.

Normally I would never buy a utensil that has only one use, which is to pit a fruit that appears only briefly each year. But if you love cherries, it's worth it. Suddenly, it's a snap to add cherries to a salad, or to make a cherry pie (although even with a pitter, I'm too crust-challenged to undertake the latter).

Even if you are pitter-equipped, I suggest that you plan to multitask while you pit, to avoid crabbiness. Catch up on your TiVo-ed episodes of *Family Guy* or at least listen to Lady Gaga. Slap on one of her CDs (if you still buy such things) and your pitting time will simply fly by. ✳ SERVES 4 TO 6

2 tablespoons balsamic vinegar

2 tablespoons red wine vinegar

1 teaspoon Dijon mustard

½ cup olive oil

½ teaspoon kosher salt

¼ teaspoon freshly ground black pepper

4 cups (loosely packed) arugula

12 ounces cherries, pitted and halved

¼ cup dried cherries

½ cup crumbled feta cheese

½ red onion (or to taste), thinly sliced

½ cup sliced almonds, roasted (see Note)

1. First make the dressing. Whisk together the vinegars and mustard in a small bowl. Gradually whisk in the oil, in a slow stream. Whisk in the salt and pepper and set the dressing aside.

2. In a salad bowl, combine all the other ingredients and toss gently, adding enough dressing to coat all the greens. Serve immediately.

NOTE To roast the almonds, place them on a baking sheet in a 350°F oven until they are golden and fragrant, about 10 minutes.

VARIATIONS If you want to make this a one-dish meal, add some leftover pork tenderloin or roasted turkey.

Minty Cuke Salad

I WILL OFTEN BUY A CUCUMBER with the intention of putting it in the evening's salad, but by the time I get to the salad prep, I'm too crabby from making the rest of the dinner so I ditch the cucumber, telling it (I admit that I sometimes speak apologetically to neglected vegetables) that I'll use it the next day. But then I'm too crabby that day too, so the cucumber tends to languish in the refrigerator until it's time to guiltily throw it out.

If you find yourself apologizing to your neglected cucumber, I suggest you try this recipe as soon as possible, before either the cucumber perishes or your family has you committed. It's easy, but if you're a crabby cook like me, make it on a night when the rest of the meal is just leftovers. (It's great with cold roast lamb.) ✳ SERVES 4

1 head butter lettuce, damaged outer leaves discarded
1 hothouse (English) cucumber
¼ cup champagne vinegar
2 teaspoons finely grated lemon zest
2 tablespoons finely chopped fresh mint
1 teaspoon honey
½ teaspoon kosher salt
Freshly ground black pepper, to taste
¾ cup extra-virgin olive oil

1. Rinse the lettuce and pat it dry with paper towels. Tear the lettuce into pieces and place them in a salad bowl.

2. Trim the ends off the cucumber, cut it into thin slices, and add them to the salad bowl.

3. In a separate bowl, whisk together the vinegar, lemon zest, mint, honey, salt, and pepper. Slowly add the olive oil, whisking until the dressing thickens. Drizzle the dressing over the salad and toss it gently, making sure all the lettuce and cucumber slices are coated. Serve immediately.

The Old Uncle's Rice Salad

I ONCE READ IN SOME INFORMATIVE ARTICLE that people tend to use the same dishwasher detergent as their moms used. This is totally true for me; I think of my mother every time I pour the Cascade.

But I believe the theory also applies to certain kitchen staples, things like salt (Morton's), cereal (Quaker Oats), and canned soup (Campbell's). And then there's rice.

In an attempt to be a mature cook, I have had some rice adventures, touring the world of basmati, wild, and the lovely jasmine. Also, due to advice from bossy nutritionists, I use brown rice more and more.

Still, I've never given up on my old Uncle Ben. I've known that cheerful orange box since childhood, so its presence comforts me. Also I know that I won't burn the house down making Uncle Ben's, which distinguishes it from other rice types. (I don't know why it is, but I have set off many smoke alarms while flirting with strange grains.)

If you have a history with some other kind of rice, or if you're in the mood for brown rice or something exotic, go ahead, substitute. But most of the time, when I make this rice salad, I reach for the Uncle. ✳ SERVES 4

For the salad

  2 cups cooked white or brown rice
  ½ cup walnut halves, chopped
  ¼ cup raisins
  ½ apple, cored and cut into small dice
  2 tablespoons finely chopped red onion
  2 tablespoons finely chopped fresh parsley
  2 tablespoons snipped fresh chives

For the dressing

  ¼ cup red wine vinegar
  2 teaspoons fresh lemon juice
  1 teaspoon minced garlic
  ½ teaspoon curry powder, or to taste
  ½ teaspoon salt

  ¼ teaspoon freshly ground black pepper
  ¼ cup olive oil

1. Combine the rice, walnuts, raisins, apple, onion, parsley, and chives in a large bowl.

2. In a separate bowl, combine the vinegar, lemon juice, garlic, curry powder, salt, and pepper. Slowly whisk in the olive oil. Pour enough dressing over the salad to moisten all the ingredients, tossing to combine everything well.

3. Cover the salad and refrigerate it for 30 minutes before serving, to allow the flavors to blend. Serve chilled or at room temperature.

Dog-Proof Caprese Salad

I WAS THRILLED WHEN I HEARD ABOUT A DEVICE called the Bowlingual. It's a gadget with two parts, one of which is a dog collar that picks up and translates your pooch's barks, sending the translation to the second component, a hand-held speaker that spits out the dog's message in a human voice.

I would love to have a Bowlingual chat with Oliver. I would probably stay away from subjects like the goings-on in Afghanistan or the unemployment numbers since I suspect the dog is bored by such things. He is, however, an avid foodie, so that would be a good conversation starter. I'd like to ask him how he felt about that roast chicken he swiped from the kitchen counter—should I have adjusted the rosemary?—or why he finds it so appealing to chew on my newly purchased teal suede pumps. I'd also like to know why, with his diverse tastes, he wouldn't go near the delicious Caprese salad that Tom left within striking range the other day. Was it the basil? Is he lactose intolerant?

The only trouble with the Bowlingual is that the current (second) generation of the device offers the translation only in Japanese: you have to hire a translator to translate the translation, which may be cost-prohibitive.

So, until I hear that the Bowlingual has gone English, Oliver and I will continue to stumble through life without understanding each other's food preferences. (Kinda like it's been with the kids for twenty years.) Meanwhile, at least I know I can leave Caprese Salad on the counter and it'll be there when I come back. ✳ SERVES 4

2½ cups grape tomatoes

8 ounces fresh mozzarella cheese

3 tablespoons olive oil

1 tablespoon balsamic vinegar

1 teaspoon minced garlic

½ teaspoon kosher salt or coarse sea salt

¼ teaspoon freshly ground black pepper

¼ cup chopped fresh basil

4 leaves butter or red-leaf lettuce

1. Cut the tomatoes in half and place them in a large bowl. Cut the mozzarella into ½-inch cubes and add them to the bowl. In a separate bowl, mix together the olive oil, vinegar, garlic, salt, and pepper; add this to the salad bowl. Gently toss the salad to combine everything well. Add the basil and toss again.

2. Place a leaf of lettuce on each of four salad plates. Top the lettuce leaves with the salad, and serve.

Kool Slaw

I'M TOLD THAT COLESLAW DATES BACK TO THE ANCIENT ROMANS, although it didn't really kick into gear until mayo was invented in the 18th century. (Can you imagine life before mayo? One more reason to be glad that, in the birth lottery, you got a later century.)

"Cole" comes from the Latin word *colis,* you will be interested to know. But the Dutch called the salad *koolsla,* which I find more appealing so I'm stealing from them.

(I think the Dutch also invented chocolate bars, and certainly popularized tulips, so they have really got it going on.)

Anyway, I like a salad that won't wilt overnight; you can make Kool Slaw on a Friday and eat it all weekend. Have it with (or inside) a sandwich, pop open a beer, and it's a kool day. ✳ SERVES 6 TO 8

1 small head Savoy cabbage
2 carrots, peeled
1 apple, cored and finely chopped
¼ cup finely chopped fresh parsley
¼ cup finely chopped fresh dill (optional)
1 cup mayonnaise
¼ cup buttermilk
1 tablespoon cider vinegar
1 tablespoon Dijon mustard
1 teaspoon honey
½ cup almonds, roasted and chopped (see Note)

1. Using the slicer blade, shred the cabbage in a food processor. Transfer the cabbage to a salad bowl. Use the grater blade to grate the carrots in the food processor. Add the carrots, apple, parsley, and the dill, if you are using it, to the cabbage and mix together well.

2. Combine the mayonnaise, buttermilk, vinegar, mustard, and honey in a separate bowl.

3. Toss the slaw with as much dressing as you like. Sprinkle the nuts on top, and serve.

NOTE To roast the almonds, place them on a baking sheet and roast in a 350°F oven for about 10 minutes, or until they are fragrant.

Corny Salad

THIS IS A GREAT CHOICE IN SUMMER, when the corn is peaking. However, you can get into trouble if you happen to be cooking for a picky group. I once made this (as a side dish with grilled swordfish) for the extended family on Cape Cod and my sister-in-law doesn't like tomatoes, so I left them out, and my niece said she wouldn't eat beans due to concerns about flatulence (she was going on a blind date later), so I ditched the beans. Then my husband sneered at the cilantro and my father-in-law reminded me that he was allergic to onions. So the salad was stripped down to corn, with basil subbing for the cilantro, but it was still good.

In other words, this salad is versatile if you are related to incredibly picky people. ✳ SERVES 6

4 ears fresh corn, husks and silk removed

1 can (15 ounces) black beans, rinsed and drained

3 plum tomatoes, seeded and chopped

¼ cup diced red onion

¼ cup chopped fresh cilantro

3 tablespoons fresh lime juice

¼ cup olive oil

½ teaspoon ground cumin

½ teaspoon kosher salt

Freshly ground black pepper, to taste

1. Bring a large pot of water to a boil, add the corn, and cook until it is just tender, 2 to 3 minutes. (Or steam the corn in a vegetable steamer if you prefer.)

2. Drain the corn and set it aside to cool. When it is cool enough to handle, scrape the kernels off the cobs with a sharp knife, letting them fall into a salad bowl.

3. Drain and rinse the beans, and pat them dry them with paper towels. Add the beans, tomatoes, onion, and cilantro to the corn.

4. Pour the lime juice into a small bowl, and gradually add the olive oil, whisking until the dressing thickens. Whisk in the cumin, salt, and pepper.

5. Pour the dressing over the corn mixture, mix well, and serve.

VARIATIONS Use basil instead of cilantro. Seed and chop a red bell pepper and substitute it for the tomatoes. Add a jalapeño pepper, seeded and finely chopped, if you want a little heat.

George Clooney Chicken Salad

THE MOST IRRITATING PART OF MAKING CHICKEN SALAD is prepping the chicken. It's not hard; it's just kind of annoying to rip the flesh from all those bones. But once that's done, the rest is a breeze, and you can make the salad ahead and it can sit in the fridge for hours, while you take a golf lesson.

Seriously, my friend Heather recently suggested I take golf lessons, which seemed like a ludicrous idea until she mentioned she'd seen George Clooney down at the driving range where she receives instruction. This made the sport sound suddenly quite appealing.

Before I went for my first lesson, I made chicken salad and popped it in the fridge. There's nothing worse than having to interrupt a close encounter with George Clooney because you have to go make dinner . . . ✳ SERVES 8 TO 10

For the chicken

4 whole bone-in, skin-on chicken breasts, split

2 tablespoons olive oil

Kosher salt and freshly ground black pepper

For the dressing

1½ cups mayonnaise

½ cup crème fraîche

6 tablespoons fresh lemon juice

3 tablespoons mango chutney

1 tablespoon curry powder

2 tablespoons chopped fresh tarragon, or 1 teaspoon dried

Pinch of freshly ground black pepper

To finish the salad

1 cup seedless purple grapes, sliced in half

2 ribs celery, cut into 1-inch-long julienne

¾ cup unsalted macadamia nuts

½ cup golden raisins

¼ cup snipped fresh chives

1. Preheat the oven to 350°F.

2. Rub the chicken breasts with the olive oil, place them, skin side up, on a baking sheet, and sprinkle with salt and pepper to taste. Bake until done, 45 to 55 minutes, depending

on the size of the breasts. Let them cool to room temperature.

3. Place the macadamia nuts on a pie plate and roast them in the oven just until they are golden and fragrant, about 8 minutes. Set the nuts aside to cool.

4. Meanwhile, mix all the dressing ingredients together in a bowl, and set it aside.

5. Place all of the grapes, celery, macadamias, raisins, and chives in a large bowl and mix gently. Remove the skin and bones from the chicken breasts, and cut the meat into bite-size chunks. Add the chicken to the mixture in the bowl. Toss the salad, adding enough dressing to coat all the ingredients well. Cover and refrigerate the salad until you are ready to serve it.

VARIATIONS Add ½ cup leftover rice. You can also use other kinds of nuts: walnuts, pecans, whatever your family likes.

WHAT HAPPENED NEXT

AFTER I MADE THE SALAD, I announced to my jock husband that I was taking up golf so that he and I could have a lively activity together, to enhance our imminent child-free golden years. I didn't mention the part about George Clooney, who, in my dreams, would also play a part in enhancing my golden years, although perhaps not on a golf course.

The first lesson was fine, except for the fact that George Clooney must have been golfing elsewhere that day. But after four lessons I realized that (a) my potential as a golfer was limited at best and (b) George Clooney was never going to show up. I faked a back injury and cancelled my ten-lesson series.

In a wee act of revenge, I told Heather that I saw Brad Pitt at the bowling alley, where she has now signed up for a lifetime pass.

TEN

The Chicken Years

I F THIS WERE A PROPER COOKBOOK, the chicken chapter would be located elsewhere, say, nestled in between the roasts and the fish. But, as you may have noticed, this is NOT a proper cookbook, but one in which family history often trumps editorial guidelines. (Just ask my poor, beleaguered editor.) So, the chicken chapter is late in the book because chicken came to dominate our dining table late in life. (Note-to-self: send editor some blondies. *Editor's note: I'm still waiting.)*

* * *

When she was little, my daughter Nora thought that "chicken" was the generic word for anything on her plate that looked like the protein element. She'd inspect the shrimp or pork chops or beef and ask, "What kind of chicken is this?"

These days, the girls are grown and gone, but my husband asks that same question. It's not, however, because he can't tell a meatball from a drumstick. It's because, due to health concerns and an aversion to most fish, he eats almost nothing but poultry. So Nora's mealtime question has taken on a new relevance, and my search for fresh and interesting chicken recipes has become desperate. I beg for them, borrow them, and yes, I even steal them.

However, when I read about the security surrounding a certain chicken recipe, I realized my desperation had its limits.

This particular recipe, scribbled in pencil on a piece of notebook paper and signed by its creator, has lived in a file cabinet in Louisville for decades. In order to access this cabinet, a recipe thief would have to enter an office building full of beefy security guards and hair-trigger alarm systems, locate and open a particular vault, then open a triple-locked door, and then the file cabinet, which has two combo-locks on it.

This would be way too much trouble. I think a recipe thief would be better advised to just surreptitiously rip a recipe from a magazine in the doctor's office. You just cough to cover the ripping sound, or you sneak the magazine to the ladies' room, which, if empty, is a discreet place to rip.

But let's get back to Louisville.

The recipe in question is, of course, Colonel Sanders' famous one for Kentucky Fried Chicken, and as its value is, well, immeasurable, some recipe thieves would find it worth the hassle of stealing.

Only two executives (whose names and ranks are undisclosed) have access to the recipe at any given time. Even the suppliers who make the stuff the chicken is dipped in divvy up the job so nobody knows what all the ingredients are. However, it *is* known that the ingredients are eleven in number.

Now, being a crabby cook, I have to say this is a recipe I would never steal. Eleven ingredients is way too many, not to mention the frying. If I'm going to steal a recipe, it's going to be an easy one, one that's worth the guilt because it's going to make my life better. If I'm in the doctor's office and the recipe in the magazine has eleven ingredients, I will not be ripping, I'll be skipping.

But regardless of what I think, the folks at KFC apparently think otherwise. They've recently decided to beef up security at corporate headquarters. Under cover of darkness, they slipped the KFC recipe into a briefcase which they handcuffed to a N.Y.P.D. officer named Bo and whisked it (and him) off to an undisclosed location so they could update their system of protecting that ratty piece of notebook paper.

So, recipe thieves beware: It just got tougher to steal that coveted document. I recommend you forget the felony and stick to the misdemeanor. When you're desperate for a new chicken recipe, do what I do: schedule a doctor's appointment.

In the meantime, try some of the tasty options in this chapter.

Roast Chicken 101

WHEN IT'S 5 P.M. and I have no idea what's for dinner and little interest in browsing through cookbooks, my default plan is to roast a chicken. It's my favorite no-brainer: You throw it in the oven and then you've got an hour to figure out what you're going to serve with it. (Or to address more compelling tasks, like making a margarita.)

Also, now that I'm just cooking for Tom and myself, roast chicken gives me my favorite thing: two meals in one. I roast it one night and use the leftovers for Saturday Salad or something. ✳ SERVES 4 (OR 2 PEOPLE TWICE)

1 chicken (4 to 5 pounds; get organic or free-range—it's much better)

Kosher salt

1 lemon, cut in half

6 garlic cloves, lightly crushed

1 bouquet garni (a bay leaf, a few sprigs of parsley, and 2 sprigs of thyme tied together with string)

2 tablespoons unsalted butter, at room temperature

½ teaspoon paprika

Freshly ground black pepper

½ cup low-sodium chicken broth

1. Preheat the oven to 425°F.

2. Rinse the chicken inside and out and dry it with paper towels. Lightly salt the cavity. Place 1 lemon half in the cavity (set the other half aside), along with the garlic and the bouquet garni. Rub the outside of the chicken with the butter, and season it with the paprika and with salt and pepper to taste.

3. Place the chicken, breast side up, in a roasting pan and roast until the skin is nicely browned and crisp and a leg moves easily in its socket, about 1 hour.

4. Remove the lemon, garlic, and bouquet garni from the cavity and place them in the roasting pan. Tip the chicken to let the juices run from the cavity into the pan. Set the chicken on a carving board to rest.

5. Squeeze the juice from both the cooked and uncooked lemon halves into the pan. Add the broth to the pan, and simmer on top of the stove over medium heat until the sauce is slightly reduced, 3 to 4 minutes. Strain the sauce into a pitcher.

6. Carve the chicken, and serve it with the sauce on the side.

VARIATIONS Slice a large onion, toss the slices in a bowl with a little olive oil, salt, and pepper, and add the slices to the pan for the last 30 minutes of cooking. The onions make a great side dish. (My family won't go near them, but I love them.)

If you're really on top of things (I'm so not), you can also throw in some potatoes to roast with the chicken. Just cut some Yukon Gold or red potatoes into chunks, rub them with a little oil, sprinkle with salt and pepper, and hurl them into the roasting pan 30 minutes before the chicken's done. Then your dinner is *so* done, except for the struggle of preparing something green to go with it.

Blue Moon Chicken

I'VE OFTEN USED THE EXPRESSION "once in a blue moon" but never knew its origin. I only knew that it implied infrequency, as in "My husband cooks only once in a blue moon," a complaint I have made a thousand times.

When I heard that there would be an actual blue moon on New Year's Eve of 2009, I did a little research. Now I know: a blue moon is the second of two full moons in one month, and you only get one about every two and a half years.

I told Tom about this, and suggested that since we were having a blue moon, it might be a fitting time for him to cook dinner. This led to a discussion of his cooking repertoire, a list which, as you know by now, includes only cream cheese and olive sandwiches, tuna melts, grilled hamburgers, and Campbell's soup. None of these seemed like festive options. Then Tom admitted that as a bachelor, he had cooked chicken in the oven, a practice he gave up the minute we exchanged vows. (I didn't realize that when I said "I do," it was short for "I do the cooking.") I asked him what his recipe was.

"Oh, you know, you just put the chicken in a pan and stick it in the oven until it's done."

Salt? Pepper? "Nah."

Oven temperature? "I don't know, medium, I guess."

Cooking time? "Like I said, till it's done."

"Okay, " I said. "Go for it." He did, and the chicken was not half bad.

Later that week, I was making the grilled chicken that follows. It requires so little effort that I made a note-to-self to give Tom the recipe next time he feels moved to cook. And I did the math: The next blue moon is in mid-2012. ✳ SERVES 8, OR 4 TODAY AND 4 TOMORROW

½ cup fresh lemon juice

¼ cup Dijon mustard

1 tablespoon chopped fresh thyme or chopped fresh rosemary

1 tablespoon olive oil, plus extra for the grill pan

½ teaspoon salt

¼ teaspoon freshly ground black pepper

8 boneless, skinless chicken breast halves

1. In a bowl that is large enough to hold all the chicken, combine the lemon juice, mustard, thyme, olive oil, salt, and pepper. Add the chicken breasts and turn them so they're coated on all sides with the marinade. Cover the bowl and marinate in the refrigerator for 1 to 4 hours.

2. When you're ready to cook the chicken, lightly oil a grill pan and heat it over medium heat. When the pan is hot, grill the chicken until the juices run clear, 7 to 8 minutes on each side.

3. Serve hot or at room temperature.

VARIATIONS Use other herbs if you want, like chopped basil or dill. If you're dealing with herb-resistant children, omit the herbs altogether—it's still great.

Chicken Nuggets

I CONFESS THAT WHEN MY CHILDREN WERE YOUNG and I was a kitchen desperado, Tom and I used to take them to a certain fast-food joint (my husband called it Mickey Dee's) on most Saturdays. It made the girls incredibly happy to frolic on the play structure while chomping on those gnarly Chicken McNuggets and (pretty great) French fries. I'd tell myself that since we didn't resort to it more than once a week, the girls would survive this moment of dubious nutrition, and it was worth it, given all that joy.

As they grew older, the kids lost interest in the toys that came with those meals, and then in the meals themselves. This was right about the time the press was going nuts on the subject of trans fats, so it was a good moment to rethink the nugget.

I found something like this recipe and played with it until it passed muster with my girls, and we all began to eat these guilt-free nuggets on a regular basis.

Now when I serve these to Tom, I add some roasted spuds as a sub for those fabulous fries (although I do not provide a toy), and we can almost feel like it's 1995 and we're back at Mickey Dee's (in a good way). ✳ SERVES 4

Cooking oil, for the baking sheet
½ cup mayonnaise
3 tablespoons milk
½ teaspoon ground cumin
¼ teaspoon freshly ground black pepper
1 clove garlic
¾ cup unseasoned dry bread crumbs or panko (Japanese bread crumbs)
1 pound boneless, skinless chicken breasts, cut into 2-inch chunks

1. Preheat the oven to 425°F. Lightly oil a baking sheet, and set it aside.

2. In a small bowl, mix the mayonnaise, milk, cumin, and pepper together. Put the garlic through a garlic press, letting it drop into the bowl, and mix it well with the other ingredients.

3. Place the bread crumbs on a pie plate. Dip each chunk of chicken in the mayonnaise mixture, and then roll it in the bread crumbs to coat it completely. Place the nuggets on the oiled baking sheet and bake until they're sizzling and golden, 15 to 20 minutes.

VARIATIONS If you like, make a dip for these: Mix ½ cup mayo with ½ cup of the salsa on page 52.

Picnic Chicken

ONE OF THE GREAT THINGS ABOUT LOS ANGELES is the Hollywood
Bowl. I love the Bowl, but I love it for the wrong reason.

I don't love it because it's a beautiful outdoor venue where you
(and nearly 18,000 other patrons) can sit under the stars and hear the
L.A. Philharmonic or Beck while crickets chirp and you dine on picnic
food. I love it because, thanks to the Hollywood Bowl dining tradition,
many takeout places and restaurants in L.A. offer picnic baskets to
go, all summer long. For those of us who are honing our cooking-
avoidance skills, this is fabulous.

I got on to this recently when Tom and I cancelled our plans to
go to the Bowl one night. In an attempt to expand our new child-free
life, my husband and I have been trying to get out more, to explore the
city we live in. But that night, Tom had a volatile situation at the office,
the traffic was insane, and the scheduled concert turned out to be a
celebration of the L.A. Dodgers, a team neither of us has an allegiance to.

We ditched the show, but the good news was that I'd ordered and
picked up a picnic for us at a restaurant, which we ate *al fresco* on the
patio, with our own private stars and crickets and 17,998 fewer people.

From now on, I plan to pretend to go to the Hollywood Bowl
on a regular basis. I'll order a picnic basket, and at pickup time I'll
exchange lively banter with the purveyor about who's playing the
Bowl that night and how bad the traffic's likely to
be, and then I'll sneak home, light candles, put on
my L.A. Phil CD, and dinner will be so done.

If the town you live in does not have a
Bowl, or takeout picnics, here's a relatively
painless chicken that makes a great picnic

basket item. It's like fried chicken without the frying. Make it the morning of your picnic, throw it in a basket with some chips, pickles, and grapes (and Wet-Naps), and go sit on the patio. ✳ SERVES 4

½ cup Dijon mustard

1 clove garlic, mashed

½ teaspoon dried thyme

1 cup panko (Japanese bread crumbs)

¾ cup freshly grated Parmigiano-Reggiano cheese

1 teaspoon paprika

2 bone-in, skin-on chicken breasts, split (4 pieces; about 8 ounces each), or 1 whole chicken (3 to 3½ pounds) cut into 4 pieces

1. Preheat the oven to 375°F.

2. Mix the mustard, garlic, and thyme together in a bowl. On a pie plate, mix the bread crumbs, cheese, and paprika together. Coat a piece of the chicken with the mustard mixture (I do this with my hands), and then place the chicken in the breadcrumb mixture and turn it to fully coat it with crumbs on all sides. Repeat this with all the chicken pieces.

3. Place the chicken pieces on a rimmed baking sheet and bake until they are golden brown, crispy, and cooked through, 50 to 55 minutes, depending on their size.

4. Serve the chicken hot, or let it cool and take it on a picnic with some Spud Salad (page 199), Corny Salad (page 209), or The Old Uncle's Rice Salad (page 205).

Chicken Curry

MY FRIEND SUZANNE is one lucky woman. She recently sent me an e-mail that began, "Tonight Adam and his buddies are making the following meal for themselves."

Okay, I had to pause there for a second. Adam is Suzanne's fifteen-year-old son, just so you know, so already I was choking with envy. I have thus far never had the opportunity to write a sentence like that regarding my own children. Plus, aren't teenage boys supposed to be out zooming around on motorcycles, rebelling without a cause? What's up with this?

It gets worse. Here's what Adam and friends were making: "Sweet potato and plantain soup with smoked chile crème and fried plantain, Cotija-crusted quesadillas with basil, red chiles, and charred corn relish, pan-roasted pork chops with yellow pepper mole sauce, and warm chocolate cake with dulce de leche." Not only was Suzanne's son cooking dinner, it was a gourmet one, including an ingredient I had to Google: Cotija. (It's a cheese. Who knew?)

How did Suzanne get so lucky? Was it nature or nurture? Did Adam just get the Emeril gene or did Suzanne give him cooking utensils as crib toys? Whatever the answer, I fear it's too late for me. My kids are older than Adam, have gone off to college, and on their rare visits home they show no signs of using a spatula for anything but a fly swatter. Just recently, in fact, when Elizabeth was home, I asked if she'd like to learn how to make chicken curry. I hyped it as a simple but exotic recipe, good for novice cooks, but she wandered off to watch TV just as I was extolling the virtues of coconut milk. (How can a kid who is so uninterested in cooking be so obsessed with *Top Chef*?)

If you can rope your teenager into cooking dinner, I envy you. If you can't, try this recipe yourself. It has no ingredients you have to Google. ✳ SERVES 4

3 tablespoons unsalted butter

2 tablespoons olive oil

4 boneless, skinless chicken breast halves (about 6 ounces each)

Coarse salt and freshly ground black pepper

1 large onion, chopped

2 cloves garlic, minced

1 tablespoon curry powder

1 can (14 ounces) diced tomatoes, with their juices

½ cup coconut milk (see Note)

Hot cooked rice, for serving

1. Melt 2 tablespoons of the butter in 1 tablespoon of the olive oil in a large skillet over medium-low heat. Sprinkle the chicken breasts lightly with salt and pepper, and cook until they are browned and cooked through, 7 to 8 minutes on each side. Transfer the chicken to a plate and tent it with aluminum foil.

2. Wipe out the skillet and add the remaining 1 tablespoon butter and 1 tablespoon olive oil. When the butter has melted, add the onion and cook until it is tender, about 10 minutes. Add the garlic and curry powder, and cook for 1 minute. Add the tomatoes and cook until their liquid has reduced and the sauce has thickened, 4 to 5 minutes.

3. Add the coconut milk to the skillet and stir to combine it well with the other ingredients. Add ¼ teaspoon each of salt and pepper, or to taste. Return the chicken breasts to the pan and cook for 2 minutes or so, just to heat them through.

4. Serve the curry over the rice.

NOTE Coconut milk can be found in most supermarkets these days. Chill the can before you open it. For this recipe, use only the creamy part of the coconut milk, which will have risen to the top of the can—do not combine it with the watery part of the milk that has collected below.

VARIATIONS You can use garam masala in place of the curry powder. If I'm feeding my kids, I stick with the curry because using the other spice is pushing their boundaries, but I would definitely recommend garam masala.

Chicken Teriyaki-ish

LUCKILY FOR ME, there are a few takeout establishments nearby that offer chicken dishes that Tom likes.

Tom loves Chinese lemon chicken, and there's no way I'm cooking it when that restaurant two miles away will do it for me. Chicken kebabs are another favorite, available from the local Persian restaurant, and I can get chicken teriyaki from the nearby Japanese restaurant, which happens to be called The Crazy Asian.

But occasionally I discover a recipe that's so easy, I have to relax my attitude. My new feeling is, if, say, it's rush hour, so it's going to take less time and stress to cook something than it would to drive somewhere to pick it up, I'll cook it. This recipe is much like the chicken teriyaki Tom likes, but cooking it myself is even easier than a 5 P.M. trip to The Crazy Asian. ✳ SERVES 4

8 bone-in, skin-on chicken thighs (about 4 pounds total)

½ cup soy sauce

½ cup (packed) brown sugar

2 tablespoons Dijon mustard

1 tablespoon grated fresh ginger

2 cloves garlic, finely minced

¼ teaspoon freshly ground black pepper

1. Place the chicken thighs in a bowl. Mix all the remaining ingredients together in another bowl, and pour the mixture over the chicken. Cover, and marinate the chicken in the refrigerator for at least 3 hours or as long as overnight.

2. About 1 hour before you want to serve the chicken, preheat the oven to 350°F.

3. Place the chicken in a baking dish or roasting pan, and bake, basting occasionally, until it is browned and cooked through, about 50 minutes.

4. Serve the chicken hot or at room temperature.

Saucy Chicken

I LIKE TO USE LEEKS IN A RECIPE because they are the one type of onion that my husband will not identify as such, so he will happily eat them, thinking he's eating wilted celery or something.

Should you ever run into Tom, please don't tell him about leeks—
that they are relatives of the onion—or I'll never be able to use them
again. Contrary to what you might be thinking, there is little chance
that he'll figure it out by reading this (or any other) cookbook.

✳ SERVES 4

2 tablespoons olive oil

4 skinless, boneless chicken breast
halves (about 6 ounces each)

Salt and freshly ground black pepper,
to taste

2 leeks (white part only), well rinsed
and patted dry

1 tablespoon unsalted butter

½ cup dry white wine

½ cup low-sodium chicken broth
(homemade if possible)

2 tablespoons heavy (whipping) cream

1 teaspoon Dijon mustard

1 teaspoon dried tarragon

1. Heat 1 tablespoon of the olive oil
in a large skillet over medium-low
heat. Sprinkle the chicken breasts
lightly with salt and pepper, and
cook until they are cooked through
and nicely browned on both sides,
about 8 minutes per side.

2. Meanwhile, cut the leeks in half
crosswise, then lengthwise into thin
strips.

3. When the chicken is done,
transfer it to a plate and tent it with
aluminum foil.

4. Wipe out the skillet and add the
remaining 1 tablespoon olive oil
and the butter. When the butter has
melted, add the leeks and cook until
they are soft, about 5 minutes. Add
the wine and the broth, raise the
heat slightly, and simmer until the
liquid is reduced by half and slightly
syrupy, about 5 minutes. Stir in the
cream, mustard, and tarragon.

5. Return the chicken to the skillet
to warm it slightly. Then serve
it immediately, with the sauce
spooned on top.

VARIATION If your family refuses
to eat leeks or if you just want to
simplify this recipe, you can omit
the leeks. When the chicken's done,
just skip right to the addition of the
wine and proceed.

Home Run Chicken

SINCE THE KIDS HAVE GONE TO COLLEGE, I am trying extra-hard to have quality time with my husband. This is why I have taken up watching sports on television. It's a good way to share a little couch time with a man who goes to Planet ESPN whenever he possibly can.

Sometimes I'm genuinely enthusiastic about whatever the game is; I like basketball and tennis, and I was surprised to notice how well I tolerated the Masters golf tournament recently. But I have trouble with baseball. I just can't get behind the great American pastime; I doze off around inning four.

However, when baseball season rolls around again, which will mean a fair amount of TV exposure to the antics of the Baltimore Orioles, I've decided to go the extra mile. I've learned some baseball lingo I can throw at my husband so he will think I'm not just a slacker, but rather a savvy, sports-connected babe.

When the first guy comes out with a bat, I will, of course, shout, "Batter up!" just to let Tom know I'm enthusiastic. I'll follow up by referring to a good fastball as a "cheese" and then I'll casually ask if a certain player "has a Mendoza line," which means a batting average of around 200, which I think is not so good. (I should probably Google that guy Mendoza in case there's questioning.)

But I'm going to save the big guns for the very moment when somebody hits a home run. I can't wait to see Tom's face when I spout, "Wow, that fireman threw a meatball, which, if the outfield guy had used his wheels, mighta been a circus catch but instead was a tater!"

Roughly translated, this means the pitcher who came in late threw a lousy pitch and if the guy who stands around way out by the wall had run faster he'd have caught it but he didn't so it's a home run (and he's a loser who probably has a Mendoza line).

After that display of lingo expertise, I'll bring out a six-pack and a cheese ball (that's not a baseball term—it's an appetizer). During the seventh inning stretch, I'll grill some chicken with a chimichurri sauce. (Hot dogs would be the more obvious choice, but this is a zesty substitute if you live a wiener-free life.) Then I'll sit back, relax, eat, drink, and maybe even belch. ✳ SERVES 4

¾ cup olive oil

½ cup chopped fresh flat-leaf parsley

2 tablespoons sherry vinegar

2 tablespoons fresh lemon juice

1 tablespoon chopped fresh oregano, or 1 teaspoon dried

2 cloves garlic, minced

½ teaspoon crushed red pepper flakes

½ teaspoon salt

¼ teaspoon freshly ground black pepper

4 boneless, skinless chicken breast halves (about 6 ounces each)

1. Combine the olive oil, parsley, vinegar, lemon juice, oregano, garlic, red pepper flakes, salt, and pepper in a food processor. Process for about 5 seconds, until this chimichurri sauce is well blended.

2. Place the chicken breasts in a bowl. Add about ¼ cup of the chimichurri sauce and turn the chicken to coat it on all sides. Cover the bowl and let the chicken marinate at room temperature for 30 minutes. Set the remaining chimichurri sauce aside.

3. When you're ready to cook, heat a grill pan over medium heat. Grill the chicken until it is cooked through, 7 to 8 minutes per side. Serve with the reserved chimichurri sauce on the side.

VARIATIONS You can add more garlic to the sauce if you are not planning to breathe on anybody after dinner. You might also add ¼ cup chopped cilantro or mint to make things more interesting. Some people add finely chopped onion or tomato, too, but I'm too lazy to do this. The sauce is also great with grilled shrimp or steak.

My Favorite Chicken

MY KITCHEN is not glamorously equipped.

My favorite thing is a 9 x 13-inch Pyrex baking dish that I've used for years to roast chickens and bake cakes. (I also once used it to soak a wounded toe.) I don't know what I'd do without that dish, or the Le Creuset casseroley thing (I always forget proper names of pots) that I use for stew, mulling cider (I did that once), and catching rain when my office window leaks. Those, and a wedding-gift pasta pot that's missing a handle, are my most-used pans. My feeling is, why have eight fancy, shiny, matching, adorable vessels when a few simple ones will suffice?

However, I recently went to Surfas, a cookware shop in Los Angeles, with the intention of spiffing up my sorry collection of pans. The store was stocked with stacks of stainless steel pans, racks of odd utensils that looked like instruments of torture, sacks of unusual flours, and armies of salt shakers. Anything a cook's heart desired could be found in this dazzling shop.

But I just can't get my mind around cooking equipment. Set me loose in a shoe store and I'm a house on fire, but in the presence of all that cookware, my eyes glaze over and I feel like I'm shrinking. I went in expecting to change my culinary life and I left with a biscuit cutter, a tin of paprika, a talking kitchen scale, and some paper flowers meant, I think, to line a cake plate, although I'm not really sure.

Much later, I went online and finally bought a new roasting pan. A friend had told me exactly what to get. I typed it in and clicked and three days later I was rewarded with the pan's arrival at my doorstep.

Having discovered the ease of shopping for cookware online, I might just go wild and buy a new pasta pot. Meanwhile, I'm using my new pan almost daily, including when I make one of my new favorite recipes, chicken with apples. ✳ SERVES 4

1 whole chicken (3 to 3½ pounds),
cut into 4 pieces, or 4 skin-on,
bone-in chicken breast halves
(about 8 ounces each)
1 cup unseasoned dry bread crumbs
½ teaspoon paprika
¼ teaspoon coarse salt
½ cup Dijon mustard
¼ teaspoon dried thyme
Freshly ground black pepper
7 garlic cloves
2 Granny Smith apples, peeled, cored,
and sliced
1 tablespoon olive oil
¼ teaspoon ground cinnamon
1 tablespoon unsalted butter

1. Preheat the oven to 350°F.

2. Rinse the chicken pieces and pat them dry with paper towels.

3. Mix the bread crumbs, paprika, and salt together on a pie plate.

4. In a bowl, mix together the mustard, thyme, and pepper to taste. Put one of the garlic cloves through a garlic press and add it to the mustard mixture. Blend well.

5. In a separate bowl, toss the apple slices with the olive oil, cinnamon, and about 6 twists of the peppermill. Stir in the remaining 6 garlic cloves. Spread the apples and garlic on the bottom of a roasting pan.

6. Spread some of the mustard mixture over a piece of chicken, covering it completely. Place the chicken on the bread crumbs and press down lightly; then turn the chicken over and coat the other side with crumbs. Place the chicken on top of the apples and garlic in the pan. Repeat this with the other chicken pieces.

7. Dot the chicken with the butter, and bake until it is browned and crispy and the apples are tender, about 50 minutes. Serve it hot.

A Postscript

BY THE WAY, that talking kitchen scale I got at Surfas actually comes in handy. With the girls gone, it is the only female voice in my house besides my own. I turn the thing on and a low-registered, warm voice says, "Hello," which is rather pleasant in the profound silence of my recently emptied nest. Then she pauses for a second, presumably to make internal adjustments, and says, "I'm ready."

This is an eerie echo of what Nora said at the end of last summer, when she was itching to follow in her sister's footsteps and get to college. Now she's gone, and when we got back from dropping her, after all the packing, schlepping, shopping, and shipping, her room looked and felt like Dorothy's, post-tornado: a mess, and dead still.

I didn't dare enter it for a couple of days; I knew it was an emotional minefield. When I finally wandered in and picked my way through Nora's detritus, I remained calm even when handling her abandoned fairy wings. Nor was my composure rocked by the sight of the worn schoolbooks and the ancient teddy bear. It was the picture on the wall of young Nora, one that captures her spunky spirit—she's leaping and laughing, just kind of glorious—that did me in.

After the weeping, I knew I needed task therapy, and maybe some comfort food. It seemed like a good moment to roast a chicken. I hauled a giant bird from the fridge and plunked it on the kitchen scale. I flipped the switch: "Hello." Pause. "I'm ready."

"Easy for you to say," I said.

ELEVEN

Just Desserts

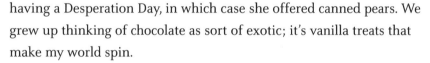

I T SEEMS TO ME the world can be divided into two main groups: the vanilla-heads and the chocolate-heads. It's all about your upbringing.

Throughout my childhood, we ate vanilla desserts—vanilla pudding, floating island, vanilla ice cream, and vanilla cookies, unless my mother was having a Desperation Day, in which case she offered canned pears. We grew up thinking of chocolate as sort of exotic; it's vanilla treats that make my world spin.

Tom, on the other hand, grew up with a chocolate cake permanently perched on his mother's kitchen counter, and with an abundance of Oreos and chocolate ice cream. So now my husband is a chocolate-head and I am a vanilla-head, and thanks to our mixed marriage, our children swing both ways.

However, Elizabeth was, for the first year or so of her life, deprived of all sweets, vanilla *or* chocolate. My husband and I kept our sugar addictions covert, sneaking chocolate chip cookies, Junior Mints, and Ben & Jerry's ice cream when our kid was napping.

On Elizabeth's first birthday, I made a cake that was loaded with nutrients and as light as a brick. I recently revisited some photos of my one-year-old merrily eating handfuls of that nasty cake, which was so full of soy flour, raisins, and molasses, it had only managed to rise about three quarters of an inch. Although I know my intentions were good, the picture made me feel that I'd been a bad parent, not a good one. I'd denied my own child one of the world's greatest pleasures, a treat to which everyone is entitled: a real, honest-to-goodness, sugar-crammed birthday cake.

My health conscious frenzy continued into Elizabeth's second year. I bought my daughter cookies from Whole Foods that were like Fig Newtons from hell. While I found them inedible, my poor, innocent child ate them happily, along with soy pudding, carrot-y doughnuts, and other disgusting but nutritionally correct treats.

She was to discover my betrayal soon enough. When she was about a year and a half old, Elizabeth became social, and she attended her first normal birthday party. By "normal" I mean the table was loaded with soda, chips, M&Ms, and, of course, a big, fat chocolate cake and vanilla ice cream. Maybe I was reading her wrong, but after she took her first bite, I thought the look she gave me said, "Why didn't you tell me about this, you loser?"

From then on, there was no turning back. By the time she was two, Elizabeth had been to enough parties to know the drill: There were to be no Birthday Brick Cakes for her ever again. This chapter contains recipes that have made her (and her family's) life a lot sweeter.

Tom's Birthday Cake

ALTHOUGH WE DO HAVE MANY LOCAL BAKERIES that make delicious cakes, my kids and my husband have always preferred homemade. (Well, sort of homemade. A cake mix is often involved.) If it's Tom's birthday, it has to be chocolate.

My husband is never happier than when he is eating chocolate cake. He is a chocoholic, unable to exercise restraint; he'll eat six pieces of cake if they are available. So, to preserve his health, I don't bake a cake often. But when I do, his favorite is this one, topped generously with Scharffen Berger chocolate buttercream icing.

✳ SERVES UP TO 12 PEOPLE IF TOM IS NOT PRESENT. IF TOM IS PRESENT, IT SERVES HIM AND MAYBE A COUPLE OTHER PEOPLE IF THEY ACT FAST.

1 box chocolate cake mix (see Note)

4 ounces Scharffen Berger semisweet chocolate, chopped into small pieces

8 tablespoons (1 stick) unsalted butter, at room temperature

2 cups confectioners' sugar

1 teaspoon vanilla extract

¼ teaspoon salt

1. Bake the cake in a 9 x 13-inch pan, following the directions on the package. Let it cool to room temperature.

2. Heat water in the bottom of a double boiler until it is just steaming (no hotter). Add the chocolate to the top pot, set it over the hot water, and heat it until it has melted. Set it aside to cool slightly.

3. Combine the unsalted butter, confectioners' sugar, vanilla, and salt in a food processor, and process until the mixture is smooth. Gently stir in the chocolate by hand until it's well blended.

4. Spread the icing on the cake, cut it into squares, and serve.

NOTE I don't have a favorite brand of cake mix, but I'm drawn to the ones that only ask you to butter the *bottom* (not the sides) of the pan. (I know, I'm such a lazy-ass.) The ingredients you need for most mixes are eggs and vegetable oil (and water), but make sure you check the box (and your cupboard) before you get started. More than once, I've had to stop mid-cake and go buy oil.

VARIATIONS If you like the combination of chocolate and peanut butter, make the cake with peanut butter icing: Combine 1 cup creamy peanut butter, 1 cup confectioners' sugar, 4 tablespoons room-temperature butter, and 1 teaspoon vanilla extract in the food processor. Delish.

Criminal Coconut Cake

COCONUT CAKE IS MY FAVORITE. It's tough to explain the origins of this preference, since I never ate it as a child. My father loathes coconut; cake flavors in our house were limited to vanilla and chocolate.

I think it was my acquaintance with the Mounds bar that made me a coconut-hugger. The bar and I were probably introduced on some Halloween, and I've been a devotee ever since. My twin brother, Billy, and I were, in fact, so devoted to Mounds bars that, at the tender age of six, we stole one from the supermarket.

I like to think that it was Billy's idea, but I was certainly a willing accomplice. I can remember the adrenalin rush I got when Billy plucked the gorgeous bar from the shelf and stuffed it into his pants while our mother was busy buying something more nutritious.

After a guilty, silent ride home, Billy and I hid behind the garage and ate the Mounds bar in Guinness record time—say, eight seconds. But Mom, who was not so oblivious as we thought, found us before we finished chewing.

After we were apprehended, we tried to attribute our criminal behavior to sugar deprivation. Our mother didn't believe in stocking the house with treats; we had no access to Coca-Cola, ice cream bars, or chocolate chip cookies. We little perps were driven to theft to satisfy our needs.

Mom heard our defense but was unsympathetic. Just to make sure the shame was indelibly etched in our souls, she took us back to the market for some face time with the manager. This was among the most humiliating moments of my childhood, topped only by the time I wet my pants during a card game with strangers.

After the Mounds incident, I switched to Zagnut and Clark bars, always careful to actually pay for them. But recently, a friend who often travels to Florida brought me some of the state's famous coconut patties and my interest in the whole genre was revived.

This cake is sort of like a giant Mounds bar without the chocolate, all sweet and coconutty. It's based on an old southern recipe that my Alabaman friend Cynthia grew up eating in a house where treats were in abundance, so the crime rate was low.

A caveat: You start making this cake three days before you eat it, so you must do the thing that's challenging for crabby cooks: plan ahead! ✳ SERVES 8 TO 12

2 cups sour cream

2 cups granulated sugar

2 cups sweetened shredded coconut

1½ teaspoons vanilla extract

1 box vanilla cake mix
  (see Note, page 233)

1 teaspoon almond extract

1 cup heavy (whipping) cream

1 tablespoon confectioners' sugar

1. Mix the sour cream, granulated sugar, coconut, and 1 teaspoon of the vanilla extract together in a bowl. Cover the coconut icing and refrigerate it overnight.

2. Prepare the cake batter, following the directions on the package. Stir in ½ teaspoon of the almond extract. Divide the batter between two buttered 8-inch round cake pans, and bake as instructed on the package. Let the cakes cool completely in the pans.

3. Remove one cake from its pan. Using a large serrated knife, cut the cake in half horizontally. Place the bottom half on a cake plate and frost it with about one fourth of the coconut icing. Place the second layer on top. With your knife, carefully slice off the rounded top of the cake to make a flat surface. Frost that with a similar amount of icing.

4. Cut the second cake in half, and place the bottom layer on top of the assembled cake. Spread half of the remaining icing over it. Place the top layer on top of that. Cover and refrigerate the cake and the remaining icing for 2 days.

5. Whip the cream in a bowl until soft peaks form. Add the remaining ½ teaspoon vanilla, the remaining ½ teaspoon almond extract, and the confectioners' sugar, and whip until the peaks are fairly stiff. By hand, gently fold the remaining coconut icing into the whipped cream. Spread this mixture over the top and sides of the assembled cake, and serve.

No Patience Coconut Cookies

THE OTHER DAY, I heard a lady on the radio whose name was Patience Wait. (I am not kidding.) She was participating in a news quiz, and she sounded like a very patient person. I guess she'd have to be patient, growing up with all those knuckleheads cackling about her name. I wonder if, had I been named Patience Wait, I'd have grown into that sort of person, instead of one who irritably paces her kitchen. I guess we'll never know.

If you have a coconut craving and do not have the Patience to Wait for Cyn's three-day cake (see page 234), try these incredibly easy cookies. Just be sure to let them cool before you chow down. Patience. Wait. ✳ MAKES ABOUT 3 DOZEN COOKIES

Unsalted butter, at room temperature, for the parchment

2 cups sweetened shredded coconut

1 can (7 ounces) sweetened condensed milk

1 teaspoon vanilla extract

½ teaspoon almond extract

⅛ teaspoon salt

1. Preheat the oven to 325°F. Line a baking sheet with parchment paper, and butter the parchment.

2. Combine the shredded coconut and all the remaining ingredients in a bowl, and stir together well.

3. Place teaspoonfuls of the mixture on the prepared baking sheet, spacing them about 2 inches apart. Bake the cookies until the edges turn golden brown, about 15 minutes.

4. Let the cookies cool on the baking sheet for 5 minutes; then transfer them to a wire rack to cool completely. These cookies are best eaten the day they are baked.

Boston Cream Cupcakes

ALTHOUGH THESE ARE A LITTLE LABOR-INTENSIVE due to the injection of filling, they are great for a kids' party because they are finger food, so you don't have to mess with plates. Plus they appeal to both vanilla-heads and chocolate-heads, preempting any flavor tantrums. ✳ MAKES 24 CUPCAKES IF YOU FILL THE LINERS TWO-THIRDS FULL, OR FEWER IF YOU FILL THEM ALMOST TO THE TOP, WHICH IS WHAT I USUALLY DO.

For the custard filling
1½ cups whole milk
⅓ cup sugar
⅛ teaspoon salt
3 tablespoons cornstarch
1 tablespoon unsalted butter, at room temperature
1 teaspoon vanilla extract

For the cupcakes
1 box yellow cake mix (see Note, page 233)

For the chocolate glaze
8 ounces good-quality semisweet chocolate, coarsely chopped
4 tablespoons (½ stick) unsalted butter, at room temperature
1 tablespoon light corn syrup

1. Prepare the custard first: Mix 1¼ cups of the milk, the sugar, and the salt in a small saucepan set over medium-low heat. In a bowl, mix the remaining ¼ cup milk with the cornstarch and blend well, making sure there are no lumps; then add this to the saucepan. Cook the mixture, stirring almost constantly, until it starts to bubble and thicken, about 5 minutes.

2. Remove the pan from the heat, stir in the butter and the vanilla, and mix until the butter melts. Pour the mixture into a bowl, cover, and refrigerate it for 2 to 24 hours.

3. While the custard is chilling, bake the cupcakes following the directions on the package, using paper liners in your muffin tin. Let the cupcakes cool completely on a wire rack.

4. When you are ready to assemble the cupcakes, fill a pastry bag with the custard mixture and fit it with a filling tip. Using an apple corer, make a cavity in the top of a cupcake, reaching almost to the bottom of the cupcake. When you remove the corer from the cupcake, carefully remove the cake that comes out with it and set it aside to use as a "plug." Squirt some custard into the cavity, almost to the top, and place the top half of the recovered cake "plug" on top to seal it. Repeat this with all the cupcakes.

5. Make the glaze: Place the chocolate, butter, and corn syrup in the top of a double boiler set over hot (not boiling) water, and stir occasionally until the chocolate has melted.

6. Pour a tablespoon or so of the warm glaze over each cupcake—just enough to cover the top. Chill the cupcakes until the glaze is set, about 30 minutes.

7. If you're not serving them immediately, keep the cupcakes in the refrigerator until 30 minutes before serving.

Girlfriends Pear Cake

I LOVE THIS CAKE. I think of it as a dessert for minor events, like when a couple of girlfriends come over or I'm having an insignificant birthday, say, turning forty-three. (Okay, fine, that happened a while ago.)

This is an easy recipe, and it's very forgiving. Once when I made this cake in a fit of impatience, I threw all the wet ingredients in the food processor, even the milk, which normally requires a delicate entry. Although the batter looked pathetic, the cake was entirely edible. ✳

SERVES 6 TO 8

8 tablespoons (1 stick) unsalted butter, at room temperature, plus extra for the pan

¾ cup plus 1 tablespoon sugar

2 eggs

1 teaspoon vanilla extract

1 cup all-purpose flour

1 teaspoon baking powder

½ teaspoon salt

½ cup whole milk

2 pears (I like Bosc)

1 tablespoon fresh lemon juice

½ teaspoon ground cinnamon

½ cup pine nuts, toasted (see Note; optional)

Whipped cream or vanilla ice cream, for serving (optional)

1. Preheat the oven to 350°F. Generously butter a 9-inch square cake pan.

2. Using a hand-held electric mixer, cream the butter and ¾ cup of the sugar together in a bowl until well blended. Add the eggs, one at a time, beating each addition until well combined. Stir in the vanilla.

3. In a separate bowl, mix the flour, baking powder, and salt together. Add half the flour to the butter mixture and blend well. Add ¼ cup of the milk to the batter and mix well. Then add the rest of the flour, mix, and stir in the remaining ¼ cup milk. Spoon the batter into the prepared cake pan and set it aside.

4. Peel the pears and quarter them lengthwise. Core them and cut the quarters crosswise into ¼-inch-thick slices. Place the sliced pears in a bowl and toss with the lemon juice, the remaining 1 tablespoon sugar, the cinnamon, and the pine nuts if you're using them. Spread the pear mixture evenly on top of the batter.

5. Bake until the top of the cake is golden brown and a knife inserted in the middle comes out clean, 55 to 60 minutes.

6. Serve warm or at room temperature, preferably with whipped cream or vanilla ice cream.

NOTE To toast the pine nuts, place them in a dry skillet over medium heat and toast, stirring or shaking frequently, for just a few minutes, until they are fragrant and golden. Let them cool completely in a bowl.

VARIATIONS You can use apples, plums, apricots, peaches, or other fruit in place of the pears. You can also substitute walnuts or chopped almonds for the pine nuts.

Tom's Brownies

MY HUSBAND AND I DO NOT NEED BROWNIES; we've eaten enough of them already to meet our lifetime quota and to account for certain body changes that I will not describe here. But because Tom is a hopeless chocoholic, when I make brownies to curry favor with my kids' friends, I have to keep an eye on them.

For a long time, when brownies disappeared from the cooling rack and my husband seemed the obvious perpetrator, he would issue a denial and look meaningfully in the direction of Oliver. So I thought the golden retriever was amazingly athletic (how did he reach the brownies I had placed behind the kitchen sink?) and had a remarkable tolerance for chocolate, a substance that is notorious for making dogs ill.

But then, on a recent occasion, I left a hot brownie batch on the counter to cool and took Oliver for a walk. When I returned and noticed that the baking pan was half empty, I did a breathalyzer test on napping Tom. Sure enough: chocolate breath. (And a messy crime scene: brown crumbs on the sofa.)

Since then, I have become more creative with my hiding places, putting cooling racks in the car or in the guest bathroom.

So far, so good: Tom has lost five pounds. ✳ MAKES 12 BROWNIES

8 tablespoons (1 stick) unsalted butter, plus extra for the baking dish

1 cup sugar

2 eggs

1 teaspoon vanilla extract

½ cup plus 2 tablespoons all-purpose flour

⅓ cup good-quality unsweetened cocoa powder (I like Scharffen Berger)

½ teaspoon baking powder

½ teaspoon kosher salt

½ cup roasted, salted peanuts (for example Planters cocktail peanuts)

½ cup semisweet chocolate chips

1. Preheat the oven to 350°F. Butter an 8-inch square baking pan, line it with parchment, and butter the parchment.

2. Melt the butter in a small saucepan over low heat and set it aside to cool. Place the sugar and eggs in a large bowl. Using a whisk or an electric hand mixer, beat them until they are well blended, light and pale yellow, about 2 minutes,. Gradually beat in the melted butter, then stir in the vanilla.

3. In a separate bowl, combine the flour, cocoa, baking powder, and salt. Mix well, then fold the flour mixture into the butter and egg mixture until just combined. Fold in the nuts and chocolate chips. Spread the batter in the prepared baking pan and bake until the top is crusty and cracking around the edges, and a toothpick inserted in the center of the brownies comes out with a little batter on it, about 30 minutes.

4. Let the brownies cool completely in the pan, then cut them into 12 pieces and serve.

My Blondies

I'M HOPING THAT I GET TO GO TO HEAVEN, because I'm told they've got a dessert bar there that offers your favorite sweets, 24/7. The chef just knows what you like: you walk up, she hands it to you. She'd hand me (a devout vanilla-head) one of these blondies, still warm from the oven, with a scoop of vanilla ice cream on top.

The other good news about heaven is that you can eat all you want and not get fat or redundantly drop dead. Until I get there, however, I have to exercise restraint and make these blondies only once in a while, because if I ate as many of them as I wanted, I would end up in heaven prematurely. ✳ MAKES 9 TO 12 BLONDIES

¾ cup unsalted macadamia nuts

8 tablespoons (1 stick) unsalted butter, plus extra for the pan

1 cup (packed) light brown sugar

1 egg

1½ teaspoons vanilla extract

1 cup all-purpose flour

1 teaspoon baking powder

½ teaspoon salt

½ cup white chocolate chips

½ cup unsweetened shredded coconut

Vanilla ice cream, for serving (optional)

1. Preheat the oven to 350°F. Butter an 8-inch square baking pan; then line it with parchment paper and butter that. Set the pan aside.

2. Place the macadamia nuts on a baking sheet and toast them in the oven until they are golden and fragrant, about 10 minutes. Allow them to cool slightly, then chop them coarsely and set them aside.

3. Melt the butter in a small saucepan over low heat. Stir in the brown sugar and let it dissolve slightly. Allow this mixture to cool for about 5 minutes. Then beat in the egg and the vanilla.

4. Mix the flour, baking powder, and salt together in a large bowl. Fold in the butter mixture just until the ingredients are combined. Fold in the macadamia nuts, white chocolate chips, and coconut.

5. Spoon the batter into the prepared baking pan, spreading it out evenly. Bake until the top is shiny and a toothpick inserted in the middle comes out with just a little batter on it, 25 to 30 minutes.

6. Let the blondies cool in the pan. Then cut them into squares and serve them warm (with a scoop of vanilla ice cream if you're really going for it) or at room temperature.

Vanilla Pudding, Skin Optional

WHEN I WAS GROWING UP, our family dinners were always chaotic. Six kids shouting, spitting, and spilling pretty much precluded good digestion, but I didn't really mind the mayhem. It gave me the cover I needed to discreetly dispose of the evening's green vegetable.

The chaos at our dinner table intensified when pudding was on the menu. This was due to the competition for pudding skin. Four kids were Skin Eaters, fond of that rubbery layer that forms on top of pudding if the chef is too frantic or crabby to take preventive measures. So when Mom made pudding, the pace of dinner accelerated: the Skin Eaters were anxious to get their share. Not being a Skin Eater myself (I preferred the mushy stuff below), my anxiety with regard to pudding was only moderate. But the other kids would speed-feed their spaghetti and tear off to the kitchen, yapping like coyotes at a kill. When they had scored their skin, my sister (a fellow Mush Eater) and I would happily slurp up the squishy leavings at a leisurely pace.

Here's the skinny on pudding skin: If you don't like it, the trick is to lay some plastic wrap right on the surface of the pudding while it cools. If you do like pudding skin, don't let the plastic wrap touch the pudding. Then get ready for the wars. ✳ SERVES 6 TO 8

2½ cups whole milk
⅔ cup sugar
Pinch of salt
¼ cup cornstarch
2 tablespoons unsalted butter, at room temperature
1 teaspoon vanilla extract
Whipped cream, for serving (optional)

1. Combine 2 cups of the milk, the sugar, and the salt in a saucepan set over medium-low heat. Mix the remaining ½ cup milk with the cornstarch in a bowl and blend well, making sure there are no lumps, then add this to the saucepan. Cook the mixture, stirring almost constantly, until it thickens, about 10 minutes.

2. Stir in the butter and the vanilla, and mix well. Remove the pan from the heat.

3. Pour the pudding into six to eight 4-ounce ramekins or into one large bowl, and refrigerate it—covered directly or indirectly with plastic wrap—until it's thoroughly chilled, at least 2 hours.

4. Top with a little whipped cream, if desired, and serve.

VARIATIONS If you have a family full of chocolate-heads, you can easily turn this into chocolate pudding: Add 2 ounces semisweet chocolate chips to the pudding when you add the butter and vanilla, and stir until the chocolate melts.

If your family swings both ways (some vanilla-heads, some chocolate-), as mine does, fill half the ramekins with vanilla pudding; then mix in some chocolate and fill the rest, so everyone is happy.

Pumpkin-Head Pudding

OKAY, SO WE'VE ADDRESSED THE NEEDS of the chocolate-heads and the vanilla-heads. This recipe focuses on the pumpkin-heads.

Many people are indifferent to pumpkin, but there are those who are crazy about it, including me and my daughters. We became pumpkin-huggers due to exposure to pumpkin pie, a dessert that usually appears on Thanksgiving and then goes into hiding for twelve months. Like roast turkey and stuffing, it seems almost out of place when served in, say, July.

I compensate during the year by making pumpkin pancakes, pumpkin muffins, and pumpkin soup. And then there's this easy little dessert, which is almost like pumpkin pie without the crust. It serves as an excellent teaser throughout the months when we're deprived of (or too crabby to make) that T-day treat. ✳ SERVES 6

4 eggs

1 cup heavy (whipping) cream

1 cup canned pumpkin puree

⅔ cup (packed) dark brown sugar

1 teaspoon vanilla extract

½ teaspoon salt

½ teaspoon ground cinnamon

¼ teaspoon ground ginger

⅛ teaspoon ground allspice

Whipped cream, for serving

1. Preheat the oven to 350°F.

2. Whisk the eggs lightly in a large bowl. Then add the cream, pumpkin, brown sugar, vanilla, salt, and spices. Whisk until well combined.

3. Pour the mixture into six 4-ounce ramekins and place them in a large baking pan. Pour hot water into the pan, enough to reach halfway up the sides of the ramekins. Place the baking pan in the oven and bake for about 30 minutes, until the top of a custard feels slightly springy to the touch. (The custard will still be quite soft, but it will firm up in the fridge.)

4. Remove the ramekins from the water with tongs, and let them cool on a wire rack. Then cover and refrigerate them for at least 2 hours or for up to 3 days.

5. Serve chilled, with whipped cream.

No-Pie-Zone Berry Crisp

IT SEEMS TO ME that in the movies and TV shows I grew up watching, women were always making pies. They'd do it effortlessly. You'd never see Donna Reed or Joan Crawford or Barbara Billingsley dusted with flour, makeup-free, sweating, and swearing over a rolling pin. They'd just suddenly produce a pie, smiling, clothes and lipstick perfect, making it look like a task any female should be able to pull off.

When I grew up and tried to emulate these icons, I was astounded to find that making a pie crust was not in my skill package. Whenever I made one, it would either stick to the counter or become so hard you'd throw your back out trying to roll it. If I did manage to get the pie assembled and bake it, the crust would emerge from the oven tasting like either Play-Doh or old socks.

Well, after several failed attempts at pie-making, I picked myself up, dusted myself off, and made an executive decision: In my house we'd eat crumble (or cobbler or crisp) instead of pie. It's almost the same, without the agony of creating a good crust. Who has the time, energy, or self-esteem to meet the Pie Crust Challenge, especially when there's such a delicious and easy alternative? I suggest you try this recipe and kiss the pie good-bye. ✳ SERVES 6

For the filling

6 cups mixed fresh berries (blueberries, raspberries, blackberries, and strawberries)

3 tablespoons granulated sugar

1 tablespoon fresh lemon juice

1 tablespoon pearl tapioca

For the topping

½ cup all-purpose flour

⅓ cup quick-cooking oats

¼ cup granulated sugar

¼ cup (packed) dark brown sugar

½ teaspoon ground cinnamon

¼ teaspoon salt

½ cup finely chopped almonds

12 tablespoons (1½ sticks) unsalted butter, plus extra for the pan

Whipped cream or vanilla ice cream, for serving

1. Preheat the oven to 350°F. Butter a 9-inch square baking dish.

2. For the filling: Mix the berries, sugar, lemon juice, and tapioca together in a bowl, and spoon the mixture into the prepared baking dish.

3. For the topping: Mix the flour, oats, both sugars, cinnamon, salt, and almonds together in a bowl. Cut the butter into small chunks, and work it into the flour mixture with your fingers until the topping is well blended and crumbly. Spread the topping over the berries.

4. Bake the crisp until the top is beginning to brown and the fruit is bubbly, 55 to 60 minutes.

5. Serve it warm, with whipped cream or vanilla ice cream.

Berry Easy

LET'S SAY YOU HAVE A BUNCH OF BERRIES you were intending to use in a crisp, but then at the last minute you decide you are too crabby for a task of that magnitude. (This happens to me all the time.) Here's an easy dessert solution. Just throw those berries in some bowls and add some of this topping, which takes two minutes to make. People will be almost as happy as they would've been with a crisp (if you hadn't been such a lazy-ass). ✳ SERVES 4

8 ounces Greek yogurt

4 ounces mascarpone cheese

2 to 3 tablespoons Cointreau, to taste

2 tablespoons confectioners' sugar

1 teaspoon grated orange zest

½ teaspoon vanilla extract

⅛ teaspoon salt

3 cups mixed fresh berries

1. Combine all the ingredients except the berries in the bowl of your food processor. Process briefly until the sauce is smooth. Chill the sauce for at least 1 hour or as long as overnight.

2. Divide the berries among four bowls, add a dollop of sauce to each one, and serve.

VARIATIONS If you're serving kids, use fresh-squeezed orange juice instead of the Cointreau, or leave out the orange flavoring altogether.

Tiramisù

THIS IS JUST THE BEST DESSERT AROUND if you lose your mind and decide to have a dinner party. It's easy and you make it the night before, just adding the whipped cream at the last minute.

You might think that, with the espresso and the alcoholic ingredients, your guests will get wired and drunk from eating this, and then they'll trash the dining room and stay till 3 A.M. This has not been my experience, I promise, but you might want to use decaffeinated espresso. ✳ SERVES 8

6 egg yolks (see Note)
½ cup sugar
1½ pounds mascarpone cheese
½ cup sweet Marsala wine
1½ cups brewed espresso
½ cup Kahlúa liqueur
30 Italian ladyfingers (savoiardi)
1 cup heavy (whipping) cream
1 tablespoon confectioners' sugar
1 teaspoon vanilla extract
2 tablespoons unsweetened cocoa
   powder

1. Using a standing or hand-held electric mixer, beat the egg yolks and sugar together in a bowl until light and fluffy, 4 to 5 minutes. Add the mascarpone and the Marsala, and beat until everything is well combined.

2. Mix the espresso and Kahlúa together in a small bowl. Roll each ladyfinger briefly in the Kahlúa mixture. (They should be moist but not soggy.) Arrange half of the ladyfingers in rows to cover the bottom of a 9 x 13-inch (or equivalent) serving dish. Pour half of the mascarpone mixture over the ladyfingers, carefully spreading it with a spatula to distribute it evenly. Arrange another layer of dipped ladyfingers on top of that. Finish with the remaining mascarpone mixture. Then cover the dish with plastic wrap and refrigerate it overnight.

3. Within a couple hours of serving time, whip the cream with a hand-held electric mixer until soft peaks form. Add the confectioners' sugar and vanilla, and continue to beat the cream until the peaks are a

little stiffer. Spread a thin (½-inch) layer of whipped cream over the top of the tiramisù.

4. Dust the tiramisù lightly with the cocoa powder, and serve.

NOTE This recipe contains raw eggs, so make sure your eggs are very fresh and have been kept refrigerated.

Nora's Cookies

WHEN NORA WAS EIGHT, she took an after-school cooking class every Tuesday. Her teacher provided the children with ultra-simple recipes and lots of hands-on attention, and the kids brought home the results of their efforts.

I loved Tuesdays. Freed for a day from the rigors of dinner prep, I accomplished meaningful things, like rollerblading and buying a vacuum cleaner. I'd pick up Nora at the end of the afternoon and happily chirp words I never thought I would say to a member of my immediate family: "What's for dinner, honey?" She'd proudly present the Chinese chicken salad or the spaghetti and meatballs and I'd whoop for joy.

After the class ended, I still experienced a little *frisson* of anticipation when I woke up on Tuesdays. This was followed by a stab of disappointment when reality kicked in: Nora had handed the toque back to me.

She has not so much as wielded a whisk since then.

On the good side, I found a cookie recipe, a remnant of her cooking class, crumpled up in Nora's backpack. We made them at home, with a few adjustments, and they became an instant classic and Nora's favorite. Everyone loves them, except people like my annoying husband, who won't eat a dessert that does not involve chocolate. ✳ MAKES 16 TO 18 COOKIES, DEPENDING ON THE SIZE OF YOUR COOKIE CUTTER

For the cookies

1 cup (2 sticks) unsalted butter, at room temperature
½ cup confectioners' sugar
1 teaspoon vanilla extract
2 cups all-purpose flour
⅛ teaspoon salt

For the icing

1 egg white
1 cup confectioners' sugar
Food coloring (optional)
Sprinkles (optional)

1. Using a hand-held electric mixer, cream the butter and confectioners' sugar together until they're well blended. Mix in the vanilla.

2. Stir the flour and salt together in a separate bowl. Add this to the butter mixture and blend well.

3. Roll the dough out between two sheets of wax paper to about ¼-inch thickness. Place the dough, still sandwiched between the sheets of wax paper, in the fridge and chill for 30 minutes.

4. While the dough is chilling, preheat the oven to 350°F.

5. Remove the dough from the refrigerator and peel off the top layer of wax paper. Using cookie cutters (or an inverted juice glass), cut the dough into shapes. Collect the scraps to re-roll and cut into another small batch. Arrange the cookies, 2 inches apart, on an ungreased baking sheet, and bake until they're just turning golden, about 20 minutes.

6. Let the cookies cool on the baking sheet for 5 minutes. Then carefully transfer them to a wire rack and let them cool completely.

7. To ice the cookies, mix the egg white and the confectioners' sugar together in a small bowl, and stir in a drop of food coloring if you want. Spread the icing over the cooled cookies. Add sprinkles if you like, and set the cookies aside until the icing sets, 20 to 30 minutes.

VARIATIONS If you want to make these cookies really lively, use pink food coloring in the icing and sprinkle the cookies with multicolored sprinkles. I call these "Happy Cookies" as they are intended to cheer people up.

Or, if you want to accommodate a chocolate-head, make "Jackson Pollock" cookies: Melt 6 ounces semisweet chocolate and 6 tablespoons unsalted butter in a double boiler set over hot water, whisking until it melts. Drizzle the chocolate mixture over the cooled cookies in a random, scribbly way. Chill the cookies to set the chocolate.

The Chip Variations

I HEARD RECENTLY THAT THE SECRET to perfect chocolate chip cookies is to allow the dough to rest for thirty-six hours before you bake them.

This is swell in theory, but in reality it's quite impossible. For crabby cooks, making anything in advance is challenging; we usually cook on an as-needed-right-now basis.

There's also the fact that I make C.C.C.'s when I'm in emergency mode—when I need them immediately, not in three days. I need them when the kids are having friends over, and you don't get three days' notice on such occasions—you're lucky if you get three minutes. The house fills, quite suddenly, with hungry teenagers and in a rush of goodwill, you agree to make them cookies. Before you have time to say "What was I thinking?" you've got out the flour and the butter. Half an hour later, you've got happy teens and a great-smelling house.

So, don't worry if you can't let the dough rest for thirty-six hours. Just make the cookies when you need 'em, and then *you* go rest for thirty-six hours.

Here are three favorite recipes for cookies with chocolate chips.

Nutty Chocolate Chunk Cookies

THESE ARE Tom's favorite, natch. ✳ MAKES ABOUT 4 DOZEN COOKIES

1 cup (2 sticks) unsalted butter,
   at room temperature
1½ cups (packed) light brown sugar
½ cup granulated sugar
2 eggs
1 teaspoon vanilla extract
¼ cup unsweetened cocoa powder
2¼ cups all-purpose flour
1 teaspoon baking soda
½ teaspoon kosher salt
1 package (12 ounces) semisweet
   chocolate chips
1 cup coarsely chopped unsalted
   hazelnuts, lightly roasted (see Note)

1. Preheat the oven to 350°F. Line a baking sheet with parchment paper.

2. Using a hand-held electric mixer, beat the butter and both sugars together in a large bowl until smooth. Then add the eggs, one at a time, beating after each addition. Add the vanilla and the cocoa powder, and mix well.

3. Mix the flour, baking soda, and salt together in a medium bowl.

Gradually add the dry mixture to the butter mixture, and mix until everything is well combined. Stir in the chocolate chips and the hazelnuts.

4. Place tablespoon-size clumps of dough on the lined baking sheet, spacing them 2 inches apart. Bake the cookies until they look done but are still slightly soft to the touch, about 12 minutes. Let them cool for 5 minutes on the sheet before you move them to a wire rack to cool completely. Repeat, using up the remaining dough.

NOTE To roast the hazelnuts, place them on a baking sheet and roast in a 350°F oven until they are golden and fragrant, 8 to 10 minutes.

VARIATIONS You can use pecans instead of hazelnuts, and you can skip roasting the nuts if it's just one step too many.

Diana's Oatmeal Cookies

THESE ARE MY FAVORITE, based on my sister Diana's recipe. She lives in Alaska, where such comfort foods are in great demand, especially in, say, February. ✳ MAKES 28 TO 30 COOKIES

1 cup (2 sticks) unsalted butter,
   at room temperature
1 cup granulated sugar
1 cup (packed) dark brown sugar
2 eggs
1 teaspoon vanilla extract
2 cups all-purpose flour
1 teaspoon baking soda
1 teaspoon baking powder
1 teaspoon ground cinnamon
1 teaspoon salt
3 cups old-fashioned rolled oats
1 cup white chocolate chips
1 cup dried sweetened cranberries
1 cup coarsely chopped pecans

1. Preheat the oven to 350°F. Line a baking sheet with parchment paper.

2. Using a hand-held electric mixer, cream the butter and both sugars together in a bowl until well blended. Add the eggs one at a time, beating well after each addition. Add the vanilla, and mix well.

3. In a separate bowl, combine the flour, baking soda, baking powder, cinnamon, and salt, and mix well. Add the flour mixture and the oats to the butter mixture, and mix well. Add the white chocolate chips, cranberries, and pecans, and mix until they are well distributed in the batter.

4. Place 2-tablespoon-size clumps of the dough on the lined baking sheet, spacing them about 2 inches apart, and flatten them slightly with your hand. Bake the cookies until they are just golden but still somewhat soft, about 15 minutes. Let the cookies cool on the baking sheet for 5 minutes, and then transfer them to a wire rack to cool completely. Repeat, using up the remaining dough.

P. B. C. C.'s

THESE ARE THE KIDS' FAVORITE, occasionally making an appearance in a college care package. ✳ MAKES ABOUT 2 DOZEN COOKIES

8 tablespoons (1 stick) unsalted butter, at room temperature
½ cup granulated sugar
½ cup (packed) light brown sugar
1 cup chunky natural peanut butter (I like Santa Cruz brand)
1 egg
1 teaspoon vanilla extract
1½ cups all-purpose flour
1 teaspoon baking soda
½ teaspoon salt
1 cup milk chocolate chips

1. Preheat the oven to 350°F. Line a baking sheet with parchment paper.

2. Using a hand-held electric mixer, cream the butter and both sugars together in a bowl until well blended. Add the peanut butter and mix well. Add the egg and vanilla, and stir to combine.

3. In a separate bowl, combine the flour, baking soda, and salt, and mix well. Add the flour mixture to the peanut butter mixture, and combine well. Stir in the chocolate chips until they are well distributed in the dough.

4. Place tablespoon-size clumps of the dough on the lined baking sheet, spacing them about 2 inches apart. Using a fork, press down lightly on the cookies, making a mark with the fork. Press lightly again, crosswise. Bake the cookies until they are golden, about 15 minutes. Allow them to cool on the baking sheet for 5 minutes, and then move them to a wire rack to cool completely. Repeat, using up the remaining dough.

A Postscript

I'D NEVER HEARD OF GOLDEN BIRTHDAYS until a couple of years ago, when Elizabeth announced that hers was imminent—she was turning nineteen on the nineteenth—and asked that we treat it as an extraordinary occasion.

Since I was born on the third day of the month, my G.B. went by long ago and was unidentified as Golden. And since I had a twin, all birthdays were challenging enough for my parents without adding the Golden touch. But my mother tells me that, although Billy and I were oblivious of the special quality of our third birthday, we were quite demanding. I asked Mom to make ballerina figures out of pipe cleaners for all the female guests, while Billy wanted a cowboy costume and toy guns for the boys.

The good news for Mom was that feeding a mass of three-year-olds was literally a piece of cake, or, as a friend of mine whose first language is not English says, "piece from cake." You time your party for mid-afternoon and all they're interested in is cake and ice cream. This had been my agenda for every birthday party I'd ever thrown for either of my kids.

But for her Golden Birthday, Elizabeth had other ideas: she wanted an upgrade. She wanted everything to be gold—balloons, clothing, even food—and she envisioned a sophisticated dinner party for twelve people. Since my daughter is now away at college most of the time, I like to indulge her when she's home, but these instructions triggered my Hostess Anxiety Syndrome.

Luckily, I had a good six weeks' notice to prepare for this event, with plenty of time to obsess over the menu: what food is sort of gold in color and easy to cook?

My daughter refused to go with the giant takeout mac 'n cheese

I've resorted to on other occasions. I thought of chicken tenders, but the idea of making enough for twelve, plus side dishes, made me feel faint. Chili was too red, beef too brown, salad too green.

After thinking about this way too much, I relaxed my gold standards. I made Chinese noodles with peanut sauce, which were tan in color, in the gold family. I supplemented that with Chinese chicken salad, which was not golden, not even close, but the takeout place from whence it came *was* close, as in nearby.

It was not a fabulous menu, but then there was the fabulous chocolate cake, which I did *not* make. Covered in gold detail and utterly delicious, it erased all memories of the dubious main course.

Nora will have a Golden Birthday when she turns twenty, so I have over a year to obsess about what to cook for that occasion. But now, since the girls are away and my cooking chores have been so reduced, I feel like I'm undergoing an attitudinal shift. Apparently absence makes the heart grow fonder of cooking. This past Thanksgiving I prepared that entire massive meal without yelling at anybody. I was calm, even without a Crantini, and all that week I enjoyed feeding the girls. They'd been eating cafeteria food for weeks, while I'd accumulated a lot of cooking (and maternal) energy. I made Baked French Toast and Pain-in-the-Ass Minestrone and Tony's Rigatoni and Ham I Am and Tom's Brownies and I wallowed in their appreciation.

I don't want to speak too soon, but I'm thinking this might be a trend, this new food-i-tude. By the time Nora goes Golden, it could be that, when she requests corn chowder, hummus, rutabagas, butterscotch pudding, polenta, and other gold-ish foods for a dozen guests, I will not falter, curse, or turn pale. I might just smile, nod, and say, "Piece from cake."

WEIGHT CONVERSIONS

U.S.	METRIC	U.S.	METRIC
½ oz	15 g	7 oz	200 g
1 oz	30 g	8 oz	250 g
1½ oz	45 g	9 oz	275 g
2 oz	60 g	10 oz	300 g
2½ oz	75 g	11 oz	325 g
3 oz	90 g	12 oz	350 g
3½ oz	100 g	13 oz	375 g
4 oz	125 g	14 oz	400 g
5 oz	150 g	15 oz	450 g
6 oz	175 g	1 lb	500 g

APPROXIMATE EQUIVALENTS

1 stick butter = 8 tbs = 4 oz = ½ cup

1 cup all-purpose presifted flour or
    dried bread crumbs = 5 oz

1 cup granulated sugar = 8 oz

1 cup (packed) brown sugar = 6 oz

1 cup confectioners' sugar = 4½ oz

1 cup honey or syrup = 12 oz

1 cup grated cheese = 4 oz

1 cup dried beans = 6 oz

1 large egg = about 2 oz or about 3 tbs

1 egg yolk = about 1 tbs

1 egg white = about 2 tbs

Please note that all conversions are approximate but close enough to be useful when converting from one system to another.

LIQUID CONVERSIONS

U.S.	IMPERIAL	METRIC
2 tbs	1 fl oz	30 ml
3 tbs	1½ fl oz	45 ml
¼ cup	2 fl oz	60 ml
⅓ cup	2½ fl oz	75 ml
⅓ cup + 1 tbs	3 fl oz	90 ml
⅓ cup + 2 tbs	3½ fl oz	100 ml
½ cup	4 fl oz	125 ml
⅔ cup	5 fl oz	150 ml
¾ cup	6 fl oz	175 ml
¾ cup + 2 tbs	7 fl oz	200 ml
1 cup	8 fl oz	250 ml
1 cup + 2 tbs	9 fl oz	275 ml
1¼ cups	10 fl oz	300 ml
1⅓ cups	11 fl oz	325 ml
1½ cups	12 fl oz	350 ml
1⅔ cups	13 fl oz	375 ml
1¾ cups	14 fl oz	400 ml
1¾ cups + 2 tbs	15 fl oz	450 ml
2 cups (1 pint)	16 fl oz	500 ml
2½ cups	20 fl oz (1 pint)	600 ml
3¾ cups	1½ pints	900 ml
4 cups	1¾ pints	1 liter

OVEN TEMPERATURES

°F	GAS MARK	°C	°F	GAS MARK	°C
250	½	120	400	6	200
275	1	140	425	7	220
300	2	150	450	8	230
325	3	160	475	9	240
350	4	180	500	10	260
375	5	190			

Note: Reduce the temperature by 68°F (20°C) for fan-assisted ovens.

INDEX